Fundamentals of Journalism

Reporting, Writing and Editing

OTHER BOOKS OF INTEREST FROM MARQUETTE BOOKS

Tomasz Pludowski (ed.), *How the World's News Media Reacted to 9/11: Essays from Around the Globe* (2007). ISBN: 978-0-922993-66-6 (paper); 978-0-922993-73-4 (cloth)

Stephen D. Cooper, *Watching the Watchdog: Bloggers as the Fifth Estate* (2006). ISBN: 0-922993-46-7 (cloth); 0-922993-47-5 (paper)

Ralph D. Berenger (ed.), *Cybermedia Go to War: Role of Convergent Media Before and During the 2003 Iraq War* (2006). ISBN: 0-922993-48-1 (cloth); 0-922993-49-1 (paper)

Jami Fullerton and Alice Kendrick, *Advertising's War on Terrorism: The Story of the Shared Values Initiative* (2006). ISBN: 0-922993-43-2 (cloth); 0-922993-44-0 (paper)

Mitchell Land and Bill W. Hornaday, *Contemporary Media Ethics: A Practical Guide for Students, Scholars and Professionals* (2006). ISBN: 0-922993-41-6 (cloth); 0-922993-42-4 (paper)

Joey Reagan, *Applied Research Methods for Mass Communicators* (2006). ISBN: 0-922993-45-9 (paper)

David Demers, *Dictionary of Mass Communication & Media Research: A Guide for Students, Scholars and Professionals* (2005). ISBN: 0-922993-35-1 (cloth); 0-922993-25-4 (paper)

John C. Merrill, Ralph D. Berenger and Charles J. Merrill, *Media Musings: Interviews with Great Thinkers* (2004). ISBN: 0-922993-15-7 (paper)

Ralph D. Berenger (ed.), *Global Media Go to War: Role of Entertainment and News During the 2003 Iraq War* (2004). ISBN: 0-922993-10-6 (paper)

Melvin L. DeFleur and Margaret H. DeFleur, *Learning to Hate Americans: How U.S. Media Shape Negative Attitudes Among Teenagers in Twelve Countries* (2003). ISBN: 0-922993-05-X

Fundamentals of Journalism

Reporting, Writing and Editing

R. Thomas Berner

Marquette Books LLC
Spokane, Washington

Copyright © 2007 Marquette Books LLC

All rights reserved. No part of this publication may be reproduced, stored in a retrieval system, or transmitted in any form or by any means, electronic, mechanical, photocopying, microfilming, recording, or otherwise, without permission of the publisher.

Printed in the United States of America

OTHER RECENT BOOKS BY R. THOMAS BERNER

FICTION
Extra! Extra! Read All About It! Jimmy Olson Saves Las Vegas
(Aventine Press)

NONFICTION
The Literature of Journalism: Text and Context (Strata Publishing, Inc.)
The Best Times We Spent Together: Stories from China (Aventine Press)

PHOTOBOOKS
A Smart Eye in China (www.lulu.com)
Peeping Tom: The Street Photography of R. Thomas Berner (www.lulu.com)
Visions of Santa Fe (Contributor) (Squarebooks Publishing)

Library of Congress Cataloging-in-Publication Data

Berner, R. Thomas.
  Fundamentals of journalism : reporting, writing, and editing / R. Thomas Berner.
    p. cm.
  Includes bibliographical references and index.
  ISBN 978-0-922993-76-5 (pbk. : alk. paper)
  1. Reporters and reporting. 2. Journalism--Authorship. 3. Journalism--Editing. I. Title.
PN4781.B39 2007
070.4'3--dc22

                        2007009030

Edited by Darcy Creviston
Cover Photo Copyright © Lori Sparkia, Fotolia.com

MARQUETTE BOOKS LLC
3107 East 62nd Avenue
Spokane, Washington 99223
509-443-7057 (voice) / 509-448-2191 (fax)
books@marquettebooks.com / www.MarquetteBooks.com

Dedication

For all those students
in all those years
in all those countries

Table of Contents

Preface, 13

Introduction — NEWS, 17
    Role of News Media in Society, 17 / News Values and Beats, 22 /
    News as a Construct, 25 / News Values and Content, 27

PART I — REPORTING

    Chapter 1 — REPORTING, 33
        The Value of Curiosity for Reporters, 33 / Sources of Stories, 39

    Chapter 2 — GATHERING INFORMATION, 45
        Interviews, 45 / Observation, 50 / Documents, 53 / Note-Taking, 55

    Chapter 3 — NEWS EVALUATION, 59
        What Makes News, 59 / The Story Conference and Copy Flow, 64 /
        Putting Theory into Practice, 65 / Hard vs. Soft, 67 / The Want to
        Know vs. The Need to Know, 68 / A First Amendment Obligation, 69

PART II — WRITING

    Chapter 4 — ELEMENTS OF A NEWS STORY, 71
        A Story's Elements, 71 / Writing the Lead, 77

    Chapter 5 — THE FUNDAMENTALS OF WRITING NEWS, 83
        The Writing Process, 83 / Leads, No-News Leads and News
        Judgment, 85 / Backing into Stories, 87 / Blind Leads, 89 / Length of
        Lead, 90 / Dependent Clause Problems, 92 / Emphasis, 92 / One
        Issue per Lead, 93 / The Why Element, 93 / Follow the Lead, 94/
        Developing a Story, 95

Chapter 6 — OTHER STORY TYPES, 103
   Feature Stories, 103 / Profiles, 108 / Obituaries, 119 / In-depth Articles, 123

Chapter 7 — NARRATIVE NONFICTION, 129
   What Is Narrative Nonfiction? 129 / Elements and Techniques of Narrative Nonfiction, 131 / Beginning, Middle and End, 135

PART III — EDITING

Chapter 8 — EDITORS, 141
   The Role of Copy Editors, 141 / A Variety of Editors and Their Duties, 144 / The Newsroom Hierarchy, 147

Chapter 9 — THE EDITING FUNCTION I, 151
   Do No Harm, 151 / Maintain Copy Flow, 152 / Meet Deadlines, 153 / Deflate Pomposity, 154 / Put Life into Breathless Prose, 155 / Fill in the Holes, 156 / Question Facts, 157 / Get the Facts Straight, 158 / Watch for New Words Made by "Typos", 159 / Gang Up on Double Entendres, 160 / Challenge Profanity, 161 / Put Precision into Sentences, 161 / Do the Arithmetic, 162 / Verify Names, 164 / Verify Dates, 164 / Use Foreign Words Correctly, 165

Chapter 10 — THE EDITING FUNCTION II, 169
   Don't Trust the Wires, 170 / Keep Style Consistent, 170 / Protect Against Libel, 171 / Respect Privacy, 174 / Remember Your Audience's Tastes, 177 / Cool Off Copy, 178 / Test Sources, 180 / Strive for Balance, 181 / Stamp Out Stereotypes, 182 / Be a Self-Checker, 186

Chapter 11 — THE WRITTEN WORD, 189
   The Need for Graceful Prose, 189 / The News Story, 191 / Leads, 191 / The Body of the Story, 197 / Endings, 199 / News Style, 200 / Context, 200 / Viewpoint, 201 / Attribution, 201 / Tone, 204 / Sentences and Paragraphs, 205 / Transition, 206 / No Story Is a Formula, 208

Chapter 12 — TIGHTENING COPY, 211
   Spare the Reader, 211 / Remove Verbosity, 213 / Make Sentences Direct, 213 / Eliminate Conventional Information, 214 / Strengthen Weak Verbs, 214 / Cut Weak Phrases, 215 / Get the Right Word, 215 / Watch for Redundancies, 217 / Compress Wordy Phrases, 218 / Evaluate Detail with a Cutting Eye, 218 / Omit the Obvious, 219 / Unpile Prepositional Phrases, 219 / Knock Down Stone Walls, 220 / Edit Elliptically, 220 / Drop Unnecessary Pronouns, 221 / A Closing Note, 221

Chapter 13 — HEADLINES AND CAPTIONS, 223
   Headlines: Aid to Readers, 223 / A Guide to Writing Headlines, 224 / Headline Rules, 228 / In Error They Glare, 234 / Writing Seductive Headlines, 237 / Caption Writing, 240

PART IV — LAW AND ETHICS

Chapter 14 — RESPONSIBLE JOURNALISM, 245
   A Primer on Ethics, 245 / Cover the News, 248 / Plagiarism, 248 / Sensitive Stories, 252 / Race and Sex, 253 / Age, 254 / Anonymous or Unidentified Sources, 254 / Just the Facts, 255 / Photographs, 255 / A Primer on Libel, 259

APPENDICES

Appendix A — SENTENCES AND PARAGRAPHS, 267
   Traditional and Nontraditional Sentence Patterns, 267 / The Simple Sentence, 269 / The Compound Sentence, 271 / The Complex Sentence, 273 / The Compound-Complex Sentence, 275 / Positioning for Clarity, 276

Appendix B — CONVENTIONAL GRAMMAR, 281
   Nouns and Pronouns, 281 / Effect on Verbs, 281 / Effect on Pronouns, 282 / Unclear Antecedent, 284 / Missing Antecedent, 284 / Overworked Pronouns, 285 / Pronouns in Attribution, 286 / False Antecedent, 286 / Indefinite Use, 286 / Other Antecedents, 287 / Pronoun Forms, 287 / Sexism and Pronouns, 290

Appendix C — MODIFICATION, 293
   Positioning Modifiers Correctly, 293 / Dangling and Misplaced Modifiers, 296 / Other Faults, 298

Appendix D — PUNCTUATION, 301
   Establishing Relationships, 301 / The Period, 303 / The Question Mark, 305 / Exclamation Mark, 305 / The Comma, 306/ The Semicolon, 321 / The Colon, 323 / The Hyphen, 324 / The Dash, 329 / Parentheses, 331 / Brackets, 333 / The Apostrophe, 334 / Quotation Marks, 335

Appendix E — A CONDENSED STYLEBOOK, 339

Appendix F — GLOSSARY, 345

Index, 349

Preface

This book was developed for use in three journalism skills courses: newswriting and reporting, feature writing, and copy editing. It distills much of the content in other books I wrote during my 28 years teaching at Pennsylvania State University, including *The Process of Writing News, Writing Literary Features, The Literature of Journalism: Text and Context, The Process of Editing,* and *Language Skills for Journalists.*

When I pitched the idea to David Demers, publisher of Marquette Books, I pointed out that journalism students often pay far too much for their books, only to sell them back for a lot less at the end of the semester. Why not publish and sell one for a reasonable price? For his day job, Professor Demers is a member of the journalism faculty at Washington State University. He understood the situation immediately and agreed that I could take a stab at such a book. And so here it is.

As the subtitle to this book indicates, the first three chapters focus on the role of the reporter. Chapters 4 through 7 focus on writing. And chapters 8 through 13 focus on editing.[1] The last chapter briefly examines ethical and legal issues. The appendices on language and style can be used on an as-needed basis. In fact, should there be a required course in language skills, Appendices A through D would provide the core of such a course.

One of the major changes that has taken place in the journalism field and in journalism education has been the rise of designers and photo editors at newspapers and related courses in journalism programs. My earlier editing textbooks assumed that copy editors performed those functions (I certainly did when I was a city editor.). Today copy editors don't design pages and size photographs as routinely as they did in my day, and so I have not picked up any of that material from my earlier editing books. Although the editing section mentions the role of other editors, it focuses on copy editing, and headline and caption writing.

---

[1] Chapter 3 also contains information helpful to editors.

You will also notice that I reference *The New York Times* a lot. It has had problems in recent years, some of them bad enough to result in the dismissal of top editors. But no matter, the *Times* remains the No. 1 newspaper in the world. If you watch the evening news, note how many times the newscaster credits the *Times* for originally reporting a certain story. Or, if you tune into television or radio talk shows, you will notice that the subject frequently will be something first reported in the *Times*. Because of the scope of its coverage, the *Times* remains the benchmark. (And in fairness, when the *Times* follows up on a story from another newspaper or television station, it credits the original source.)

GOAL OF THIS BOOK

I'm a news junkie. I check the news online, on the air and in print throughout the day.

A lot of people are like me. They expect to be provided with fair, unbiased, clear, concise and interesting news. They want to know why things happen and how events might affect them. They want to learn about other people and gain perspective about how others deal with the good and the bad in their lives.

Granted, I teach online mass media courses (even though I'm retired), so I must keep up with the news. But many people who don't have any such obligation do the same thing I do every day for the same underlying reason: They want to understand the world around them. Curious by nature, they crave reliable information about what's going on at the state, national and international levels and how that ultimately relates to them at the local level.

If you are a journalism student, these news junkies will be your major audience. If you are a journalism teacher, you are teaching young people to feed the addiction of these junkies. This book intends to present components that can be packaged in different ways for different courses with the same basic goal: to produce capable, savvy, ethical and vibrant young reporters and editors who will serve the public — news junkies and all — well. I hope it accomplishes that task.

R. Thomas Berner, Santa Fe, New Mexico
JournProf@comcast.net / CoalCracker@psu.edu

Introduction

NEWS

For two millennia, writing has been a medium through which the public has gotten its news. Historians credit Julius Caesar with publishing a newssheet, titled *Acta Diurna*, that gave the public a summary of happenings in the Roman Senate. *Acta Diurna* means "Daily Acts," and the Latin word for daily, *diurnal*, is the antecedent for the word *journalism*. Two-thousand-plus years later news media are still telling readers, listeners and viewers what is happening in their world.

ROLE OF NEWS MEDIA IN SOCIETY

"We in the press," editorial writer Jean W. Otto once said, "create one of this nation's common denominators — shared information. We unify. We create the base upon which our nation's diversities can co-exist without destroying themselves and each other."[1] Viewed in that light, journalism has a mission. Journalists generally do not see themselves as holding down a job but as following a calling, much the way someone who takes religious vows might. Journalists seek to convey a larger truth about the world, to shed light where there are shadows, to make the sun shine through the clouds of obfuscation, to give a voice to the voiceless.

With the rise of the printing press in western culture came the rise of censorship,[2] which involves attempts by government to silence journalists and other dissenting voices. In England during the reigns of Mary and Elizabeth I, the crown established a monopoly on printing through the Stationers Company and then proceeded to censor content. Elizabeth also

---

[1] Jean H. Otto, "The Meek Shall Not Inherit," The John Peter Zenger Award for Freedom of the Press and the People's Right to Know (given at the University of Arizona, Tucson, Nov. 11, 1988).

[2] Censorship is frequently misunderstood by the public. It is not censorship when an editor refuses to publish a story, column or letter. That is an editor's prerogative. It's called editing. Censorship occurs when the government attempts to suppress information.

established the infamous Star Chamber, which prosecuted, among others, printers who failed to submit to her editing pencil. The licensing system that attempted to keep printers and others in line and to keep negative information away from the public lasted for a century.

In the American colonies attached to England, some people attempted to provide information not controlled by the crown or its agents. One of the first newspapers was the *News-Letter*. Published in Boston, it proclaimed it published "for the Publick Good, to give a true Account of All Foreign & Domestick Occurrences, and to prevent a great many false reports of the same."

One of the best known journalists in the colonies was Benjamin Franklin, who established the *Pennsylvania Gazette* in colonial Philadelphia. In the early days of journalism, the owners of the newspapers did everything. They gathered information, set type, ran the presses, delivered the papers, sold advertising and kept the books in order. As technology advanced, those jobs were split among many people. Today, interestingly enough, one person with a personal computer can effectively once again follow in the steps of Franklin, for the personal computer allows someone to write and correct the information, design and print the pages (if necessary), distribute the information electronically (if desired), and, with a spreadsheet program, keep the accounts.

Franklin was one of many bold journalists. "If all printers were determined not to print anything until they were sure it would offend nobody," he once wrote, "there would be very little printed." Franklin made that comment in the days before the First Amendment protected the freedom of the press and speech.

In some countries, boldness came with a price. Napoleon once had a printer executed. Still later, another newspaper condemned the general, leading him to refer to the press as "the fifth great power." Around the same time in England, Edmund Burke referred to the press as the Fourth Estate,[3] and Thomas Macauley saw the press as the equal of the three estates of the realm: the Lords Spiritual, the Lords Temporal and the Lords Common. Neither Burke nor Macauley was happy with the power of the press. And Napoleon observed: "A journalist is a grumbler, a censurer, a giver of advice, a regent of sovereigns, a tutor of nations. Four hostile

---

[3]"There are three estates in Parliament but in the Reporters' Gallery yonder there sits a Fourth Estate more important far than they all. It is not a figure of speech or witty saying; it is a literal fact, very momentous to us in these times." From: "Speaking of a Free Press" published by the American Newspaper Publishers Association in 1987.

newspapers are more to be feared than a thousand bayonets."

In the newly formed United States, newspapers began as extensions of political parties, their distribution through the mail subsidized by the federal government, and it was not until the 1830s that newspapers shifted from party ownership to private ownership, signaling what is considered the rise of the penny press. Communications scholar Michael Schudson says it was then that fact gained prominence over opinion in news stories. Schudson also notes changes in the names of newspapers, away from commercial names such as *Advertiser* to functional ones such as *Herald* or *Tribune*.[4]

Schudson also credits the press with taking advantage of the technology of the time. One major advance was the steam press, which enabled publishers to reproduce thousands of copies of a multiple-page newspaper in a short amount of time. Before the steam press, newspapers were still printed on presses with moveable type, which Gutenberg introduced around 1450. They didn't have many pages, yet printing them consumed much of the publisher's labor.

Also popular with the press was the telegraph, which enabled newspapers to get information quickly and across great distances. The telegraph first proved its worth to newspapers during the Civil War, when correspondents at the site of battles could quickly send their stories to waiting editors in the major cities.

As the 19th century closed, newspapers had become more democratic, more egalitarian and more middle class. The mass distribution of newspapers meant that many people not only read the news stories but also the advertisements. Thus was born the mass market. A larger audience shared information. Furthermore, Schudson notes, the newspaper changed "from something to be borrowed or read at a club or library to a product one bought for home consumption."

Also born at the 19th century's close, according to Schudson, was the formal position of reporter. The division of labor common for most of the 20th century had arrived. Some workers, such as the printers, become unionized, usually under the International Typographical Union, which has been subsumed by the Communications Workers of America. Where once travelers provided information to the local editor, reporters were now hired full time to gather news and write stories. Some of those early reporters went on to become masters in American literature. Realism was

---

[4]Michael Schudson, *Discovering the News* (New York: Basic Books, Inc., 1978), p. 17.

a major element in the American novel at that time, and scholars today trace that to the journalistic work that predated the novels.

With World War I ended and the Depression just beginning, American journalism broadened its outlets. One such addition was *TIME Magazine*, a combination of news and interpretation in each story. One of *Time's* founders, Henry R. Luce, disdained those who spoke of objectivity: "Show me a man who thinks he's objective, and I'll show you a man who's deceiving himself." Other magazines followed.

Then came the rise of the radio. Suddenly, Americans could hear for themselves the words of the president of the United States or of a dictator from a foreign land. Broadcast stations created networks and hired their own reporters. Edward R. Murrow assembled a team to cover the war in Europe. Murrow would broadcast live to the United States during German bombing raids on London.

Murrow went on to present equally intensive and exciting journalism on television. The newscast evolved from someone sitting behind a desk reading the news to a 15-minute program with two anchors to half-hour or longer programs that we see and hear today. Live coverage of both parties' presidential conventions helped advance the careers of some broadcast journalists.

Today, information junkies have much to choose from. If they have the time, they can read in print at least three newspapers distributed nationally — *The Wall Street Journal*, *The New York Times* and *USA Today* — as well as a local newspaper and any other newspaper that appears on the World Wide Web. If our information junkies live in an area served by cable, they probably watch news from NBC, CBS, ABC, CNN, PBS, and Fox and at least one C-SPAN channel. They probably also have access to a couple of regional television stations that provide some local news. And don't forget local radio stations.

All of these outlets are telling people about current events. But they are also doing what Jean Otto talked about — they are creating an environment of shared information from which we, a diverse people, draw.

Also, there's local flavor. In a study of what makes smaller newspapers excellent, journalism professor Thomas Connery identified, among other things, thorough coverage of the community, original reporting, in-depth reporting and a strong editorial voice. One editor told Connery:

> Our job is to make our readers care. Not just about government, but about the way people live, about the way the world lives. Our job is to

see that they know the facts and figures, but the human stories, too, and to do it honestly and responsibly.[5]

Implicit in the editor's statement is a view of the press that derives from a 1947 study funded by Luce of *TIME Magazine* and conducted by a group of scholars led by chairman Robert M. Hutchins.[6] The Commission on Freedom of the Press said it had five expectations for communications media:

1. A truthful, comprehensive and intelligent account of the day's events in a context which gives the meaning.
2. A forum for the exchange of comment and criticism.
3. The projection of a representative picture of the constituent groups in the society.
4. The presentation and clarification of the goals and values of the society.
5. Full access to the day's intelligence.

This came to be called the social responsibility theory of the press. Although news media at the time gave little news coverage to the commission's report, it nevertheless had an impact on journalism programs, which passed the commission's ideas on to their students. Some critics argue that the industry has been slow to adopt these ideas. But news media are not monolithic, not even when referred to as "the press" or when *media*, the plural form of *medium*, is used erroneously as a singular noun. The lack of a monolithic structure means that each outlet — each newspaper, radio station, television station, related and unrelated Web sites — behaves the way it wants. And that means that each outlet does not necessarily measure up to the expectations of the Hutchins Commission.

Still, the Hutchins commission's expectations continue to state succinctly and explicitly what the role of the news media ought to be in a democratic society. The underlying assumptions in this book are that the commission's expectations are worthy ideals for modern journalists to follow.

---

[5]Thomas Connery, "Management Commitment & the Small Daily," *Newspaper Research Journal* (Summer/Fall 1989), p. 64.
[6]Commission on Freedom of the Press, *A Free and Responsible Press* (Chicago: University of Chicago Press,1947).

NEWS VALUES AND BEATS

Defining news is not easy. In the world of the beginning newswriter, news can refer to such things as rising tuition and dormitory fees, unwanted pregnancy, sexually transmitted diseases, a noisy dorm floor, a cutback in library hours, the scheduled appearance of a favorite musical group on campus, downtime on the server, and the success or failure of an athletic team. For others, news can be increasing taxes, the rising cost of medical care, the stability and future of Social Security, the inefficiency of the trash collection system, the infrequency of police patrols in a neighborhood, and plans for a new — and expensive — school.

Lord Northcliffe once described news as "something someone wants to suppress." Another, even more classic definition, says that when a dog bites a man, that isn't news; but when a man bites a dog, that is. And perhaps the simplest definition: News is what is printed in a newspaper (or broadcast on a radio or television station or on the Internet). Although interesting, these definitions aren't very useful in terms of helping journalists decide what to print. Thus, journalists often talk about values that influence the selection process.

Among them are these, which Professor Wallace B. Eberhard of the University of Georgia found after examining 14 newswriting textbooks: timeliness, proximity-nearness, prominence-eminence, change, action, audience, impact, unusualness, conflict, significance, magnitude, human interest, consequence-probable consequence, sex, children, animals, tragedy, oddities-bizarreness-novelty-rarity, interest, importance, economic impact, familiarity, humor, pathos-pathos/bathos, currency, emotional stimulus-emotion, accuracy, certainty, explanation, clarity, sensationalism, suspense, objectivity, conciseness, irony, drama, surprise, identification, concreteness, personality, progress, disaster, news balance.[7] Although news stories often contain one or more of these values, journalists in the real world don't sit around filling out scorecards on lists of terms. With experience, they develop a sense of what their readers need and want to know.

For example, five U.S. soldiers killed in a foreign conflict might rate five paragraphs on an inside page, but if one of the soldiers lived within the newspaper's circulation area, the story would lead that day's paper with photographs of the dead soldier and a sidebar containing interviews

---

[7]Wallace B. Eberhard, "'News Value' Treatments Are Far from Consistent Among Newswriting Texts," *Journalism Educator* (Spring 1982), pp. 9-11, 50.

with survivors, other relatives and friends. A second sidebar might enumerate the deaths of other local residents in faraway wars. In one such situation, the return of the body of a local soldier from Iraq received higher billing on page one than the visit of the president of the United States in Montana on the same day in November 2006. Another example: A fatal nursing home fire in California might mean nothing to newspapers in other states, except when those states have issues with nursing homes violating fire codes. Newspapers there might very well play the California story on the front page and add comment from local fire officials.

Although journalists must ultimately decide what to publish or broadcast, values are not the only thing influencing the news selection process. Another factor is how news organizations are integrated into a community. Most news organizations create news beats — such as city council, the mayor's office, the police station and the courts — where reporters routinely collect news and information. Larger news organizations have staff that cover the governor's office, the state legislature, the three branches of federal government, and sometimes federal agencies (FBI, EPA).

These beats are not randomly distributed in a community. Not all organizations have an equal chance of being covered regularly. Most beats are linked to powerful institutions or organizations, and the people who run those organizations — leaders or elites — help define the news. They conduct public meetings, issue press releases and pass ordinances and laws that affect everyday life. In other words, leaders or elites who work in powerful institutions play a disproportionate role in creating and defining the news.

There is nothing sinister about beats and the way journalist cover them. Powerful people and institutions generally are considered to be credible sources of news, and people want to know what they are doing, because their actions affect people's lives. But overdependence on such powerful sources and on some values, such as conflict, has a downside. It means that less powerful groups have more difficulty making the news, and sometimes they have to create conflict to make the news.

The late John Chancellor of NBC News defined news as "a chronicle of conflict and change." Implicit in that definition — perhaps "description" is a better word — is that peace and stability are not news. News organizations seem to detail war more than peace, just as history courses focus more on wars than on the peace between the wars. Given Chancellor's description, one can understand why some under-represented groups in our society (e.g., minorities, labor movements, environmentalists) have found it necessary to become confrontational and hostile — that was the best and sometimes only way to get the news media's attention.

In fact, political scientist Lance Bennett wonders if news isn't an advertisement for the system. In other words, news reinforces the status quo.[8] A great deal of social science research actually supports this theory.

But it would be wrong to conclude that journalism is simply a lap dog of powerful elites. It often publishes content that is critical of them and their actions, and, historically, the evidence suggests that journalism has given increased coverage to social movements. News rooms are much more diverse today than in the past. Editors realized that ethnic and gender variety in the newsroom helped diversify the news and create a newspaper or broadcast program that was more relevant to the population. Stories were no longer defined through the narrow prism of one ethnic group or one gender.

Thanks to an increasing number of women in the newsroom, editors began assigning stories on childcare and women-in-the-workplace. The arrival of ethnic minorities gave rise to broader reporting of social issues. Does welfare work? What are the conditions among the disenfranchised? How does racism hold people back? Is the education system working? How accessible is the community? What are mental health services really like? The news media are often criticized for focusing on personalities rather than issues and for covering what is familiar rather than going into new places and finding new sources.

News, then, can be defined as a social product that is shaped by values (journalistic as well as societal) and by the way news organizations are integrated into a community. News reflects the power structure, but it can also be critical of it. In fact, one scholar even argues that journalism produced by corporate news organizations is much more critical of the status quo, and that, historically, the news is becoming more, not less, critical of the status quo.[9]

The upshot of this is that journalists should seek to be as inclusive as possible when covering the news. Journalists also can help by producing more in-depth stories about community issues rather than filling the paper and the airwaves with reports from the police and other routine news beats.

---

[8]Status quo is defined here as the current state of affairs, especially in terms of political and social power.

[9]David Demers, *The Menace of the Corporate Newspaper: Fact or Fiction?* (Ames: Iowa State University Press, 1996).

NEWS AS A CONSTRUCT

Anyone who has examined the process of writing news soon realizes that news really is a construct — that, far from being something inherent in nature (as some journalists seem to believe), news is whatever the journalist writes and the editor prints or the producer broadcasts and the audience consumes. That's not necessarily bad when everyone, including readers and viewers, recognizes the process. News gets tangled in a web of disputes when some try to make it something it is not. While news is based on fact, it does not replace truth, and it is not an objective account of something, although journalists strive to be fair and balanced in their writing and disinterested in the outcome of any dispute on which they are reporting.

Some journalists have claimed that the news media merely reflect society, but the truth is that many journalists often write stories for other journalists (especially for editors), journalists often conform to stereotypes, and journalists often come to a news event predisposed to a storyline rather than with an open mind. Journalists are hardly the objective fact-gatherers and presenters that they claim to be. News is not an inherent part of nature, but is something constructed by journalists for their readers. Depending on the audience, the story is constructed differently. Writing about broadcast news executives, Gans says: "They more or less operated on the assumption that a news story could be shot, edited and narrated in a number of different ways, and that the producer was responsible for reconstructing it along lines that met the standards and policies of the network."

The same is true of newspapers. I have in my files stories about the governor of New York testifying before a House committee about tax revisions. *The New York Times* version includes references to Governor Cuomo's "sharp tongue," has him making declarations and refers to him as "the star of the show."[10] *The Wall Street Journal*, on the other hand, has Cuomo pleading and asserting, but also makes reference to Gov. Richard Thornburgh of Pennsylvania, as a champion of the tax revisions.[11]

What lessons can a beginning journalist draw from this? Consider how each journalist portrayed the people in the story. Although both

---

[10]David E. Rosenbaum, "Cuomo Takes Case to House," *The New York Times* (July 18, 1985), p. D1.

[11]Jeffrey H. Birnbaum, "Cuomo, Others Plead With House Panel for State, Local Tax Break to Be Kept," *The Wall Street Journal* (July 18, 1985), p. 14.

stories acknowledge Cuomo's prominence, the *Times'* account casts the governor in the role of someone who is showing up those scoundrels in Washington. It helps that Cuomo is the governor of New York, home of the *New York Times*.

The *Journal's* account, on the other hand, strikes a more even-handed pose, even comes across somewhat dryly. Cuomo rates an "asserted" and Thornburgh gets a "champion" in a story otherwise powered by relatively neutral verbs.

Both stories were written with the audiences of the newspapers in mind. If New York is the highest tax state in the nation and the deductibility of local taxes is in jeopardy, then what the New York governor says is of importance and interest to *New York Times'* readers. In fact, the story appears at the bottom of the first business page with a photograph, whereas the *Journal's* account appears on page 14 and without a photograph.[12] The *Journal's* audience is made up of business persons from around the country, from low-tax states as well as high-tax states, and people who probably favor lower taxes period. Knowing that, the *Journal* reporter isn't about to paint Cuomo as a David up against a Goliath. The *Times*, on the other hand, gets an interesting story for its audience by adopting that storyline. Conflict is newsworthy.

Both newspapers are considering the interests of their audience. When a newspaper does that, it considers the make-up of its readership. What is the educational level of its readers? Where do they work (in a steel mill or for a defense contractor)? Where do they live (suburban area or an urban area)? What is the racial make-up? What are their leisure time interests? Is religion important? Is church attendance high or low? What are their politics? What is the mix of all of the preceding?

What journalists need to remember is that the audience plays a major role in reading the story. Stories are not merely something laid down by a journalist and then received with the same intensity or understanding by all readers. Readers bring to stories their prejudices and predispositions. What might appear positive to one reader could be negative to another.

In a locale where hunting is popular, for example, a newspaper will publish photographs of hunters and their kill. Not everyone in the newspaper's audience approves; some people in the audience oppose hunting and suggest that the newspaper is condoning the practice because it publishes the photographs. But the editor might reply that since hunting

---

[12] At the time, the *Journal* was not publishing photographs.

is important to many in his audience, he is responding to his audience. Curiously, though, the editor has never skipped a year of publishing the photographs to see if the hunters really care as much about their absence as the nonhunters do about their presence.

Sociologist Herbert Gans says news is "often the highlights of highlights,"[13] but the important message from Gans for readers and viewers is not to rely on one outlet and one medium for your news, but get involved and dig deeper. Journalists are the ones who decide what the highlights of the highlights will be. The mayor of a city in Pennsylvania, one of the few in the nation with independent competing newspapers, once observed that new ownership of one of the newspapers had resulted in increased coverage of local government. It wasn't that local government had done anything more newsworthy; it was that the new blood in an old competitive situation had redefined news in this city.

NEWS VALUES AND CONTENT

Now that you have heard the nuances, it is time to discuss news values, starting with content. Let's discuss the content of one edition of a 25,000-circulation newspaper that publishes seven days a week. The newspaper is divided into four sections, which in itself makes a statement about what is news. Each section enables the editors to emphasize aspects of the community they think are newsworthy. Thus, the newspaper that begins a section with business news but buries sports in a section that leads off with arts is making a statement about its news values.

The bulk of section one is devoted to what some people would call "wire news" — that is, nonlocal. But an exception appears on page one. It is a feature story about a local gunsmith who makes replicas of muzzleloaders. It's a human interest story, a typical feature story. Otherwise, the front page contains stories distributed by the Associated Press, *The Washington Post*, the *Los Angeles Times*, the *Philadelphia Inquirer* and Knight Ridder Newspapers.[14] Three of the stories focus on current events. In two instances, the events are elections; the third event is a demonstration in Moscow. All three stories are international.

The last two stories are not about events. One is a feature story on the demise of a sport called "cornerball," which is played by the Amish and

---

[13] Herbert J. Gans, *Deciding What's News*. (New York: Pantheon Books, 1979), p. 92.

[14] In 2006, The McClatchy Company purchased Knight Ridder.

Mennonites, and the other story tells about Congress' use of mailing privileges (called "franking"). Neither the cornerball story nor the mailing story is tied to a specific event and could have just as easily been published the day before or three days from today. So why are they newsworthy?

The cornerball story fits several categories on Eberhard's list. It has human interest and is about change and novelty. The mail story, despite the apparent lack of a current event, was current because it was an election year and candidates for Congress were announcing for office. The mail story represents an attempt to monitor the system. This is something the news media do.

Inside, a story details a meeting in the United States between the president of the United States and the chancellor of West Germany (at the time, soon to be unified with East Germany and become Germany). Another story announces that the planned launch of a U.S. space shuttle has been delayed. One more story uses a recent controversy over cigarette smoking to focus on the first year of service by the secretary of Health and Human Services. Similar in purpose to the mail story on page one, this particular story recounts the secretary's first year in office and the problems he has had and makes the case that he has finally found a popular issue in condemning cigarettes. Twenty-five percent of one page is devoted to the weather forecasts — local, national and international. The weather is always of interest.

The second section, which is the local news section, contains a story, with photograph, about the owners of a local airport contesting a proposed development at the end of their runway. Controversy makes news, and this is all the juicier since one of the developers is also a state senator. Is he receiving favored treatment? The story outlines the concerns of the airport's owners and their suggested resolution. The story also reveals that the airport's owners have not contacted the developers about their concerns. The newspaper has become a mediator, publicly relaying messages between the squabbling parties.

Another story tells that an unidentified woman crawled out of an elevator stalled between floors and fell 20 feet to the bottom of the elevator shaft. She was in critical condition with a head injury. A third story is what is known as an "advance." It announces that two municipalities' planning commissions are going to hold a joint work session to discuss proposed land use regulations. Consultants working on the regulations will be at the meeting, the story says, and the public is urged to attend and offer comments.

On the next two inside pages appears routine accident and police reports, a listing of municipal meetings for the week ahead and the milestone-type information — births, hospital admissions and discharges, deaths and funerals. (Some newspapers have started publishing the obituaries of pets.) Later on in this local section can be found state, business and entertainment news.

Section three carries an advice column, a profile of a YMCA director, and information for senior citizens. Inside is more information, most of it about library activities in the county.

Section four is the sports section. This particular day, a Monday, devotes most of its space to the results of Sunday's professional, collegiate and high school games and meets. Half of one page is given over to box scores, other results and standings — all in minute type. This is the page for the truly devoted, who will read it in detail.

The last page of the paper will receive equal attention, but probably from a different segment of the audience. This is the page that carries the television listings and reviews of shows on television that night.

Larger newspapers have more sections or divide the paper along different lines. Some newspapers devote an entire section to business, for example, and others give more space than one page to arts and entertainment. Examine any metropolitan newspaper's Website and you'll see how news is broken into sections and cross-referenced — a process made simple because of the technology. Examine your local newspaper and see how it breaks out the content, then look at another newspaper from another state.

A reporter covering an event that includes several topics must decide what is newsworthy and what is not. At the least, the reporter must select the one point of a story that's newsworthy enough to make the first paragraph.

One reporter, faced with four actions by a board of elected officials, had to choose from among routine appointments to advisory boards, an announcement by the township manager that construction of a new township building was on schedule, a vote on protecting water-well sites not just in the one municipality but across the region, and approval of plans to develop an industrial park, which had been reviewed by various advisory boards in public with no objections.

The reporter chose the appointments to advisory boards but was redirected by his editor to rewrite the story and lead with the discussion on water. Why? Well, the newspaper's circulation area included at least 65 municipal boards, all of which routinely appointed people to advisory boards. The appointments were of no interest outside the one municipality. Water, on the other hand, cuts across municipal boundaries, and at this time was a topic of concern among several municipalities in the newspaper's coverage.[15] They all drew their water from the same aquifer. By highlighting water, the reporter was developing the story to have broader appeal. The water story would function as a unifier within the newspaper's audience.

In sum, news is something journalists construct. They aim to provide information they believe their readers and viewers should have or want to have. That information is usually timely and is pegged to current events. Sometimes news is what is said locally about something that happened hundreds or thousands of miles away. Sometimes news is about local government or local problems. Sometimes news is a human interest story about someone residing in the newspaper's circulation area. Sometimes news is a human interest story about a subculture not residing in the newspaper's circulation area. News is what journalists believe will interest their readers and viewers. News is a disruption in the rhythm of a community, a state or a nation. News, in the words of historian Mitchell Stephens, is "what's on a society's mind."[16] News is what makes people talk.

---

[15]Based on my travels throughout the world, water is a story everywhere.
[16]Mitchell Stephens, *A History of News* (New York: Viking Penguin, 1988), p. 9.

Chapter 1

REPORTING

News stories are based on facts gathered by reporters. Journalists do not make things up out of thin air. No journalist can fashion a news story without gathering relevant information, getting details, finding examples and then planning the story. The factual base of news stories distinguishes them from fiction.

THE VALUE OF CURIOSITY FOR REPORTERS

Norman Mailer won one of journalism's highest honors, a Pulitzer Prize for his book *Armies of the Night*. Subsequently, he wrote a book about the Apollo space program, and in it was a discussion of the accolades he had received for his journalistic work. He considered receiving the journalism honor ironic because he knew how hard journalists worked and did not feel he could live up to that standard. But he also said something I have always considered a defining point about journalists:

> They had, first of all, to have enormous curiosity, and therefore be unable to rest until they found out the secret behind even the smallest event.

Curiosity may have killed the cat, but it defines a good journalist.

On a more mundane level, editors throughout the country were asked a few decades ago what they wanted in beginning reporters. Language and writing skills were high on everyone's list. But somewhere in the body of the article, the author listed some of the comments editors had offered, comments that had not found their way onto the list. One editor said what he wanted in a reporter was someone who took a different route to work every day. In other words, a curious person.

Good editors also like reporters who don't hang around the office waiting for the phone to ring. Curious reporters are usually out of the office digging up news. They may use the phone to schedule interviews or to check a random fact. But usually they get out on the street and feel life just like the cop walking the neighborhood beat. Inexperienced reporters sometimes try to write about matters they haven't seen. A reporter assigned to write a story about a particular traffic problem should go to the scene of the problem. See it first hand. There's no substitute for being there.

It is true that many news stories come from the police beat or from town council and school board meetings, or from the planning commission and zoning board. It is true that many news stories come from a reporter's beat or specialty, from labor, health, education, sports, the legal system, business, science, technology, religion or politics. But what really drives every successful story is curiosity. Good reporters want to know everything. They won't take "no" for an answer. They search everywhere; they're never satisfied. They know that little stories lead to big stories.

A good reporter goes beyond the routine information from the beat to see if there's a better story. For example, one day Vanessa Winans of the *York* (Pa.) *Daily Record* read on the police blotter that the bookkeeper for the York YMCA was robbed while taking the Y's money to the bank for deposit. She could have written a four-paragraph story from the information the police gave her. But instead she called the victim and got a better story. And to find the woman, Winans had to dial several phone numbers because the police did not have the woman's home address or her husband's name, which would have made finding her phone number a snap. One of the questions Winans asked the victim: What went through your mind as you were struggling with the robber? Here's the story:

ROBBERY VICTIM GOES DOWN FIGHTING[1]
YMCA Bookkeeper Struggles with Thief Who Took *Cash*, Checks

By Vanessa Winans

> Judy Reed did not give up without a fight when she was robbed while on the way to make a bank deposit in the rain Monday.
>
> Mrs. Reed, the bookkeeper for the York YMCA, was walking in the 100 block of west Market Street at 10:15 a.m. when she saw a man pass her, she said Monday night. She saw him stop at a parking lot, turn, and wait for her to pass.
>
> Moments later, she felt a pull at the white satchel that contained the

---

[1]Vanessa Winans, "Robbery Victim Goes Down Fighting," *York Daily Record* (Aug. 21, 1990). Copyright 1990 by the *York Daily Record*. All rights reserved.

YMCA's weekend receipts — $1,100 in cash and $2,300 in checks, she said.

Tightening her grip on the satchel, the 5-foot, 51-year-old woman whirled to face the much-taller robber. She said she tried to jab the man with the point of her umbrella, but at the moment of truth, it blew inside out. So she tried to hang on to the satchel.

"I was tugging and he was tugging," she recalled. "Eventually, he was stronger, and he pulled it out of my hand. I fell down and started yelling, 'Police! Police!'"

Her attacker said nothing as they struggled.

The man, who did not show her a weapon, ran north through the Columbia Gas Co. parking lot, city police reported. Police had not caught the thief Monday night.

The robber was black, about 5 feet 8 inches to 5 feet 10 inches tall, wearing dark or neutral clothes, in his 20s, with a thin to medium build and close-cropped hair, Mrs. Reed said.

The woman said she tried to fight the man because the idea of being robbed angered her.

"I was just mad," she said. "I wasn't going to give in to him completely."

In retrospect, she was glad she fought, despite her bruised left hip and left elbow and three broken fingernails. She takes classes at the YMCA and considers herself fit. But if another robber had a gun or knife, she wouldn't argue again, she said.

Norman L. Walters, YMCA president, said the deposit robbery was the YMCA's first.

YMCA officials plan to change the way employees take deposits to the bank, Mr. Walters said. The money taken Monday was insured and the checks were all marked for deposit.

"You would guard against that in the evening or the early morning, but you'd think at that time of day, you'd be safe," he said. "It's supposedly the safest corridor to the bank we've got."

Mrs. Reed, who has walked the route for the 22 months she has been the YMCA's book keeper, said the attack upset her.

"I get shaky when I think about it."

Elsewhere, two reporters for the *Post and Courier* in the Port of Charleston, S.C., saw a police blotter item about an officer who had pulled his gun on a dockworker during an argument. Shots were not fired. No one was hurt.

But the two reporters were curious. First, they wanted to know what the officer's record was like. They learned he had a temper that had shown up in other police jobs. The next question: Why was he hired by yet another department? Did anyone track potentially dangerous police officers? Was this problem larger than their circulation area?

Glenn Smith and Ron Menchaca spent a year gathering information and produced a three-part series titled "Tarnished Badges" which revealed a systemic failure that was not keeping dangerous officers from moving from one job to another. They received a statewide $5,000 award for investigative journalism — just because they were curious. This is how the series began[2]:

> Port of Charleston police officer Patrick O'Neal leveled his pistol at the stunned crowd of dockworkers, barking orders as he straddled a longshoreman who lay handcuffed and bleeding at his feet.
> Moments before, dockworker Richard Brown made the mistake of walking away from O'Neal during an argument over a parking ticket. O'Neal jammed his gun into Brown's neck and slammed the burly longshoreman to the ground, witnesses said.
> Brown lay flat on his stomach, struggling to see, his eyes burning from a close-range blast of the officer's pepper spray.
> "He was crazy," Brown said of the June 19, 2004, incident. "I've never seen nobody like that."
> Others had.
> O'Neal's explosive temper had surfaced earlier in his law enforcement career, but State Ports Authority officials didn't know this when they hired him to guard one of the nation's busiest ports.

If that story makes you curious, then you've got some of what it takes to be a good reporter, too.

Stories grow from other stories. A few years ago, Gary Rummler of the *Milwaukee Journal* wrote a series on teenagers who were dealing with abuse. After the series appeared, Rummler received phone calls from adults who had suffered abuse as children. His curiosity whetted, Rummler interviewed several adults, talked to an expert or two and read three books, then wrote a six-part series.

The curious reporter has a perspective that goes beyond the community. The reporter is able to compare and contrast local issues with issues elsewhere. Some of that can be done merely by accessing other newspaper's Web sites and searching for stories on the same or related issues. Such stories provide the reporter with sources to call or visit (as the budget allows).

In Florida, some editors at the *Orlando Sentinel* wanted to know the impact of the state's early release program for prisoners. The program was

---

[2] Glenn Smith and Ron Menchaca, "Problem Cops: A Systemic Failure," *Post and Courier* (March 5, 2005).

designed to ease overcrowding in prisons, but instead, the *Sentinel* discovered, the program recycled criminals, some of whom graduated to a higher level of criminal activity. Not even state corrections officials were aware of the immensity and enormity of the problem.

A reporter new to an area was impressed by how efficiently the local transportation system operated during a heavy snowstorm. Curious about its efficiency in those circumstances, he checked with the transportation authority, drivers, passengers, meteorologists, and other interested parties and produced a 350-word story. It was a nice news feature that kept the public informed. And it came about because someone was curious.

At one newspaper, reporters on beats are required to meet with other beat reporters to informally discuss what is going on. The reporter in one municipality revealed that plans for a new shopping center had hit a snag because it hadn't been designed with public transit in mind. So the regional transportation authority intervened informally and got the municipality to make some changes.

How could that planning mistake be avoided in the future? The transportation beat reporter interviewed the authority's manager and learned that he was preparing legislation requiring authority review of all plans in those municipalities using the regional bus system. The transportation manager felt money and time could be saved if the authority were involved early in the process. The transportation reporter wrote a story, using the shopping center as her example of why the regionwide legislation was needed.

Local government tends to be a major source of stories for reporters. Lazy reporters write nothing beyond the town council meeting or the item on the police blotter. They don't see the larger story. They aren't curious. Good reporters, on the other hand, see each meeting and each blotter item as an opportunity to pursue information further and write a unique story. They look for trends. They maintain good files. They ask questions. They're curious.

Good reporting includes getting specific information. Nothing raises an editor's eyebrows more than to read an account of a city council meeting and see a direct quotation attributed to "a member of the audience." Wasn't the reporter curious enough to find the person's name and address and other particulars? Track down those speakers in the audience. Get their complete names and addresses. Don't give your editor room to doubt your abilities.

Some reporters who cover meetings believe that their job is that of recording secretary. It is not. Questions may arise during a meeting that should be answered in a story. For example, during a planning commission meeting the members of the commission express concern that the local university, which is leasing space off campus, may pull back suddenly and create economic problems in the downtown. Even though no one on the planning commission gave a figure of how much space was being leased and how much in rent the university was paying, that information should have been in the story the next morning.

Where would it come from? After the meeting, the reporter could check with the planning commission chair or the staff planner. Either one might have a good idea. If they don't, call the university's spokesperson. If that fails, call the university official who oversees leases. And if that fails, call a real estate agent who leases to the university. The agent might give you a figure. Make sure the source for the figures is clear in the story.

The same curiosity should drive a reporter in verifying all claims in a story. If A says something about B, call B and ask. If B contradicts A, call A back.

On a larger scale, Jean Ward and Kathleen A. Hansen[3] offer advice on verification — advice they link to the traditional tests of evidence. In addition to the verification advice already given, Ward and Hansen urge reporters to make sure information is internally and externally consistent. Is information from different sources used within a story consistent? Does information derived from one source agree with other sources? When dealing with different pieces of information, Ward and Hansen urge that they be compared for quality.

Not all sources are equal, and the reporter who believes he has written a balanced story merely by quoting all sides of an issue could be wrong. A reporter has to evaluate all sources for knowledge and credibility. What is the source's reputation? A congenital liar is useless. Ward and Hansen also suggest that the reporter ensure that the information has been provided in its true context and that any statistics be validly derived. That means checking the original document. Also, does the information have one unmistakable meaning? Is it recent? Is it relevant?

A reporter must interview not only the people who speak up the most or the loudest, but also the people who are silent. Beware of people who claim to represent a segment of the community and who sound as though they might. Check with other people in the community to see if the spokesperson is self-appointed or really representative.

---

[3]Jean Ward and Kathleen A. Hansen, *Search Strategies in Mass Communication* (New York: Longman, 1987), 35.

In researching stories, reporters need to appreciate that their best sources may not be the people at the top but the people at the middle level. People at the top feel the need to hoard and guard information, for they believe that to share it is to diminish their power and authority. A reporter who relies on such people will be their servant, which is not a good position for a journalist to be in.

Reporters also need to cultivate sources on their beat. Talk to people without interviewing them. Develop a rapport. Every conversation doesn't need to result in a story. The reporter whose every contact with someone results in a story will give the source the feeling that the reporter is using the source. Cultivate sources the way you would a garden. Do a little work everyday but don't try to harvest crops everyday.

News stories begin with background work. Not doing background work is akin to starting a novel in the middle. Sources appreciate a reporter who has done some background work. A good reporter checks the clip files so she knows something about the story and so she can fine-tune her questions. Approaching a source with too broad a question could result in a rebuff.

One beginning journalist found himself losing an interview with the administrator of a hospital because his first question was: "Tell me everything you know about the open meetings law." Granted, the interview had to do with whether the hospital's board came under the law, but the question was the reporter's way of finding out what the law was. He should have read the law and background clips in order to have specific questions for the interview. Remember, specific questions usually beget specific answers. (The next chapter discusses what to do when they don't.)

SOURCES OF STORIES

Stories can be found in many places. Curious reporters listen during conversations at social events. They read specialized journals. Meetings, of course, generate follow-up story ideas. Journalists also ask themselves what might interest readers and what readers need to know. The classified advertising section of a newspaper, especially the legal advertisements, yields tips on stories. It never hurts when bumping into someone you see only occasionally to greet him or her with a "What's new?" and then to stand back and listen. Try that in a beauty shop or barber shop. Both businesses traffic in information (some people call it gossip, or unverified information).

News releases also offer story ideas. The announcement that a company has a new CEO (chief executive officer) may mean the previous one was fired. Is the company having problems? Or a new CEO may suggest a news feature or personality profile. A news release announcing shorter hours at the local library could lead an inquisitive reporter to find out what's behind the change. Perhaps a change in state funding caused a shortfall in the library's budget and forced the cutback. The taxpayers and library's users need to know about this.

Then there is investigative reporting. Andrew Schneider of the *Pittsburgh Press* once gave a talk titled "Eight steps toward successful investigative reporting,"[4] and, while this chapter focuses on the more basic reporting concepts, Schneider's ideas can still be applied. A story, he said, starts with an idea. Step two is research and identification of sources. In steps three, four and five, determine the scope and timeline of the story and develop a budget. Step six is figuring out the objectives and step seven is preparing the story. (Step eight is layout, which is beyond the scope of this book.)

Schneider says that the reporter is the best source for a story idea, since a reporter exploring her own idea will be doing something she wants to do. But he also notes, as previously mentioned, that ideas can come from editors and fellow reporters.

Idea in mind, a reporter next does some research and identifies sources. The reporter wants to make sure she's not going over old ground. She's looking for a fresh approach. Then she wants to know what and who her sources are going to be and where the information she wants can be found.

Now the reporter must determine the scope of her story. "In your initial planning," Schneider says, "you've got to know where you're going." The problem Schneider is warning against is the one of a reporter picking a topic that is too wide in scope. Such stories become unwieldy. If the reporter lacks a hypothesis, she will have difficulty doing research and determining the scope of her story. Narrowing a general area like "the city jail" to specific questions like "Are they starving the prisoners?" is an essential step in shaping good news stories, according to one editor, who adds that a journalist needs to know the difference between an area (city

---

[4]Andrew Schneider, "Eight Steps toward Successful Investigative Reporting," speech given at the Roy W. Howard Public Affairs Reporting Seminar, Bloomington, IN (September 3-4, 1988).

jail) and a story (Are they starving the prisoners?)[5]

At some newspapers, the timeline, as Schneider calls it, does matter. Some reporters have been turned loose and allowed to do research for an extended period before starting to write, although this is less likely to occur at smaller news outlets. Editors need to know how long a reporter might be researching a story so they can deploy other newsroom resources accordingly. Good stories take time, and editors know that and will allow for it.

When it comes to a budget for a story, editors need to know what kind of travel the reporter is planning. This dovetails with the earlier step of identifying sources. Some sources may be in the state capital or in Washington, D.C. Will Freedom of Information requests need to be filed? Will an attorney be needed to help in the process?

The objectives stage encompasses many of the preceding stages. Schneider says reporters need to know

- what it is they want to write or photograph,
- what has been done before,
- who are possible sources,
- what are the ground rules (Will your editors allow off-the-record interviews, etc.?),
- how long will it take and how many people are involved,
- and how much will it cost?

Story preparation caps off the reporter's work. This is where the fruit of the reporter's research pays off. Schneider warns that writing a story about something being wrong isn't of much use if the story doesn't include information on how something should be done right.

Schneider's approach isn't the only one. Ward and Hansen note the amount of back and forth that occurs between and among a reporter's sources on a particular story. The process they describe emphasizes that what a reporter learns in an interview may lead her to a library source and a source subsequently found in the library may lead the reporter back to the person interviewed. The Ward-Hansen model begins with developing the right questions and ends with the selection and synthesis of the information gathered, a process that results in a story.

Another approach comes from Robert I. Berkman, the author of *Find*

---

[5]Frank Caperton, "Finding the Story in an Idea and Other Advice to Journalism Students," speech given at the Roy W. Howard Public Affairs Reporting Seminar, Bloomington, IN (September 3-4, 1988).

It Fast: How to Uncover Expert Information on Any Subject, a book that every reporter should have.[6] Berkman starts by defining the goal of a search, locating the basic sources, obtaining the technical sources, talking to experts, redirecting focus (as needed) and getting expert review.

PERSONAL BIAS CAN AFFECT REPORTING

All manner of biases can affect the work of journalists. S. Holly Stocking and Paget H. Gross have compiled a list of problem areas that journalists and journalism students need to be aware of.[7] They note, among other things, that journalists can rely on an eyewitness, although eyewitnesses are not necessarily reliable. They warn against making too much of a compelling anecdote that contradicts scientifically collected statistics. Contrary to the oft-stated remark that exceptions prove the rule, exceptions *don't* prove anything. Stocking and Gross caution against a reporter's predisposition leading him only to those sources that confirm the story the reporter believes exists. And they advise journalists to be careful about false correlations.

Citing earlier research, Stocking and Gross warn about problems with eyewitnesses. "Observations can vary and err as a function of a variety of factors such as prejudice, temporary expectations, the types of details being observed, and stress," they write. Several years ago, clerks from stores that had been robbed picked the robber from a line-up. The news media had a field day because the person identified was a Catholic priest. So confident were they of their eyewitnesses, that the police never checked the priest's alibi. Six months later, the real robber confessed. Not surprisingly to specialists, the robber and the priest didn't even come close to looking alike. The eyewitnesses were unreliable for a variety of reasons, among them stress. When you're looking down the barrel of a pistol, you're not focusing on the person holding the gun but on the gun itself.[8]

Stocking and Gross say people fail to appreciate the validity of statistical information against the randomness of a compelling anecdote. Journalists, they say, need to be cautious that the anecdote they use fits the statistical information. People tend to generalize from anecdotes even

---

[6] It's now in the fifth edition.

[7] Holly S. Stocking and Paget H. Gross, "Understanding Errors, Biases That Can Affect Journalists," *Journalism Educator*, 43(1): 4-11 (Spring 1989).

[8] The priest, Bernard T. Pagano, died in 2006 at the age of 81. Alas, the lead on his obituary cited the mistaken identity. No doubt Father Pagano would have preferred something else.

when the anecdotes and the statistics disagree. If the anecdote doesn't fit, don't use it.

Journalists need to be cautious when seeking out sources to test a theory. They shouldn't discount sources that refute the theory. There is nothing wrong with a journalist researching a story from a particular hypothesis, but the journalist needs to work as hard at disproving the hypothesis as proving it. Some journalists, Stocking and Gross note, will discount as shoddy the sources that contradict their hypothesis.

As suggested earlier, sources need to be evaluated for their biases. A group of Republicans will most likely respond positively to a speech by a Republican president than a Democratic one. Generalizing their response to the population as a whole fails to take into account the biased nature of the source.

Correlation problems occur when, for example, a characteristic and an event are associated in meaning by someone. Stocking and Gross cite the example of associating men with long hair and demonstrations, noting that once that correlation is made journalists covering a demonstration may overestimate the number of long-haired men at an event. A reporter could also associate a long-haired man with a certain political leaning and then assume all long-haired men have the same politics. Likewise, there's the assumption that all college professors are liberals. They aren't. (Although research shows that they, like journalists, are more likely to be liberal.)

Reporting requires journalists to be aware of themselves and their sources. Good reporters are curious; they want to know everything. They examine many sources. The next chapter continues to examine the techniques reporters use and some of the sources.

Chapter 2

GATHERING INFORMATION

News comes from a variety of sources, and reporters mine those sources using a variety of techniques. Three major sources of information are interviews, reporter observation and documents.

INTERVIEWS

Interviews can range from a quick question after a town council meeting to a scheduled rendezvous. Whatever the level, a reporter needs to be prepared. The preparation can range from just thinking about the questions that need to be asked to delving into the newspaper's library or electronic database and doing extensive research on the person to be interviewed. Even Google might yield information worth having, but make sure the person uncovered in Google is the same person you're going to interview.

The best interviews often are conducted in person rather than over the telephone, via fax or e-mail. The in-person interview gives a reporter a chance to meet the subject face to face, to see the subject as the subject responds to particular questions and to observe the interview subject in his or her environment. Other technologies can be useful as reporting tools, but none is a substitute for being there in person.

The face-to-face interview suggests a greater commitment on part of the source and the journalist, and it gives the journalist the opportunity to try several approaches to getting answers to questions. The face-to-face interview sometimes means the journalist goes to the source's office, which also provides the opportunity for a journalist to learn something by chance.

Interviews also provide reporters with the possibility of getting some useful direct quotations. They allow

- people to tell the story in their own words, which can sometimes be better than the reporter's,

- reporters to gather anecdotes, which enable them to put abstract ideas into human terms,
- a reporter the opportunity to get the subject of the interview to reveal herself or himself.

Never go into an interview without having done as much research as possible about the person and the subject matter. Granted, the purpose of the interview is to learn something, but in many cases, reporters who have done their homework use interviews to confirm what they already know. Furthermore, a source will have a difficult time toying with the facts if the reporter has prepared in advance. And how does the source know? By the questions asked. The questions are evidence that a reporter has prepared herself. And if that isn't enough — if a source answers a question that is inconsistent with the reporter's research — she can always say: "According to what I've read ..." and go on to correct the record.

In preparing for an interview, a reporter will come up with a series of questions. An unskilled interviewer makes the mistake of asking only prepared questions rather than picking up cues that may lead to different questions. Listen for the unexpected and follow the trail from there. Don't stick to a script when a better story is unexpectedly unfolding.

Be careful not to interrupt someone in the middle of an answer. That could sidetrack the person and destroy the response. If, during an answer, a good question comes up, jot it down in the margin of your notepad, highlight it, and get back to it later.

Related to this advice is the saying "dumb is smart." Don't assume anything. If the subject of an interview starts to explain something you think you already understand, don't say, "Oh, I know what you mean. Here's my next question." Let the person explain, because the person may end up saying something you don't know. He or she may give you the unexpected.

Frequently, the best questions in an interview come after the formal interview is over and the reporter has put the notebook away. During the chit-chat that follows, the reporter may ask a question that catches the source off guard and results in a candid answer.

The master of this was a television detective named "Lieutenant Columbo." Played by Peter Falk, Columbo was adept at seemingly having ended an interview and being on his way out the door when he would turn around and catch the unaware suspect with this: "Just one more question, if you don't mind." Caught off guard, the respondent (who was also the murderer and had rehearsed his answers) would say something he had not planned on saying, and it provided Columbo with the insight he needed to solve the crime.

If at all possible, conduct more than one interview, especially when you don't know the subject. Stranger to stranger does not make for the best of interview conditions. Once the interview subject knows the reporter, he or she probably will be looser the next time and provide a better interview. This is especially crucial in profiles, where a reporter is trying to capture the essence of someone. If more than one interview is impossible, a reporter would do well to begin the interview with casual conversation just to set the subject at ease. Remember: Most people are not adept at dealing with the news media.

The reporter should begin the interview by stating its purpose. "I'm writing a story on the parking situation in town, Mayor Bailey, and I want to get your feelings on the matter." This is a focusing statement, both for you and for the mayor. It functions just like a headline on a story and can be useful should the subject start to stray from the topic. The reporter can always restate the opening statement as a polite way of bringing the interviewee back to the topic.

> What you're saying is interesting, Mayor Bailey, but I want to get back to the purpose of the interview — the parking situation — because your time is valuable.

The reporter sets the tone for the interview, and the wrong tone from the outset can destroy the interview. For that reason, don't ask touchy questions first. Starting off with soft questions not only relaxes the interview subject but also allows the reporter to establish a set of answers against which later answers can be compared. It is the same approach an attorney uses in court when questioning a hostile witness.

When the tough questions need to be asked, the reporter should make every effort not to antagonize the subject by acting as though the questions originated with the reporter. The reporter is not an advocate for a particular cause and should not sound like one. When tough questions need to be asked, the reporter can deflect antagonism by casting them in a way that does not offend the subject. In other words, don't put the subject of an interview on the defensive.

For example, let's say you're interviewing a controversial local politician who has not cooperated with the news media and, in fact, has been hostile. Furthermore, she doesn't like your newspaper because your newspaper has criticized her in editorials. She doesn't understand the separation between the newsroom and the editorial page, between news and commentary on the news. She thinks you're out to get her, period.

You need to preface the touchy questions in a way that makes someone else the source of the questions. Try this:

> Mayor Bailey, let me play devil's advocate[1] on this parking issue. I want to outline some different approaches to solving the parking problem and see what you think of them.

With this approach, the mayor's position is being challenged, but not by you. The mayor may react negatively, but not toward you. If that approach doesn't work, wait a few questions and then come back.

> Mayor Bailey, some people would say that the better way to solve the parking problem is not by building a new garage but by instituting a park-and-ride program. How do you feel about that?

What the reporter is trying to do is distance herself from the parking issue. The reporter is trying to get a variety of views on the issue, including the mayor's, but the reporter should not imply through her questions how she feels about the issue.

Most questions should be cast as neutrally as possible. Remember some of the comments in the last chapter about reporter bias? Imagine the reporter whose question leads the interview subject to an answer.

> Tell us about the terrible parking situation in your city, Mayor Bailey.

That question presumes the parking situation is terrible. It may be, but let the mayor tell you that. You've done your homework and you know the facts.

> Mayor Bailey, how would you describe the parking situation?
> *Not bad.*
> But, Mayor, people are complaining that there's no place to park.
> *It's their imagination.*
> But, Mayor, I checked with the police department the other day and they tell me that they've issued 50 percent more tickets for illegal parking

---

[1] In journalism, someone who politely asks questions that challenge the beliefs of the person being interviewed. In the Catholic Church, the devil's advocate was a priest who was called upon to report — warts and all — on someone who had been nominated for beatification or canonization. The position was abolished in the late 20th century.

this year than for the same period last year.
Fifty percent?
Yes.
That sounds pretty bad to me.

The tone of questions needs to fluctuate. If all of your questions are neutral, the person being interviewed will be given a platform to say anything. As the previous example shows, when the neutral question elicits an answer that doesn't square with the facts, the reporter can change the tone of the questions. Avoid questions that can be answered "yes" or "no," but when they can't be avoided, follow up with: "Can you elaborate on that?" or "Why did you say that?"

In another approach, the reporter keeps repeating the question "Why?" after every answer. You see, answers are like the descending rings to hell in Dante's *Inferno,* and if you keep asking "Why?" the subject of the interview will keep digging deeper to answer the question. A variation of "Why?" is "Why's that?" The repetition approach suggests that people answer questions superficially. They're not trying to deceive; they believe they have answered the question. When a reporter keeps asking "Why?" the person being questioned works a little harder on the answer and a better answer usually results. The repeated question suggests that the reporter is looking for a precise answer. The source appreciates that. After all, imprecision reflects badly on the source.

Make sure that the subject of an interview labels fact, opinion and second-hand observation. Mayor Bailey may say that the police have issued 25 percent more parking tickets this year, and while that sounds like a fact, the reporter should confirm the figure with the police. Trust but verify. Just as a matter of routine, a reporter should attempt to verify all facts or, as the legendary advice from a Chicago newsroom goes: "If your mother says she loves you, check it out."

Make sure that you understand the answer to a question, and if you don't, tell the subject of the interview that you don't. The person should be willing to recast the answer so it's clear to you. If it isn't clear to you, you're not going to explain it well in your story. Furthermore, if you get an answer that doesn't seem to fit, ask how the answer relates to the situation being discussed. This can be done agreeably simply by saying: "I don't see how that fits. Would you tie it in for me, please?"

During the interview, if at all possible, don't tip your hand. Don't tell anyone your interview schedule. Let the subjects of interviews infer where you've been and where you're going, but never confirm unless you need to challenge a statement. For example, a banker once said to a reporter during an interview: "Well, you'll see this in the court documents anyway." The reporter, who was new to the job, didn't let on that he hadn't thought of looking at the court documents, but you can be sure that he was in the courthouse at 8 a.m. the next day. By acting dumb, he was led to a gold mine.

A reporter can lead the subject of an interview in more ways than one. Neutral questions, of course, are one way of avoiding this problem. Reporters must also be aware of other signals they send — signals that could be misinterpreted by the subject of an interview. For example, reporters should be consistent in their note-taking. Don't convey to someone that what he is saying isn't important by suddenly stopping the note-taking process. Even if you're writing down trivia, write it down. Besides, it may not be trivia later.

Also, reporters can use various cues to keep the subject of an interview talking. Saying "uh-huh" or "OK" or nodding your head reinforces the person being interviewed and he wants to keep talking. Broadcast journalists frequently nod their heads to keep someone talking and reduce the necessity of cutting into an interview to keep it going. This technique aids the videographer, but it has practical advantages for the print journalist as well.

Another effective approach is silence. Most people abhor a verbal vacuum and will keep talking to fill it. As long as they stay on the topic, let them talk. Who knows what they'll say?

OBSERVATION

Here is the beginning of the first of seven stories on people who were discharged from mental asylums under the guise of social reform. The series was written by Donald C. Drake and published in the *Philadelphia Inquirer*.[2]

> Dawn was just beginning to brighten the eastern sky. It was a sunrise that went unnoticed by the man asleep on the steam grate opposite Rittenhouse Square, folded up between a concrete trash receptacle and a newspaper vending machine.
>
> An electric digital display in a nearby bank window gave the time: 5:54.
>
> The sleeping man was wearing baggy corduroy pants, a wool hat, a shirt and a dirty blanket worn over his shoulders like a shawl.

---

[2]Donald C. Drake, "The Forsaken: How America Has Abandoned Thousands in the Name of Social Progress," *The Philadelphia Inquirer* (July 18, 1982), p. 1.

His eyes still closed, the man reached into his open shirt to scratch at the lice, as he had been doing all night. A bread truck roared by on Walnut Street, followed a few minutes later by a milk truck. Then it was quiet again.

The sidewalk, which in two hours would be crowded with people hurrying to their jobs, was deserted now. The only signs of life were the man and a lone car that waited obediently at an empty intersection for the light to change.

The man started to stir and, still without opening his eyes, pushed himself up to a sitting position, leaning back against the concrete trash receptacle. Joggers began to appear across the street, resolutely circling the park, too intent on their exercise to notice the solitary man.

It took a long time, maybe 15 or 20 minutes, for the man to wake up fully, but by 6:15 his eyes were open wide, staring down the elegant street that had been his home for three years. At first he did nothing but sit, stare and scratch.

Another day was beginning for Jim Logue Crawford, 69, former mental hospital patient.

How do you suppose Drake captured that vignette? Do you think that perhaps he awoke at 7 a.m. and went to his office, then walked to Rittenhouse Square, found Jim Crawford and interviewed him? Or do you think he was in Rittenhouse Square observing Crawford when he awoke?

You're right. Drake was in Rittenhouse Square on his 18-month tracking of released mental patients in Philadelphia. He wanted to know how they lived, so he observed them. It is part of Drake's approach to be, in his words, "more than a facts and figure reporter."

Reporters should use observation in all manner of stories, from the most basic to the most extensive. Take a fire, for example. Is the account of a fire all facts and figures? Well, it can be. Somewhere the time of the alarm is recorded and the number of trucks and firefighters dispatched is known. It's often not hard to find the owners of the property. The insurance company, among others, can give an estimate of the damage. Those are facts and figures, and should be reported. But what about the reporter's observations? They're valid also and can be made part of the story.

Here, for example, is a story about a fire. (The complete story is in Chapter 4.). The reporter's observations are *italicized:*

> A *quick-burning* fire roared through the body and parts shop of D&M Chrysler Plymouth Inc. Sunday morning, destroying seven cars and *reducing the concrete-block building to a blackened shell.*
>
> Fire officials are estimating the loss to the business at $800,000. The

owners of the dealership, Daniel and Michael Faretta, had only $290,000 insurance on the building and its contents, according to City Fire Chief Reynold D. Santone. ...

Good reporters include in their notes not only what they heard and read, but also what they saw. Good reporters draw heavily on all of their senses. Not only does a journalist record what he sees, but what he hears and smells.

Recording observations requires a reporter to function more like a vacuum cleaner than an editor. Throw out your biases, your stereotypes, your predispositions. Keep an open mind. Rather than making a judgment that an observation is not worth recording, a reporter should include it in his notes. Later, especially when working with a writing coach, the reporter may discover in his notebook the telling observation that binds the story.

What should a reporter observe?

Tom Wolfe suggests paying attention to people's status in life.[3] Look at their furniture, how they decorate their house, what color scheme they used. Others suggest reporting body language. In one memorable political campaign, two opponents sat next to each other during a candidates' night. One was running a dirty campaign. Throughout the night, the other, a woman, sat legs crossed and knees pointing almost at a right angle away from her opponent. It was clear she did not like the person.

Also report physical characteristics. You don't have to say someone is big. You might say that when the person sits, he fills a chair with no room to spare. Look for touching. Some people touch others unconsciously. Other people abhor touching and recoil if touched. Touching can also suggest intimacy between two people, an intimacy they may be trying to keep private. Look for the way people interact — how something is said rather than what is said.

How people dress is worth observing. But, as with any observation, don't make judgments; merely report. Let the reader make the judgments. Let the reader decide if the person with a green shirt and red tie and argyle socks and gray suit is badly dressed. (Find out first if the person isn't color blind. "Excuse me, Mayor, but I can't help noticing the color scheme you chose today.")

Also remember that your observations are exactly that — yours — and that any event comes with multiple perspectives. The observations of

---

[3]Tom Wolfe, *The New Journalism,* with an anthology edited by Tom Wolfe and E. W. Johnson (New York: Harper & Row, 1973).

others are worth getting because they can reinforce yours or help fill out the picture you are trying to draw.

Just as a notepad and recorder have been useful for journalists, so has the camera. Film cameras, however, were clumsy to use because the journalist needed to get film developed and prints made. But the contents of a digital camera can be transferred to a computer for instant viewing and review by the writer. An inexpensive digital camera is a great reporting tool.

Observation requires the reporter to behave like a fly on the wall — unnoticed and unobtrusive. Don't annoy anyone. Just watch. Take it all in, and then use it to be more than a facts and figures reporter.

DOCUMENTS

Documents are a great source of information. A valuable document can be something as simple as a one-page memo to an annual budget or an income report by a nonprofit group to the federal government. A document, assuming it is not a forgery, is proof of something. It may prove a past action, or it may suggest a future action. Journalists love documents in any form — parchment, paper, film, digital.

One of the most basic of all documents is the telephone book. There a reporter can find a name, an address, verify a spelling, check an area or zip code, or locate a business. Another useful directory is a city directory in which the town is divided block by block. Such a directory tells who lives side by side and who lives across the street. Such a directory gives the phone numbers of each person, and it also has a cross listing that allows a reporter to locate someone by address or alphabetically. One reporter covered a fire by telephone in a town 40 miles away merely by finding people who lived near the scene of the fire, calling them on the telephone and interviewing them.

Still another standard document is the map. Good maps are divided into grids and list street names and grid coordinates. Maps help people see relationships. Some maps show physical characteristics, such as forests and mountains and the highways and byways. Roads are designated by ownership and responsibility, so it's useful to have a quick source to figure out if a particular road is a U.S. route, a state route or a municipal street.

Government offices are repositories of documents. On the local level are planning and zoning documents, official correspondence, contracts, the results of health and code inspections, and so on. Courthouses offer, in addition to court decisions, copies of wills and deeds, listings of property ownership and the assessed value of the property. Many legal transactions must be recorded with some office in the courthouse, and with the possible exception of sealed court decisions or court actions regarding juveniles, these transactions are available for public consumption.

One immediate source of documents is the newspaper's library. A good newspaper, even a small one, attempts to have on hand certain local documents that are referred to from time to time. Within this category are the newspaper's own clip and computer files. What the reporter can glean from the library is whether or not the story has already been done or what related stories might have been done locally. Checking other newspaper Web sites to see what they've done on a particular subject is useful.

Good reporters, by the way, are not lulled into believing that what they retrieve from an electronic database is gospel. Information in many databases is only as good as the sources it was derived from. Just because Google provides a link to a search term doesn't mean the link is accurate. The digital age has allowed anyone to create a Web site.

Good sources are those that are overseen by experts. A good example would be the *Encyclopedia Britannica*, which has been compiled by experts known for their depth of knowledge about a particular subject. A good example of a source to stay away from is Wikipedia, which bills itself as a free encyclopedia. It's an encyclopedia in name only. Anything free should be automatically suspect. Wikipedia is problematic because just about anyone can edit any entry and instances of erroneous information appearing have been noted in the news media from time to time.[4]

A library that is a repository for state and federal documents — known as a Federal Depository Library — is an excellent place to do research, especially if the topic is national and the reporter is adapting it to the local situation. Such a library holds copies of congressional hearings, which offer not only a great deal of background but also the names of people the reporter can call. Market and corporate information is probably available in such a library. Also available are thousands of reference books, magazines and reviews. And while a particular book may not focus directly on the issue being researched, its index and bibliography might allow the reporter to find more specific sources. One of the best resources

---

[4]In what is perhaps the most egregious case, someone edited an entry about a respected journalist to suggest he had been involved in the assassination of President Kennedy and his brother Bobby. The entry also said the journalist had been a Nazi and lived in the Soviet Union for a period. One can imagine the lead on the journalist's obituary based on the false entry in Wikipedia. Fortunately he was able to get it corrected.

in any library is the librarian himself. Librarians are experts at finding credible information or knowing how to find such information and being able to distinguish between credible sources and questionable sources.

NOTE-TAKING

Taking accurate notes is a critical part of good reporting. The best reporting effort in the world can be undermined by inaccurate or illegible notes.

The computer and the photocopying machine have reduced the chance for error, simply because no human hand intercedes in the note-taking process. But when covering a meeting or interviewing someone, a reporter relies on a notebook and a pencil or pen.

Note-taking is an individual art, and as long as the notes are clear and accurate when the reporter sits down to write, the particular approach to taking notes does not matter. One reporter's methods may not work for another reporter.

Unless you have learned shorthand, you will need to make up your own. Look for words that readily lend themselves to abbreviation or a short form and develop a standardized shorthand. For example:

Shorthand	Meaning	Shorthand	Meaning
/w	with	gov	government
/wo	without	fed	federal
thru	through	demo	demonstration
&	and	rel	related
devel	develop	bus	business
devels	developers	orig	original
b4	before	alt	alternate
hier	higher	pt	point
hi	high	st	state
½	one-half	pop	population
rec	recommendation	est	estimate
appx	approximate	acc	according to

So if someone said: "We need an estimate of the state and federal populations before we can make a recommendation on development," the reporter's shorthand might produce: "we need est st-fed pops b4 make rec on devel."

Each reporting situation presents unique opportunities for shorthand. For example, a reporter usually abbreviates the names of speakers at a meeting, being careful not to shorten anyone's name to a single letter so that the reporter doesn't confuse the person with someone else whose last name begins with the same letter.

Also make sure a question ends with a question mark. That may sound silly, unless you realize that note taking is not the art of writing down every word, but usually just the key words of an interview or meeting. So if City Council Member Beverly Jones asks if taxes are going to increase next year, the reporter's notebook might look like this: *J: taxes up?*

Verbatim note-taking has its drawbacks. It's more important for a reporter to understand what is being said before writing anything down. Not everything said is worth recording. Listen for stage directions and rhetorical throat-clearing that really mean nothing, except as facilitators in a meeting. If the chairman of a meeting says, "OK, what do we do next?" why write it down? And if someone says, "Let's do parking," why write it down until everyone has spoken and the group had decided what to discuss next?

Rhetorical throat-clearing may be worth getting into your notes, but not at first sound. Rhetorical throat-clearing includes words and phrases that a speaker begins a statement with as he or she gropes mentally for the right words to make the salient point he or she wants to make. For example:

> "After careful thought and in my considered opinion, I say we don't raise taxes."

The salient point is the speaker's statement not to raise taxes. That's what the reporter must get in his notes. The throat-clearing is unnecessary.

Elsewhere in a notepad are the reporter's checkmarks. They indicate items in the notebook that — after the meeting — the reporter has to check back with someone to clarify a fact or a statement. Such checking is laudatory and professional. It enables a journalist to write an accurate story and also develop credibility with sources. Some journalists might use a question mark to signal an ambiguous line in his notes, but a question mark could be read as indicating a question. The check mark says "check."

Some other tricks come to mind. One journalist uses a grid when covering some multiple-speaker events as a way of cataloguing their positions. For example, in the coverage of a candidate's night, she set up a grid with the names of the six candidates across the top and the issues, as they arose, down the left hand side. She still took thorough notes, but she used the grid to develop an instant summary of where the candidates stood on the issues. The grid became a story-organizing device, since she could organize her story by lumping together the candidates who agreed on the issues. It also enabled her to contrast statements and positions.

One favorite notebook is a 6-by-9-inch pad with a rule down the center. The center rule enables reporters, such as sportswriters, to use halves of the page to record actions by the opposing teams. For a football game, a sportswriter can go down the left side for one team's offensive drive and then switch to the other half after a score or a punt or a fumble and record the other team on that half of the page. The sportswriter can use the blank space opposite her notes to put asterisks to signify key plays that she wants to get into her story. Such an approach doubles as an outline and enables the writer to begin writing as the game is ending.

Some beginning journalists use digital recorders for the most routine events. A digital recorder is useful as a back-up in a long interview and can be played back to check a quote or a fact. But a recorder is not infallible, and its use should never supersede a notebook and several sharp pencils or fresh pens.

One of the country's best nonfiction writers, Tracy Kidder, seldom uses a tape-recorder. He doesn't like them because the tapes must be transcribed, the recorders are unwieldy and they miss subtleties. "Also," Kidder once said, "a tape-recorder tends to make me lazy, so I might stop taking notes and miss a lot."[5]

Gathering information requires journalists to explore a variety of sources and use a variety of techniques, all aimed at producing accurate stories. The best stories come from the best research.

---

[5]Michael Schumacher, "How Tracy Kidder Writes His Books," *Writer's Digest* (November 1990), p. 33.

Chapter 3

NEWS EVALUATION

No newspaper can possibly publish every story it receives through local sources and over the wires, so it falls to editors to decide which stories see print. The choice, some days, is easy; other days hard. After all, a newspaper uses perhaps no more than 10 percent of all the wire news it receives; the editor decides which 10 percent along with what local news and how long it all will be.

WHAT MAKES NEWS

Several years ago a member of the Gannett staff reviewed the front pages of all of Gannett's (then) 85[1] daily newspapers. The staff person's job was to see how diverse the editors' news judgments were. The staff person found that the 85 dailies had 42 different lead stories, of which 35 were local. All in all, the 85 dailies covered 300 different stories on their front pages. In effect, what is newsworthy varies from city to city.

As noted in the Introduction, popular wisdom about journalism says newsworthiness is perhaps best captured in the following maxim: *If a dog bites a man, that's not news; if a man bites a dog, that's news.* There might be some truth in that statement, but it certainly doesn't provide enough guidance to make good news judgments. In fact, it has led to the publication of some silly news stories, such as one about a woman who tried to bite a policeman after her dog wouldn't, or the time a man, angered by a howling dog, bit it three times. It also didn't deter the late Adlai Stevenson from once commenting: An editor is a person who separates the wheat from the chaff and prints the chaff.

Newspapers of old placed a lot of emphasis on crime, which resulted in an unending, unrelated series of stories about, for example, home burglaries without giving a reporter time to dig deeper to survey the entire scene, to tell the reader about the crime wave and how to avoid it. When

---

[1] In 2006 the number had increased to 90.

you consider how cheap it is to hire someone to merely copy down the police report daily and spit it back at readers, you can understand why the police station became such a great source of news. The analogy today is the newspaper or television station that devotes a great amount of space, time or footage to automobile accidents. Such information is easily and cheaply obtained. Thus, it is newsworthy.

Beginning newswriters and editors are often given a list of what constitutes newsworthiness. Recall the list compiled from 14 newswriting textbooks by Professor Wallace B. Eberhard of the University of Georgia and presented in the Introduction. But news is more than a list of conditions, elements and qualities. What was the news in the Pentagon Papers case of 1971? After all, the papers revealed history, not current war policy. No secrets there. What the papers really revealed was a government policy of deceit, and by providing that insight into the government, the papers also provided the citizens of the country with a better opportunity to govern, or at least generated a more watchful attitude on the part of the governed toward the government. After all, someone had abused their consent and trust; their news outlets told them that.

News can sometimes defy compartmentalization. The man-bites-dog formula that says news is black and white: either it is news or isn't. But some rules or values stand out.

Interest to Readers

To be newsworthy, a story must have interest to many of the readers of the newspaper. That can be tricky. Take the New York *Daily News* and *The New York Times*. The murder of someone in New York City might be a big story in the *News* but gets barely a mention in the *Times*. But if some official in a program to eradicate honeybees from Texas dies of a bee sting, the *Times* might consider the article worth the lead of its National page and worthy of a reference line on Page One. The *News* wouldn't use the story. The people who read the *Times* know that generally the *Times* is not interested in local news unless it relates to a larger pattern or is national or international in scope. The federal bailing out of New York City was newsworthy to the *New York Times* because of its implications for all old cities as much as because New York City is the home of the *Times*. The same problem in Detroit or Cleveland or Chicago would merit coverage by the *Times*, but not by the *News*.

Proximity

Other news categories include proximity, such as the death of a local person in a local accident or in an accident elsewhere. The dentist who cut down one of only four white ash trees in a small community so he could put in a driveway to his office parking lot was not only news in that community, he was Page One news for three days running. The dentist had offended the community by violating the tree ordinance.

Impact

Impact on readers determines a story's newsworthiness, which is why government receives a lot of coverage. The lack of impact is also newsworthy. A bad winter storm that floods Los Angeles and does nothing to San Francisco is newsworthy in both communities, for different reasons. Farmers in Illinois will read with interest about the problems of farmers in Nebraska, because Illinois farmers are trying to learn if the problem is headed their way and if a solution exists.

Timeliness

Timeliness often determines news. An event that happened last week may lack newsworthiness, but an event that is 2 years old could be worth Page One.

When the *New York Times*, for example, discovered that an unpublicized Canadian trial had concluded that an oil company had once inflated prices, the *Times* ran the story on its front page, even though the issue had been resolved two years before. It was news because the issue of price gouging during an energy crisis was a current event that the 2-year-old trial shed some light on. Similarly, confirmation of massive earthquakes in China is newsworthy even when the confirmation occurs years after the event. Any society that operates under a closed-door policy invites the curious to snoop around when that door is opened a crack.

Scientific discoveries — even the hint of some — rate coverage because of the way these discoveries may affect the lives of readers. Any seeming step toward the cure of cancer is sure to generate headlines and magazine cover stories, even if the researchers taking the step affirm that it is but a small one. The hint is newsworthy.

Archaeological events, especially those that give clarity to the present, are newsworthy. But even if they do not, revealing secrets of ancient civilizations appeals to the curiosity of many. When Mozart's first symphony was authenticated, it was front page news in *The New York Times*. Likewise, when an American archaeologist discovered chronic lead poisoning after an analysis of skeletons of Romans killed by the eruption of Mount Vesuvius in A.D. 79, that was front-page news. A story about a book challenging the work of Margaret Mead, an anthropologist of international repute, also received front-page treatment.

Weather

Weather is always newsworthy. Parents want to know how to dress their children for school tomorrow; farmers want to know if it will be dry enough to harvest or wet enough to get seeds growing. Is an early frost expected? Did the week of rain refresh the diminishing local water supply? Weather coverage, in fact, has improved in recent years. Some newspapers devote an entire page to it, whereas others at least provide information beyond today, tonight and tomorrow. Any newspaper in a mobile community knows that today's reader may be jetting to Japan and wants to know weather conditions in Tokyo as well as locally.

State and Local News

State and local news still rank as the major focal points in newspapers. Research shows that no other news outlet provides the state and local news the way newspapers do. The wire services generally provide stories on major state government initiatives, and because whatever the state government does affects everyone, that makes it newsworthy. After state and local news, other newsworthy categories include (in any order depending on the newspaper) crime, education, cultural events, health, social problems, obituaries, labor, environment, sports, disasters, tragedies, politics, business and fashion. On any given day, of course, the editors of different newspapers will rank the events differently, and what might be worth Page One in one newspaper could rate no more than the bottom of the first break (or section) page. By the same token, the editors may have so much Page One-worthy news that they create a second front page to accommodate it.

Any newspaper with television and/or radio competition finds itself doing well when it plays up state and local news — both areas not well covered by the other two media. With a state capital bureau and back-up from their wire services, newspapers can daily present state news packages that include reports on how local legislators vote. The electronic media can present some of that, but not in the convenient, unperishable form of a newspaper. The newspaper that puts its strength into local coverage (broadly defined) increases readership and fulfills an obligation to that readership. That in no way means national and international events should be ignored. Too often an international crisis springs on newspaper readers because the newspaper has not published background stories about the events leading to the crisis. The newspaper has failed to keep its readers informed, which is one of the functions of newspapers.

International News

International news is more than stories on coups and earthquakes. In fact, a great of international coverage has shifted from disasters to economics as more and more jobs in the United States have been lost to lower-paid workers in Third World countries. A television tube manufacturer that closed its plant in Pennsylvania because it could not compete with overseas plants also dismantled the structure and sold it and the equipment to China.

The use of international news varies frequently, depending on how much the international event affects people in the United States or by how much of an investment a newspaper may have made in covering foreign events. The civil war in Vietnam would have meant nothing to U.S. readers until Congress debated whether President Eisenhower should send troops to replace the defeated French. Eisenhower didn't and Vietnam remained relatively unnewsworthy (unfortunately) for another decade.

Nearly two decades after the Vietnam War ended, a page editor on deadline missed a story about the death of a U.S. military adviser in El Salvador and was upbraided for not seeing the parallels between that death and the deaths of American advisers in Vietnam in the early 1960s. Decades later, when the United States seemed bogged down in a war in Iraq, the news media were much quicker to draw parallels with Vietnam, resurrecting the word "quagmire" to compare the two wars. If any editing moral can be drawn from this, it is that good editors are steeped in history. They understand that the past is prologue. They reject the notion that today is the only day that counts.

The Story Behind the Event

Editors who daily evaluate stories for publication or broadcast realize that the spot or breaking news that was once the staple of many news organizations no longer serves the total reader. Editors realize that what makes news is often the story behind the event, the trend, be it a crime wave or a back-to-basics movement in education. Editors now look for stories that tell about people and what makes them act. Editors want stories that tell how people think.

Social questions mean a lot to the editors making news judgments. Editors want to know how stories will affect readers, involve readers, attract readers. Does the story say something important, and does it say it well? What's in the story for the reader? None of those categories defends gimmicks that attempt to trick readers into the paper; good editors know that news long on tricks but short on substance detracts from the overall news product.

Editors too realize that news can be more than bad or sensationalistic or saber rattling. They know that behind every story people exist and that the readers want to know about the people in the story as well as the story itself. This attempt to put stories in people terms does not obviate an editor's job to publish the news, nor does it change the substance of news, just the approach. The evolving process of defining news continues today; it is that tension of evolution that makes news evaluation more than just a cataloguer's job.

The Story Conference and Copy Flow

The main editors meet daily for the story conference, at which time they tell what stories they have and make a pitch to the managing editor for their biggest story to appear on Page One. The managing editor usually makes the final decision on Page One content.

The conference, known at some newspapers as the budget meeting, is usually held about four hours before deadline, or, in the case of a multiple-edition newspaper, the first deadline, which, for a morning metropolitan newspaper, is between 7 p.m. and 9 p.m. All section editors appear with enough copies of their budgets for everyone at the meeting. Stories are described in a few sentences, and where known, their length is given. Is "art" (photographs and graphics) available? The budgets tell that. The photo editor's budget, by the way, is the finished photograph.

The editors agree on where the stories will go. One of the important benefits to this coordination is to ensure that sections of the paper are not using the same or similar stories and thus competing with each other. Overlap is avoided.

Also present at this meeting are the design editors. They know what the lead stories are for each section and the relative value of all other stories in the section. Because they also know the estimated length of the stories, they can return to their desks and begin designing pages. The photo editor sits on the operations desk, deciding what size to make each photo.

Throughout the day, reporters have been filing stories with their respective assignment desks. On those desks, the editors evaluate the stories in preparation for the story conference. They also check to make sure the reporter has covered the story well and hasn't missed the lead.

The assignment editors then release the stories to their respective copy desks. The chief copy editor (known as the "slot") assigns each story to one of the several copy editors. They, in turn, read the stories carefully, make corrections, talk to reporters about unclear sentences and bad organization and then send the story back to the chief copy editor, who checks the work of the reporter and the copy editor.

Once a page is designed, photocopies of the page go to the respective copy desks. There copy editors check headline assignments on the stories they have edited. They then pull up a copy of the stories they edited and write headlines. Again, the chief copy editor checks the work before sending it to the production department for paste-up. Copy editors also write captions for all photographs and graphics and read page proofs. (Page proofs are copies of the page as it will appear in print.)

Putting Theory into Practice

Imagine yourself the editor of a 25,000-circulation daily in a 65,000-population college city in the center of the state. Your newspaper has television competition from stations in towns 45 and 65 miles away, stations that send crews into your town from time to time. You are 90 miles away from your state capital. The university's football team is always in the top 20 and the university has an otherwise solid sports program. The university has 30,000 students and is the largest public university in the state. You're the wire editor and must make sure nothing of local interest for any department is overlooked. Let us go through some items, compiled from several Associated Press news digests, which should catch your eye.

One story that should be of interest comes from Washington, D.C., with this lead: "In a case that could add to the cost of local bus service, the Supreme Court is considering whether publicly owned mass transit systems should be required to pay federal minimum wages and overtime." You pull it because you know that local government runs the bus service in your town and on campus and that it is federally subsidized. This story, by the way, cries out for a local reaction sidebar.

A federal judge in a nearby state rules that the state's recently adopted plan for inspecting cars violates the Federal Clean Air Act. Because your state is about to adopt the same plan, this story immediately catches your attention. You have an added interest because the judge making the ruling is federal, meaning that the precedent could be applied outside that judge's area. A call to the state transportation people is also in order.

From your state capital comes a story saying that the state's debt to the federal government over the state's unemployment compensation fund will continue to soar this fiscal year, according to federal sources. Certainly of interest.

From Washington, a U.S. Supreme Court agreement to decide whether several states, yours among them, will have to repay more than $60 million in education aid the federal government claims was misspent. Who would pay the bill if the court rules against the states? Does this portend a tax increase? And you live in a college town, so education stories are usually of interest. Pull this story.

Here's a story from a city 3,000 miles away. The lead: "Researchers say they have developed a low-cost, high-performance solar cell that may convert sunlight into electricity for utilities more cheaply than oil- or gas-fired turbines." Well, you're not in the Sunshine Belt, but you know that among your readers is a small but loyal environmental contingent and they would certainly want to know more about this.

A story from Battle Creek, Mich., reports that a cereal company is introducing low-sodium versions of two of its cereals in four test markets. Among other things, this is a consumer story and that should give it an automatic green flag. Of course, many residents are health conscious and this is the kind of information that might interest them. And finally, the university has a nutrition department. In fact, a reporter could get a sidebar reaction story from the head of nutrition.

Then there's the story of the woman whose boyfriend sued to halt her from having an abortion. Abortion is a big issue among your readers. Use the story.

You also see this advisory about a feature story that will come later: "At Earlham College in Indiana, a Quaker school where students can major in Peace and Global Studies, officials are coming to the aid of young men who refuse to register for the draft." Given that 48 percent of the student body at your university is male and eligible, you should use this story.

You should also use the story, in fact, packaged with the preceding, from Cleveland telling that "a Mennonite college student charged with failing to register with the Selective Service has testified in court that draft registration implies the United States is preparing for war." Be careful, by the way, not to make the mistake of thinking that Quakers and Mennonites are one in the same.

Also consider for the package, from St. Paul, Minn.: "A student group wants a federal judge to block a law forcing college students to register for the draft before they can receive financial aid until he decides its constitutionality."

Then there's the Washington story about two congressmen who have introduced a bill to finance repairs of the nation's roads and bridges. One of the congressman comes from your district. Use it.

You also encounter three stories about the National Collegiate Athletic Association, including one that says the NCAA has prepared legislation that would exempt it from federal antitrust laws and protect its monopoly on televising college football. With the university's football team a regular on television on Saturday afternoons, this story is of local interest.

And because it is the primary election season and your state is a swing state, you run the stories about the three contenders from one party crisscrossing the state just before the election. You also run some wirephotos. After all, it is not every presidential election that voters in your state might select the nominees.

Then there is a story about Japan restricting imports from South Africa in response to South Africa's apartheid laws. Your readership includes a large number of people interested in this issue.

You also discover that at the last minute of the legislative calendar, the state's governing bodies — thanks to a maneuver by your local senator — have passed a historical tax reform bill and sent it to the governor. That's probably the lead, with sidebars, including a telephone interview with the senator.

The good editor recognizes the variety of interests in the newspaper's audience and attempts to provide for all interests.

HARD VS. SOFT NEWS

One of the important changes in the content of some newspapers in the 1970s was a new emphasis on so-called "soft" news. Soft news sometimes showed up as a feature story on what to wear when sledding or as a gossipy tract on show business people. But hard news became soft news in the hands of skilled writers who put feature rather than hard leads on stories, who deferred time elements and put the emphasis on people. Typically, sportswriters excelled in this field because they had been doing it longer (although not necessarily better).

Some newspapers went overboard in soft news and turned their front-page content over to magazine-style stories. The readers, though, did not want to be puffed to death; they still wanted to know what happened in the world and they didn't want to have to hunt through a collection of stories on rock stars and recipes to find that. The newspapers had put too much soft news on their pages at the expense of hard. Editors forgot that

The National Observer, which distinguished itself with what many would consider a soft approach to news, died in the late 1970s just as many newspapers were joining the soft news parade. Some editors missed the message.

Just because a news story is not breaking news does not mean it is not important. In-depth stories, for example, provide an extra dimension for readers. They are not soft news. They can show up as an in-depth look at credit policies at local banks, an analysis of cancer research, a look at the housing market.

The lack of a breaking news focus should not detract from the value of any story. The reader has to know what city council did last night, of course, but reporters, under assignment from editors, should be examining the action for its long-term implications, and when those implications are found, editors should be as willing to display the story on Page One.

THE WANT TO KNOW VS. THE NEED TO KNOW

Readers can be a notoriously fickle bunch and can throw curve balls to editors attempting to learn what readers want in their newspaper. The 1970s preoccupation with soft news at some newspapers went over the brink and brought out readers complaining that their newspapers lacked news.

By the same token, those same readers seemed to complain about an overemphasis on some government reporting. Those who complained should not be faulted, but their editors need guidance on how to better present the news. The reader who asks, "Why am I reading this? I don't need to know it," reflects poor presentation on the part of the newspaper. Often the reader does need to know the information but has not been told that. Government stories especially can appear either as mundane outlays of words or as a gaggle of officials trading barbs, and the reader will be none the wiser to the story's value (if any). A college newspaper published a story about the questionable use of funds by a branch of the student government, and readers complained that the paper was "crucifying" the student leaders. The newspaper's stories failed to say: "The money in question came from student fees. The cost of this venture came from your pocket."

Too frequently decisions are made that affect people, but they never realize it until it is too late because the newspaper failed to make the issue clear. Any time an editor reads a story and asks, "Why does the reader want to know this?" the editor has placed the burden of proof on the newspaper. Such stories need more polish so the reader can see the obvious impact. Don't give the readers something whose value to them is not clear.

A First Amendment Obligation

Editors who complain about closed-door meetings but never send a reporter to attempt to get through the closed door do not discharge their First Amendment obligation; instead, they duck it. Such editors no doubt write editorials bemoaning the public's lack of access to government and suggest that someone should do something about it. Sadly, the editors never suggest that they themselves should take the initiative.

All news media, of course, should never presume to serve as the public's surrogate, although that has happened. Such a self-appointed role highlights inconsistencies when journalists sit in on private meetings and do not report the outcome. Who then is served — the journalist or the public? Obviously, not the public.

The news media must realize, though, that because of their resources they by default serve as the public's representative at public events. Their presence assumes an interest on the part of the public, the missing audience, not the officials conducting the event. Having taken on the surrogate role, the news media must carry through, that is their First Amendment obligation.

The news media must also provide the information each member of a democracy needs to properly discharge his or her role in society. That means the news media must provide more depth, even when there is no heat, and more light where usually only shadows exist. Some editors would complain that such proposals are expensive, but they would be the editors who have for too long filled their newsholes, in print and on the air, with easy-to-get stories that require little (if any) legwork and can be mechanically put together without much thought. The people who do such work receive low pay, and it is no wonder why. The commitment to quality goes beyond one day's news to a feeling that the flow of democracy turns on a continuing obligation to observe and report for everyone. The editors who decided to publish the Pentagon Papers were exercising their First Amendment obligation to the fullest. Seemingly lesser situations arise daily throughout the world of journalism and good editors rise to the challenge.

Chapter 4

ELEMENTS OF A NEWS STORY

A good journalist strives to provide a factual, balanced, accurate, informative account of the news.[1] The typical news story is designed to convey news quickly, clearly and unambiguously. The typical news story is not a great work of literature. Rather, it is prose with a purpose — its form dictated by function.

A STORY'S ELEMENTS

Before writing a news story, beginning journalists should know the elements of a news story. A news story usually contains these elements: the lead, a time element, specific information rather than general information, sources, attribution, direct and indirect quotations, and sentences and paragraphs.

The Lead
In a typical news story, the lead is the first paragraph. It is usually no more than one sentence. The lead concisely tells the reader or listener what the story is about. Eventually, you will see leads that are longer and leads that are subtle, but for now, focus on the basics. Here is a lead from a typical news story:

> BOGOTA, Colombia — At least 40 gunmen launched a series of attacks in two impoverished neighborhoods in North Colombia, killing

---

[1] Many mass communication researchers argue that journalists cannot be objective and that their stories are biased. This is a complex debate that goes beyond the scope of this book. For purposes here, the assumption is that journalists who follow the rules of journalism outlined in this book can achieve "relative objectivity," which means their stories can reveal truth, even if that ideal is not always achieved. For more information on the concept of "relative objectivity," see David Demers, *Global Media: Menace or Messiah?* (Cresskill, NJ: Hampton Press, 1999), pp. 113-114.

eight people and destroying a local shop with a grenade, police said Sunday.

The Time Element

The time element tells when the news happened. Usually, it is confined to a day or a period in a day, such as Sunday or Sunday night or yesterday or yesterday afternoon, depending on the newspaper's style.[2] A more specific time may appear later. In the lead, above, for example, the time element reflects when the police announced the incident, not when the incident occurred. As the story says later, the incident occurred a day earlier.

Related to the time element is the tense of most of the verbs in a typical news story. Most of the verbs are past tense. Journalists can choose from a variety of tenses, all variations of present, past and future. But since by definition news is something that happened, past tense is appropriate for most news stories.

Specific Information

Specific information allows the reader and listener to know exactly what the story is about. Specific information includes names, ages, addresses, titles, votes. Rather than say a fire caused "much damage," a journalist will ask experts for their estimate of the damage and include that information in her story. The more specific information a story contains, the more credible it will be with readers.

Sources

The experts and other people providing information in a story are called sources. A story can have one source or many sources. Sources should have names, although sometimes sources have to be anonymous. Sources can also be documents and other publications. In the lead from Colombia, the police are the source.

Attribution

When a source speaks in a story, information is attributed to that source. Attribution lets the reader or listener know where information

---

[2]Some newspapers allow the use of "yesterday" and "tomorrow" in news stories, but Associated Press style uses the day of the week (Monday, Tuesday, etc.) outside of directly quoted material. The tense of the verb in the sentence distinguishes whether the day is in the past or future. AP style does permit the use of today, tonight and this morning or afternoon.

came from. Attribution is clearly marked for the reader or listener by an attribution tag. Two of the most typical attribution tags are "(person's name) said" or "according to (person's name or document)."

Attributed information appears either as a direct quotation or an indirect quotation. This is an example of a direct quotation with attribution tag:

> "They beat them with their fists," a duty nurse said of the soldiers who broke into the hospital. She refused to give her name. "I was afraid they would shoot me, too."

As an indirect quotation, the nurse's exact words would be paraphrased, and, where the first person appears, the paraphrased statement would be shifted to third person.

> A duty nurse said soldiers broke into the hospital and beat patients with their fists. The nurse, who refused to give her name, said she was afraid the soldiers would also shoot her.

Journalists frequently call direct quotations "quotes," and when a story contains some pithy direct quotation people in newsrooms say: "That's a great quote."

However, some journalists use too many direct quotations — they rely too heavily on the source to "write" the story. Some journalists argue that a large number of direct quotes in a story shows people talking, and if the quotations are pithy, they can enliven a story. Others argue that people don't speak very precisely or concisely and that a journalist can paraphrase better. These same people argue that every time journalists use a quote they are not writing, but transcribing. My advice is to use direct quotations sparingly. Use them when they make a point better than you can.

Some people are eminently quotable, and to paraphrase them would deprive readers of delightful thought and language. In the early 1990s, one such person was Gen. H. Norman Schwarzkopf, who commanded a coalition of troops that drove Iraq out of Kuwait in 1991. Asked what he thought of Saddam Hussein, the leader of Iraq at the time, he said:

> As far as Saddam Hussein being a great military strategist, he is neither a strategist, nor is he schooled in the operational arts, nor is he a tactician, nor is he a general. Other than that, he's a great military man: I want you to know that.

Paraphrasing this ironic statement would dilute its flavor. Furthermore, the direct quotation often says something about the speaker. Take, for instance, this direct quotation from Defense Secretary Donald Rumsfeld about the 2003 Iraq War:

> There are known knowns. These are things we know that we know. There are known unknowns. That is to say, there are things that we know we don't know. But there are also unknown unknowns. There are things we don't know we don't know.

Journalists get in trouble when they misquote sources or quote sources out of context. Out-of-context problems arise when the careless journalist doesn't make clear the context in which something was said. For example, a journalist might ask a leading question such as this:

> *Journalist:* Madame Mayor, wouldn't you call your proposal sloppy?
> *Mayor:* Possibly.

That exchange might translate into a story this way:

> The mayor said the proposal was "possibly sloppy."

But that's unfair to the mayor, because "sloppy" wasn't her word; it was the reporter's, who failed to note the context in which the word appeared. The problem also arises when a speaker qualifies her statements before giving a final assessment, an assessment that, without the qualifications, sounds stronger than the speaker intended. The principle here is that accuracy should guide all journalistic endeavors.

Sentences and Paragraphs

News stories are composed of sentences and paragraphs. Simple sentences best convey the news, and the good journalist limits the number of complex and compound sentences. Sentence length varies, but, typically, sentences average 17 words, and paragraphs are usually no longer than three sentences. Sometimes a paragraph is only one sentence, especially when it's an unrelated idea, a long sentence, or a great quote. Journalists compose short sentences and paragraphs because they make the story much easier to read.

Elements in a Story

The story[3] below contains many of the just cited elements:

By Barbara Scheib
Staff Writer

The writer's name at the beginning of the story is called the byline. Bylines are not a required element.

A quick-burning fire roared through the body and parts shop of D&M Chrysler Plymouth Inc. Sunday morning, destroying seven cars and reducing the concrete-block building to a blackened shell.

The lead establishes this as a fire story. It tells generally what the fire did to whom and when. The time element is "Sunday morning."

Fire officials are estimating the loss to the business at $800,000. The owners of the dealership, Daniel and Michael Faretta, had only $290,000 insurance on the building and its contents, according to City Fire Chief Reynold D. Santone.

Specific figures attributed to sources provide more explicit information for the reader. Note here and throughout that people are identified with titles. No one appears as a name alone. Always identify people in a story as fully as possible.

Among the cars crushed and burned in the blaze was a classic 1949 Buick convertible and a new van that was on a lift for repairs, the chief said. Information about the owners of the vehicles was not available.

More specific information in the form of descriptions of the car. The information appears in an indirect quote.

By mid-morning, the structure — which sits behind D&M's new-car dealership at 1549 Pleasant Valley Blvd. — looked more like it had been bombed than burned. The roof and pieces of several walls collapsed from the fire. More walls were knocked down on

Still more specific information in the form of an address. The reporter is also describing the result of the fire.

---

[3]Barbara Scheib, "Fire Levels Auto Firm's Garage," *The Altoona Mirror* (Feb. 12, 1990), pp. 1-2. Copyright 1990 by *The Altoona Mirror*.

purpose so they would not fall on firefighters.

The cause of the fire is still under investigation, but officials say they believe it was accidental. No one was injured.

Santone said that firefighters were alerted at 7:15 a.m. By then, the building was already engulfed in flame.

Assistant Fire Chief Gordon W. McConnell said he could see a tower of smoke from the vicinity of the fire as soon as he left Fire Station 1 on Washington Avenue. Six off-duty firefighters were called in as backup.

Santone said that all engine companies and equipment were called to the scene, only to find there was little they could do initially to effectively fight the fire.

"The amount of heat generated was just unbelievable," he said. "When we got here there was no getting inside. There was just nothing we could do."

He said the fire was out of control the first 45 minutes firefighters were there, then began to burn itself down.

The fire chief said the fire was particularly intense because of paints and other highly flammable materials stored in the building.

State Police Fire Marshal James Behe said this morning that the cause of the fire is under investigation but that the problem

---

Most of the paragraphs in this story are one or two sentences.

Note not only the more specific time, but also the attribution. After someone is identified by his full name, subsequent references in print and broadcast are a matter of the medium's style. This newspaper uses last name only. Also note the additional detail and the nonsexist reference to the people fighting the fire. They are "firefighters," not "firemen."

This is the only direct quotation in the story, which is good, since some journalists over-rely on direct quotation.

Note the length of the sentence in this and the two subsequent paragraphs. The sentences range from 10 to 39 words for an average of 22, a little higher than normal.

Another source appears. This is the person who will ultimately determine the fire's cause, and the reporter will is centering on a gas-powered heater with an electric fan and fluorescent lights over the paint shop.

He said he has found no evidence to suggest that anyone entered the building or set the fire. All doors to the building were locked when firefighters arrived.

Santone said there was enough water and manpower to fight the fire. The Peoples Natural Gas Co. was called and asked to cut off gas service to the building until the flames were doused. Firefighters stayed on the scene until 3 p.m. cooling "hot spots" among the charred debris.

Firefighters were able to leave when snow showers moved into the area and cooled things down.

Traffic on Pleasant Valley and Valley View boulevards was blocked for several hours to keep vehicles away from the scene. Blair County fire police were called in to direct cars away from the fire. Traffic was moving normally by 10:30 a.m.

stay in touch with him until he announces the results of his investigation. At that time, the reporter will write a follow-up story.

More specific information.

The fire story also uses the *inverted pyramid* format, also is typical of basic news stories. This involves putting the most important information first and the least important last. One advantage of this is that the story can be "cut" from the end, paragraph by paragraph, if necessary, to fit the news hole. While inverted pyramid is the most common structure for news stories, you will learn about other story structures later.

WRITING THE LEAD

There's a famous play later made into a movie called "The Front Page," which is about Chicago newspapering in 1928. In it, the editor,

Walter Burns, is watching his ace reporter, Hildy Johnson, write a story for the *Chicago Examiner*. The crux of the story is that the *Examiner* has captured a criminal. Johnson begins the story this way:

> While hundreds of Sheriff Hartman's paid gunmen stalked through Chicago shooting innocent bystanders, spreading their reign of terror, Earl Williams was lurking less than 20 yards from the sheriff's office when ...

The editor interrupts: That's lousy! Aren't you going to mention the Examiner? Don't we take any credit?
Hildy: I'm putting that in the second paragraph.
Editor: Who the hell's going to read the second paragraph?

That is the first lesson for beginning newswriters. The lead must entice the reader to go on to the second paragraph (and find out what the *Examiner* did for law-and-order in Chicago one day, decades ago).

The lead is one story element editors and reporters talk about most. The assumption is that if the lead is good — "if it grabs the reader" — the story will be read. And if the lead isn't good enough, the reader won't go on.

You may want to curse the reader for being so lazy, but consider what the newswriter is up against. The busy reader faces many diversions, including radio or television (passive purveyors of information) or the Internet (which requires some effort on the part of a user), household chores, hobbies, screaming children, discretionary time, an engaging electronic game or a portable music player. Editors and reporters alike assume that a good lead on top of a well-written story can compete with many of life's diversions.

Essentially, the lead summarizes the story or emphasizes a major point. The major point could be the murder of someone, a fatal accident, a sex scandal, foul weather (past or future), a legislation veto, a veto overridden, or city council approving a ban on cruising.

The paragraphs that follow amplify the lead by providing detail. Thus, if the lead says a person was killed in a one-car crash, the second paragraph would tell who died, with the emphasis being on the person. (A prominent person would be named in the lead.) The third paragraph would tell how the crash occurred. Subsequent paragraphs would provide detail in a descending order of importance (completing the inverted pyramid analogy).

Most news stories answer six questions, best presented in a ditty by Rudyard Kipling:

I keep six honest serving men
(They taught me all I knew);
Their names are What and Why and When
And How and Where and Who.

Remember that it's the story, not the lead, that answers those questions. A lead that answered all six questions would be too long. A good lead focuses on the most interesting or newsworthy elements of the story, not all of the elements. For example:

What happened? Ten miners killed in a cave-in.
Who did what? Mayor's veto overridden.
Why did something happen? The U.S. Senate, unhappy with an arms control agreement, rejected the treaty.

But in the real world, reporters don't sit around trying to determine whether a story should have a "why" lead or a "what" lead, or any other type of lead. You need not become engrossed in labels at the expense of substance. It's not important to categorize a story's lead — just write it as well as you can.

When covering something, determine what action or statement would be of the most interest to the readers or listeners and put that in the lead. Some events contain more than one nugget of interest, but a reporter can't lead with all of them. A reporter must decide. Consulting with an editor often helps.

Leads are also brief, although they usually run longer than the average sentence. To write a concise lead, be specific enough to engage the reader but don't be overly detailed. For example, if three people were killed in an automobile accident, the lead would not include their names, but it would contain enough identifying information to help the reader decide whether or not to read more. For example:

Three New York City residents were killed last night near Cleveland when their car skidded on a patch of ice on Interstate 80 and went off the road.

As for subsequent paragraphs, the second one would list the victims by name, age, address, relationship to each other (if any). The remaining paragraphs would provide the possible cause of the accident, police comments, and other details.

Ohio Highway Patrol identified the victims as Joan T. Snyder, 34, the driver; her husband, John, 35, and their son, Michael, 12. They

resided in Greenwich Village.
   Police said a sudden drop in temperature after a rainstorm had left the road unexpectedly icy. Police had no other details on the accident.

   One very good piece of advice journalists often mention is to "never write a lead you could have written before the event." The advice applies particularly to planned events, such as meetings, speeches and demonstrations. For example, after the president gives the State of the Union address, the lead is not that he spoke, but what he said. Read a speech by the president and then look at the news story. Frequently, the point the president wants to make is midway through his speech, but good journalists place the point at the beginning — not the middle — of their stories. It's that simple.
   Governmental meetings fit this category, too, for reporters usually have agendas and know what a particular group is planning to discuss. Here are comparative leads on a planning commission meeting. Which one engages you?

The Centre Regional Planning Commission last night heard a summary of the third section of the Centre Region comprehensive plan from its author, planner Herbert Kauhl.	More than half of the 57,000 residents of the Centre Region are Penn State students, the Centre Regional Planning Commission learned Monday night.

   The writer of the second lead saw something interesting in the report and used it in her lead. She used it as a hook or grabber. After explaining the student population matter, she went on to report on other parts of the plan.
   One of the most interesting yet overlooked elements in many leads is "why." Why was something done? It is not enough to tell that a government body took a certain action — people want to know why. Compare these:

College Town Council voted Tuesday night to shut off the street lights on College Avenue from Atherton Street to High Street for a three-day trial period.	College Town will turn out some of its street lights on College Avenue for three days to see if lighting from Penn State provides enough illumination.

Two types of leads generally discouraged are "quote" leads and question leads. Quote leads — a lead that contains only a direct quotation — are eschewed because they often lack a context for the quote, which then makes it difficult for the reader to understand it. It is a rare situation when a newswriter cannot sum up something better than a source.

Question leads can frustrate readers who come to the news story looking for answers and doesn't want to wade through a question or series of questions to get them. As with everything else, exceptions do arise and no one should be a slave to a rule. For example, one college writer wrote this lead for a feature story:

> Have you looked at your birth certificate lately?
> For one Saginaw woman, it brought the biggest surprise since she was born.

The story went on to report that the woman not only was celebrating the wrong day for 65 years, her name was even different.

You now have an idea what the major elements of a news story are and how they come together in a basic story. The importance of the lead cannot be overemphasized. Getting the lead wrong means getting the story wrong. It is now time to talk about writing stories and what pitfalls await the writer (many of them with leads) and how they can be avoided.

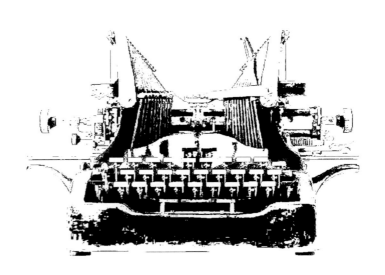

Chapter 5

THE FUNDAMENTALS OF WRITING NEWS

No two people approach writing the same way. Reporters use various approaches, some opening a can of diet soda and then spilling their words into the computer; others writing and revising a story one sentence and sip at a time. On deadline, the former is more palatable.

THE WRITING PROCESS

Journalists form stories when they write them. To help them do this, they usually take into account the information they have acquired, the audience they seek to communicate with, and what they know from previous occurrences.

They gather information from a variety of sources and then organize that information according to the outlet they're using (television, radio, newspaper, magazine). In the reporting process, journalist Paul Salsini recommends that reporters ask themselves (1) what the reader would want to know, (2) who the story's characters are and (3) what sources to talk to as well as what other research needs to be done.[1] Salsini also advises asking (4) what is needed to make an interesting story, (5) what does it mean and, finally, (6) what is the story? Some journalists go through this process by talking to someone else, be it another reporter or even an editor. Consultation is good because it helps the writer find a focus. Two minutes is plenty. The process doesn't have to take long.

Since writing reflects thinking, a journalist having a problem writing a story should think more before writing. Questions complementary to Salsini's arise: (7) What is the point of the event I just covered? That's the lead! (8) What do I want to say? More important, (9) what don't I need to

---

[1]Paul Salsini, "Reflections on the Richness of Reporting," *The Coaches' Corner* 3(1): 4-5 (March 1988).

say? (That question helps discover and thus avoid clutter.) (10) What parts of the event are related? Keep related items together; unrelated items apart.

The first paragraph out of the writer's mind should be the lead. What is this story? What's the point? Try boiling the gist of the story to three or four words. That will help you get started finding more words. Journalism professor Carole Rich suggests answering the question in 25 words or less.[2]

If you're stuck, try writing: "This is a story about a fire at an auto repair shop Sunday morning." That's a start, but since it's vague, you'll need to add more. "This is a story about a fire that badly damaged an auto repair shop Sunday morning." That's getting better because you've now used a strong verb (*damaged*). Now work on specifics: "This is a story about a fire that badly damaged an auto repair shop Sunday morning and destroyed seven cars." A few more specifics and you have the lead for the story you read in Chapter 4:

> A quick-burning fire roared through the body and parts shop of D&M Chrysler Plymouth Inc. Sunday morning, destroying seven cars and reducing the concrete-block building to a blackened shell.

The lead is critical to writing the rest of the story. The lead, according to a study by journalism professor Beverly Pitts,[3] helps the writer realize a purpose and direction for a story. Writing the lead involves a narrowing and focusing process for the journalist and, according to Pitts, can take up to a third of the time spent writing the entire story. Time spent writing a good lead is time well invested. Pitts calls the lead "a barometer by which to measure remaining parts of the story." John McPhee sees the lead as a "flashlight shining down into the story."

Pitts conceptualizes news stories as being written two or three sentences at a time — a micro approach rather than a macro approach. Journalists, she writes, "continually use memory, notes, analysis, planning, and rereading to propel them through the writing of paragraphs." What's been written, she says, helps journalists decide what to write next.

---

[2]Carole Rich, "Tips for Finding Your Lead," *The Coaches Corner*, 4(3): 9 (September 1989).

[3]Beverly Pitts, "Model Provides Description of News Writing Process," *Journalism Educator*, 43(1): 12-19, 59 (Spring 1989).

One critical element in the writing process is the writer's ability to recall events. General recall leads a writer back to his notes for detail, Pitts says. With recall so critical, then, a journalist must pay close attention when reporting a story. Taking good notes is crucial.

Once the writing is done, Pitts notes that two kinds of editing take place — editing for revision and editing for polish. Stories are checked against leads, and, if they are incompatible, a revision to one or the other takes place. Stories are also checked for continuity and, of course, mechanical (e.g., grammatical) problems.

For now, let's focus on the writing parts of the story and the problems encountered.

Leads, No-News Leads and News Judgment

The lead on a basic news story conveys some action or speaks about something specific. The lead that fails that test is known as a "no-news lead," also sometimes called the "no-content lead." The assumption is that if there's no news in the lead, there's none in the story, so why should the reader bother? It is very important for the beginning newswriter to recognize a no-news lead and to revise it. Here are some no-news leads from the same event:

> The Society of Professional Journalists sponsored a program Wednesday night on "The Ins and Outs of Court Coverage," with keynote speaker Professor Norman Collins.

> Dr. Norman Collins spoke in detail at a meeting Wednesday night sponsored by the Society of Professional Journalists about law enforcement, court coverage and the mysteries that each of these duties entail.

> A Penn State assistant professor of journalism spoke Wednesday night to the Society of Professional journalists about media court coverage.

> Wednesday night in 169 Willard about 35 people were at a lecture concerning journalists' coverage of court cases.

What was the point of the talk? Since you know that the person speaking was a journalism professor and he was talking to a group of journalists (in this case, the student chapter of the Society of Professional

Journalists), advice the speaker imparted to the students might make a good lead.

> Journalists covering a trial for the first time need to prepare if they want to do a good job, a journalism professor advised student journalists Wednesday night.

That lead has more content than the others and is far more interesting. If you think back to Chapter 4 and the advice about never writing a lead you could have written before the event, you'll see that some of the no-news leads shown fit the bill.

Action is important, but beware of generalities. Here are two leads that are too general:

> The College Town Planning Commission Thursday voiced concern regarding the University moving many downtown offices back on campus.

> Elderly residents spoke out on the latest fair housing proposal at the College Town Council meeting Thursday night.

The first lead could be improved if it contained the action the planning commission took regarding this problem rather than just saying it "voiced concern," which is a vague expression that most editors will delete. It wasn't until the story's 14th paragraph that the writer revealed what action the commission had proposed. There's the news.

> Elderly residents asked College Town Council Thursday night to raise the age limit in the latest version of a fair housing proposal.

The lead has to give the reader something to latch onto. Based on what you've just read, which of the following leads contains news?

> Richard A. Hodel, operator of Hodel Industries Inc., addressed the College Town Council Thursday night about the lack of public knowledge and the high cost of Pilsdon County's proposed solid waste plan.

> A local recycler told the College Town Council that residents are paying too much for the county's recycling program and that private recyclers could save residents money.

The lead on the left suggests something; the lead on the right says it. The lead on the right, by the way, is an example of a "blind lead," which will be discussed shortly.

A lead may contain action, but still not be much of a lead. For example:

> The College Town Planning Commission Thursday night unanimously voted in favor of a revision for the proposed YMCA.

What is missing from this lead? The revision. What was it? Here is a better lead, because it is more specific:

> The College Town Planning Commission Thursday night endorsed the YMCA's plans for a day-care center in its new headquarters at Fairlawn Drive and Oak Road.

Leads sometimes come about not because of something in the story but because of larger events affecting the story. For example, one night an expert on the role of women in Nazi Germany spoke on a college campus. The expert, Professor Claudia Koonz, spoke about her research, but she also extrapolated from her research some observations about modern society. One student reporter, rather than writing a lead about the behavior of people half a century ago, produced this timely lead:

> A political and social system that gives power to men and leaves humanity to women is dangerous, an expert on women in Nazi Germany said Thursday night.

The lead was timely and relevant because the role of women in U.S. society is an issue affecting everyone; therefore, the reader understands Koonz's insight.

When trying to think of what to lead with, it is worth remembering that (1) proposals make good leads and (2) lead with the cure, not the disease.

BACKING INTO STORIES

Related to the no-news lead problem in newswriting is "backing into the story." All that means is that the writer, instead of providing the most important details first, provide insignificant information first. The least serious infraction involves putting the attribution before the action or the interesting facts. For example:

> The Philipsburg-Osceola Area School board Monday night considered the pros and cons of entering into a contract with a television company.

Aside from being a no-news lead (i.e., lacking specific information or an outcome), this lead also starts with the attribution. An improvement is to put the attribution at the end of the lead, as such:

> The pros and cons of entering into a contract with the television company were considered Monday night at the Philipsburg-Osceola Area School board meeting.

But the lead still doesn't tell us what the board considered or whether action was taken. The problem is more serious here — the lead is buried in the story.

More specifically, a writer backs into a story usually when writing a story chronologically rather than drawing out the action or final outcome. Here is an example:

> The pros and cons of entering into a contract with a television company to provide daily newscasts in the district's classrooms were discussed at length by the Philipsburg-Osceola Area School board Monday night.
>
> Earlier this month the board had considered a three-year contract with Whittle Communications Satellite Education Network of Nashville, Tenn.
>
> Board members were in agreement with concern nationwide that today's public school students are not knowledgeable concerning daily news events.
>
> Joseph Mainello, school superintendent, said, "Students are not listening to news reports. We need to come up with a plan to correct this situation."
>
> Board members Raymond O'Brien and Michael Kochkodin were critical of what they saw as the disadvantages of the Whittle proposal. Members Howard Shaffer and Janice Walker expressed the view that even though the plan had some drawbacks, "Let's give it a try."
>
> When the issue finally came to a vote, board President Robert Hoover, Russell Tice, Elizabeth Ferguson, O'Brien and Kochkodin were opposed to the Whittle plan. Voting in favor were Barbara Wilks, Ken Wood, Shaffer and Walker. The motion was defeated.
>
> The board plans to investigate other television sources of newscasts for the students.
>
> The board went into executive session ...

The news value was the outcome of the vote (motion defeated). The story was headlined *P-O board defeats satellite news plan,* which at least gave the reader a sense of the news. But that doesn't excuse the reporter for backing into the story.

This same principle applies to paragraphs within stories that contain summary information on an issue. For example:

> The commission heard arguments regarding the necessary dimensions in parking lots. John C. Haas, an architect, contended that a width of 14.5 feet is sufficient in one-way aisles. However, zoning officer Herman Slaybaugh said 18-foot widths are necessary. At the request of the commission, Haas and Slaybaugh will attempt to reach a compromise over those measurements prior to the next town council meeting.

The lead for the paragraph is actually contained in the last sentence.

> The commission directed an architect and the zoning officer to attempt to reach a compromise in their disagreement over how wide one-way aisles in parking lots should be. [Now go on and explain the dispute and name the people.]

A lead can be improved several ways. What follows focuses on what to do and what to avoid in writing leads.

BLIND LEADS

You've been handed the current issue of the *New England Journal of Medicine* and have been asked to write a story about a study reported in the journal. The co-authors of the study are Dr. Jonathan L. Halperin of Mount Sinai Medical Center in New York City and Dr. David C. Anderson of Hennepin County Medical Center in Minneapolis. The study says that people with abnormal heartbeats can cut the risk of strokes in half by taking an aspirin a day. Strokes, which can be caused when abnormal heartbeats disrupt blood flow to the brain, are a problem that afflicts 75,000 Americans a year. You cannot get all of that into your lead, so what you have to do is use general references rather than names as a way of reducing your lead. Such a lead is called a "blind lead."

This is Daniel Q. Haney's blind lead on the Associated Press story about the aspirin study:

> An aspirin a day cuts in half the risk of strokes caused by abnormal heartbeats, devastating disruptions of blood flow to the brain that strike 75,000 Americans each year, a major new study concludes.

In this lead, the reader takes some things on faith and will wait until later in the story to learn more about the study and who conducted it.

A blind lead is one in which the main character or place in a story is identified generally rather than specifically. The usual practice, then, is to use the specific name in the second paragraph. A blind lead puts the emphasis not on the person but the result. Earlier, you saw these two leads:

	Blind lead (preferred)
Richard A. Hodel, operator of Hodel Industries Inc., addressed the College Town Council last night about the lack of public knowledge and the high cost of Pilsdon County's proposed solid waste plan.	A local recycler told the College Town Council that residents are paying too much for the county's recycling program and that private recyclers could save residents money.

The blind lead, the one on the right, puts the emphasis on what the person proposed and describes him generically rather than by name. The generic description is usually more useful to the reader, unless the person is well known. Presidents of the United States almost always get named in the lead, and the general rule of putting long attribution at the end of the lead also is waived.

Length of Lead

A good lead gets right to the point. A long lead discourages the reader because the point of the story can be lost in the verbiage. Would you want to read this story with a 49-word lead?

> The age-old problem of College Town parking intensified Tuesday night as Borough Council wrestled with a bigger issue of aesthetics vs. parking for 90 minutes before tabling the decision of whether to eliminate parking spaces for beautification purposes at the All's Quiet student apartment complex, 642 E. College Ave.

That's a lot to process. Also, in using the word "intensified," this writer also injected some opinion into the story. Unless some official said the issue was intensifying, it is better to just simply tell the reader what happened.

Here are the first two paragraphs of a story. The one on the left has too long a lead. The one on the right shows a version shortened by moving some information to the second paragraph.

Representatives of the Project Management Team said Tuesday night at the College Town Planning Commission's work session that the lack of enforcement and the weakness of current housing conversion laws have contributed to the deterioration of residential neighborhoods.

The representatives said the conversion of family homes to rental properties having three unrelated persons has led to property destruction, parking problems, noise and an exodus of families from the town's neighborhoods.

Representatives of the Project Management Team said Tuesday night that the lack of enforcement and the weakness of current housing conversion laws have contributed to the deterioration of residential neighborhoods.

The representatives told the Planning Commission at a work session that the conversion of family homes to rental properties having three unrelated persons has led to property destruction, parking problems, noise and an exodus of families from the town's neighborhoods.

The revised lead is eight words shorter than the original. The editor achieved that by moving some information into the second paragraph, information that he felt could be put off. In this case, the lead should stress the problem, not the group being told about the problem. A writer needs to know what needs to be stressed before deciding to defer information.

By the way, the second lead also could be improved by moving the attribution to the end of the lead, as such:

> The lack of enforcement and the weakness of current housing conversion laws have contributed to the deterioration of residential neighborhoods, representatives of the Project Management Team said Tuesday night.

Most writers and editors relax the rule on attribution after the lead; that is, putting the attribution first in paragraphs two and greater isn't as big a deal.

Dependent Clause Problems

A dependent clause is one that depends on the main clause for its meaning or context. Usually, it must appear somewhere in the middle or toward the end of a sentence. Placement is of more importance in a lead. Starting a story with a dependent clause is not usually a good idea because the dependent clause lacks context. The reader doesn't know what the clause modifies and therefore can't grasp its importance. Elsewhere in a story a dependent clause might work without creating the same problem that it creates in a lead. For example:

> *Defending allegations that the neighborhood action report "is trying to push students out of town,"* members of the neighborhood conservation action plan last night told the College Town Planning Commission the goal of the report is to preserve the family atmosphere of the neighborhoods.

That lead leaves everyone gasping, even without the dependent clause. Even though this lead is shorter, the dependent clause is still a problem.

> *For the first time in five years,* the Orange Grove United Way fund drive failed to reach its goal, and the deadline will be extended two weeks, officials announced today.

Rewritten with the clause in its place:

> The Orange Grove United Way fund drive failed to reach its goal *for the first time in five years,* and the deadline will be extended two weeks, officials announced today.

Emphasis

Sometimes a writer picks the wrong verb for the main clause in a lead and, thus, subordinates the news. That is the case with this lead:

> Fire *broke out* in a College Town apartment this morning, killing three high school friends giving a party for a friend bound for the Air Force.

The main verb in any lead should also be the news verb; that is, the main action of the story. In this lead, the main action is a fire killing three high school friends, not breaking out. Here's the rewrite:

> A fire in a College Town apartment this morning *killed* three high school friends giving a party for a friend bound for the Air Force.

Now the main verb represents the action of the story. By the way, the lead also could be fixed by creating a compound verb, as shown below, but many editors prefer singular verbs because the structure is simpler (and, besides, the news about the fire breaking out is far less important than the destructive impact of the fire).

> A fire *broke out* in a College Town apartment this morning and *killed* three high school friends giving a party for a friend bound for the Air Force.

ONE ISSUE PER LEAD

Leads should limit themselves to one issue, unless the issues are related. Government meetings often deal with more than one issue, so the temptation is often great.

> College Town City Council Tuesday night tabled the fair housing ordinance and authorized a study to examine alternatives for increasing parking.

Since the issues are unrelated, why yoke them in a lead? Instead, use the most interesting or pertinent issue from that meeting in the lead and add the other issue to the story or, better yet, write another separate story.

THE WHY ELEMENT

Putting unrelated issues into a lead deprives the writer of the opportunity to devote full attention to the main issue. This can be avoided by simply asking "why?"

The frequently missing critical element in many news stories, especially when an action occurs, is "why." Why did something happen? Why did the Planning Commission table action? Why did City Council raise taxes? The reporter who asks this question will write a better, more interesting story for the reader.

Follow the Lead

The first paragraph of a news story is a promise to the reader. Subsequent paragraphs deliver on that promise.

What the first paragraph usually promises is to tell the news; that is, what happened within the last 24 hours (or less). Subsequent paragraphs should fill out and further explain the action cited in the lead. Don't switch to another character in the story or to a different topic or take up history. Historical background can wait at least five paragraphs. If the lead says people have been charged with a specific crime, the next paragraph ought to tell who the people are.

If the lead says a fire badly damaged a car repair shop and destroyed some cars, the second paragraph should give a damage estimate. Remember this story? The writer followed her lead.

> A quick-burning fire roared through the body and parts shop of D&M Chrysler Plymouth Inc. Sunday morning, destroying seven cars and reducing the concrete-block building to a blackened shell.
>
> Fire officials are estimating the loss to the business at $800,000. The owners of the dealership, Daniel and Michael Faretta, had only $290,000 insurance on the building and its contents, according to City Fire Chief Reynold D. Santone.

Below is an example of a story in which the writer did not follow the lead. This issue, by the way, had been ongoing for several months and the newspaper had published several articles before this one, an account of the final decision.

> The great Spring Garden Township tree debate is over — and the trees have lost.
>
> Capping more than a year of discussion and controversy over the previously decided removal of hardwood trees on Oakdale Drive, about 15 township residents made a final attempt to save the trees at a township meeting Wednesday night.
>
> Several township officials and the developer of the area where the trees will be removed told the residents their efforts were too little and too late.
>
> Widening the road as part of a 97-acre addition to Wyndham Hills requires that more than 50 hardwood trees be removed. Most of the oak trees on the street are between 50 and 100 years old.

What throws off the reader's stride is that the first paragraph says the trees "lost" but then the second paragraph rehashes the past. When a government body acts, people will want to know how the elected officials voted on an issue and why they voted the way they did. But the four paragraphs just presented don't do that. In fact, the information appears much later in the story. It is not a good way to organize a news story. Whatever the lead, the writer must develop it.

The school board story presented earlier as an example of backing into the news also contains a second paragraph that is an example of historical lapse. The paragraph is italicized.

> The pros and cons of entering into a contract with a television company to provide daily newscasts in the district's classrooms were discussed at length by the Philipsburg-Osceola Area School board Monday night.
>
> *Earlier this month the board had considered a three-year contract with Whittle Communications Satellite Education Network of Nashville, Tenn.*
>
> Board members were in agreement with concern nationwide that today's public school students are not knowledgeable concerning daily news events.

The tip-off in this story is the paragraph's first three words: "Earlier this month." News stories generally emphasize events of the past 24 hours, not events earlier in the month. While historical information can be useful and adds to a story, it must have proper placement at the end or middle of a story, so that it does not detract from the important main action.

DEVELOPING A STORY

Some people have argued that learning to write a news story is difficult because a news story is not logical. They cite the inverted pyramid as evidence of the illogical organization of a news story.

True, a basic news story starts with a bang and ends with a whimper, but logic does play a part. It's all a matter of purpose. And with a little practice, you'll see that the structure of a hard news story is a powerful way to convey ideas and news to people.

What follows are some typical problems and solutions writers encounter in developing a story.

Transition

Transition is both the glue that holds a story together and the bridge between unrelated issues within a story. Transition links sentences to each other and paragraphs to other paragraphs. Transition can be as simple as

a repeated word or clause, or as complicated as a four- or five-paragraph anecdote. The longer the story, the more important transition becomes.
Here is a two-paragraph story in which the repetition of one word ("goal") glues the three sentences together.

> The chairman of the Orange Grove United Way fund drive announced today that the fund's deadline, originally set for today, will be extended two weeks in an attempt to reach its *goal*.
> The *goal* of $61,950 is short by about $2,000, according to H.W. Pearce. Pearce said this is the first time in five years the *goal* has not been met.

Here, in contrast, are two paragraphs that seem unrelated:

> The commission members agreed to evaluate such mixed zoning next year.
> "People like to have a place to get milk or bread two blocks away," commission member James B. Williams said, "but I'm not sure they want a place like that in their neighborhoods."

Now here is how the writer, in revising the story, linked the two paragraphs:

> The commission members agreed to evaluate such mixed zoning next year, *although one expressed skepticism about it.*
> "People like to have a place to get milk or bread two blocks away," commission member James B. Williams said, "but I'm not sure they want a place like that in their neighborhoods."

Now the quote makes sense in relation to the preceding paragraph.

A writer can signal a change in the topic with a short phrase, as this student journalist did in an article about a speech on feminism:

> Seligman said that women in other societies play very different roles. U.S. society should stop using biology as an excuse for social discrimination, she said.
> *Turning to the subject of abortion,* Seligman said that biology threatens women's freedom. She said that groups supporting the outlawing of abortion argue that women's bodies have a "higher calling," and that women should not have the right to do what they want with their own body. Seligman argued that each woman's body should be a self-determined unit.

Single words such as "but" and "however" make for good transition, when what follows them contradicts or disagrees with what precedes them.

> In America, people should be able to choose their sexual life, *but* that is not the case, gay and lesbian law specialist Rhonda Rivera said.

Transition helps the readers and the good writer uses transition in that spirit.

Emphasis in a Sentence

Sentences can be divided into three parts — a beginning, a middle and an end. In print, the most important information — or the information worth emphasizing — should appear either at the beginning of the sentence or the end. Generally, use the middle of the sentence for the attribution tag or for subordinate information.

Sentence emphasis in broadcast follows a different pattern. Generally, sentences written for broadcast end with emphasis. The beginning of a broadcast sentence is used to "warm up" the listener.

Sentence and Paragraph Length

Sentences ought to average about 17 words. Some people write sentences that go on forever. They write sentences as though they were drowning and coming to the surface occasionally. Of necessity, every time they break the surface, they gulp for air, because they never know if they're going to get another chance.

Fortunately, writing does not have to be like drowning. Writers can breathe all they want. They don't need to gulp. They can write smoothly. They needn't be afraid of short sentences.

If sentences are too long, the problem with paragraphs cuts both ways — either too long or too short. If someone comes to newswriting from a class in English composition, he or she has a tendency to write long paragraphs. Newspaper paragraphs are short because that makes them easier to read, and since the 19th century newspapers have sought to reach out to as many people as possible.

Many paragraphs are just one sentence. But they can contain more and the guiding rule is that a paragraph should be a collection of related sentences. When sentences don't relate, the writer can make a one-sentence paragraph. Remember that ideas need paragraphs to be developed, so be stingy in your use of one-sentence paragraphs.

Be Specific

In the changing news environment, the journalist comes across many new phrases daily and should be prepared to explain what they are. Daniel Haney of the Associated Press didn't hesitate to explain what strokes are.

What's a right of way? What does an arborist do?

Similarly, budget stories cry out for specifics: How big is the budget; what tax increase, if any? What's the address for a store cited as having a problem? Look it up. Better still, go to the store in person and check. Some journalists are very good at getting telling quotes and laying out issues, but not at getting the important numbers and other details that go with the quotes and the issues.

Direct Quotations

Some believe that direct quotations in a news story indicate the presence of people or authoritative sources, and the more direct quotations the merrier. Others believe in using as few direct quotes as possible, and only when they're really good. (An exception would be dialogue, which is discussed in Chapter 7.) In their haste to use direct quotes, writers abuse them. One problem is repetition. First the writer paraphrases the quote then provides in quotation marks, a condition some sarcastically call "echo quotes."

> Such as the case for the Steelers, who lost their first WPIAL Section 2 game to visiting New Castle, 46-39, mostly *because they couldn't put the ball in the basket* and may even have had problems hitting the broad side of a barn.
>
> "We just didn't put the ball in the hoop," said exasperated Steeler head coach Frank Sincek.

We know, coach. The writer just told us. Of course, it's the writer's fault, not the coach's.

Another abuse of direct quotes arises when the quote is not self-contained and the writer must insert information to make it clear. Here is one variation of the problem:

> "They (the Soviet solders) beat them (the patients) with their (the soldiers') fists," a duty nurse said.

When a writer needs bracketed matter to explain a quote, the writer should paraphrase. In this particular example, Ann Imse of the Associated Press put the explanatory information outside the quotation marks. It makes the sentence read better.

> "They beat them with their fists," a duty nurse said *of the Soviet soldiers who broke into the hospital.*

The "them" in the quote, by the way, is made clear from the paragraph preceding the quote.

In print, wherever possible, bury the attribution tag. Attribution tags can appear in three places: at the beginning of a direct or indirect quotation, in the middle, or at the end. Since the beginning and end of sentences are the strongest parts of the sentence, the best place to spot attribution is in the middle at a natural break. This usually works in sentences with clauses or in compound sentences. For example:

> "Except for a few minor items," Kurtz said, "the contractors feel we can move in on schedule."

When you have two sentences that are direct quotations, you can bury attribution between the two sentences.

> "I think that's a good idea," Nichols said. "We need more good ideas."

Generally, don't invert attribution tags. The name should go before the verb, not after. The standard structure of English sentences is subject-verb-object. Thus, when a writer inverts the order to verb-subject, the writer confuses the reader.

But there is one exception to the rule: You can invert the attribution tag when a long string of words follows. Here's an example:

> "You have to start at a small newspaper and work your way up," said the professor of journalism, who once worked for newspapers.

The reverse is very clumsy (*The professor of journalism who once worked for newspapers said.*)

Subsumption

All writing should be to the point. Sentences that meander do a disservice to readers and listeners. To write concisely, use the right verb. The right verb is the one that subsumes all other verbs in a particular action.

In order to tell someone what happened in a class, do you first have to tell that you arose at a certain hour, ate breakfast, and then walked to class? Of course not! Telling what happened in class subsumes many previous actions. Note the subsumption in this story, especially in paragraphs 2 and 3.

A Snow Shoe woman was hospitalized Wednesday morning after being hit by a truck in State College, police ~~report.~~ reported.[1]

Janice E. Meadows, 58, ~~sustained~~ was reported in good condition in Centre Community Hospital with a cracked pelvis and , several broken ribs, ~~and was admitted to Centre County Hospital.~~[2] She ~~is in good condition and~~ was expected to be discharged this morning, according to a hospital spokesperson.

The driver of the truck, Jonathan T. Hollister, 36, ~~of~~ 1214 Easy St., Pleasant Gap, ~~was the driver of the Chevrolet pick-up truck. Hollister is~~ an Assistant Professor of Music* at Penn State, ~~University. He~~ was en route to work at 7:30 a.m. when ~~he~~ his truck struck[3] Meadows on ~~E. College Ave~~ East College Avenue** at ~~the corner with~~ McAllister Street. Meadows, a janitor in the School of Nursing at Penn State, was crossing the street to get a cup of coffee.

1. Always use past tense.

2. If you tell us her condition in the hospital, we will know she was admitted. This is subsumption.

3. Instead of using a sen-tence to identify the driver, tell us what the driver did

*Titles alone or behind names are not capitalized.

**Check the stylebook.

Strong Verbs

Always attempt to write with strong verbs. Strong verbs denote action. The weakest verb is *is*. It does not denote action the way other verbs do. Try to avoid it. Every time you find yourself using it, try to replace it with a strong verb. Good writers use strong verbs.

Clichés

Clichés are words and phrases that have been used so frequently that they have become outdated or meaningless. They have lost the warmth of originality. Calling a football a "pigskin" and a football field a "gridiron" are but two of many examples. Look at clichés as second-hand prose. Don't use them. Use original language. Be unique.

Newcomers to newswriting need to find their own approach to writing a story. Most teachers agree that devoting a lot of time to writing a good lead is a help in writing a good story. Eventually, journalists in all fields must write on deadline, and anything they do to prepare themselves is of benefit.

Chapter 6

OTHER STORY TYPES

Up to this point, we've talked mostly about hard news stories. But newspapers publish other types of stories or articles, including features, profiles, obituaries, in-depth pieces (which are discussed in this chapter) and editorials, reviews and columns (see other books for more details).

FEATURE STORIES

The feature story is distinguished partly by the way it is written. The feature's tone and style are more individualized and the story is plotted. The writer's voice is apparent. A feature story is a break from the routine.

Compare the following stories. The one on the left (#1) is, except for the last paragraph, a fairly routine report of a court decision. The one on the right (#2) is a feature. You can tell the writer enjoyed writing it.

Story #1

A Howard fisherman can now tell the story of how he was the one that got away.

Kenneth W. Castleberry won an appeal of a fishing law violation Monday because of a missing word in the section of the law under which he was charged.

Castleberry was arrested for throwing a beer can into Spring Creek and charged under a section that prohibits littering "along" state streams.

At one time, the law prohibited littering "in or along" fishing streams, but the

Story #2

Consider the word "in."

As a preposition, it enables speakers of the English language to say where something is. "In court," for example.

Kenneth W. Castleberry of Howard was in court Monday because he had been found guilty of littering — of throwing a beer can (empty, of course) in Spring Creek.

In his appeal of the conviction, Castleberry argued that the law under which he had been charged did not specify a person could not litter "in" a stream.

In concurring, Cadbury

section was amended in 1974 and the word "in" was eliminated, according to Cadbury County Judge R. Paul Campbell.

In reversing the previous guilty decision, Campbell cited a Superior Court decision that says the law must be strictly interpreted.

Campbell said another section of the law "does make it a criminal offense for any person to throw any refuse or rubbish, etc., into or upon any stream."

If that section had been used, Castleberry might not have been the fisherman who got away, according to the judge.

County Judge R. Paul Campbell wrote than an earlier version of the law referred to littering "in or along streams in which the public is allowed to fish."

In later years, though, Campbell said, the word "in" was eliminated through an amendment, making it illegal to litter "along" (another preposition) but not "in" a stream.

The judge said he didn't know if the dropping of the word was inadvertent or intentional.

Regardless, Campbell said the law requires a strict interpretation, so he reversed Castleberry's conviction, noting that another section of the law could have been used because it has all the right prepositions.

The writer of story #1 put a "kicker" on his story, a play on the fish that got away. That's all right, but it doesn't measure up to the story on the right in which the writer plotted the story from beginning to end by relying on the repetition of the word "in" and a discussion on prepositions. The story on the right shows evidence of an individual writer, someone who obviously enjoyed writing the story. Of course, a feature story is not necessarily whimsy. The authors of *Reporting Processes and Practices*[1] say:

> the feature fills out the space between the lines of the standard straight news report. It adds color and flesh, considers human factors, reports meanings and motivations. The result for the reader is a different level of understanding — a richer, more refined look at the complexity of the story. As the new reporter will learn, no story is really as simple as it may seem at first. And people are endlessly complex. The feature form helps the reporter do a better job for the reader.

---

[1] Everette E. Dennis and Arnold H. Ismach. *Reporting Processes and Practices: Newswriting for Today's Readers* (Belmont, CA: Wadsworth, 1981), p. 187.

In the typical story, the hard news reporter would stick to what was said and then spit it back in 10 paragraphs, beginning with a lead and then jumping to a direct quotation in the second paragraph. She would then forge ahead with minimum transition but lots of switching back and forth between direct quotes and indirect quotes with history thrown in as needed. Informative but dull.

In the feature story, the reporter is after more than just what is being said and would most likely concentrate instead on details not found in the typical news story. Such details are likely to be environmental or scene setting. What does the place look like? How are people dressed? What sounds could you hear? What sounds couldn't you hear? An occasional adjective and adverb are allowed. Transport the readers from their livingroom to the scene. Make the story come alive. Paint a picture with words. Let the reader experience the story. Show, don't tell.

A good feature story comes with a beginning, middle and end. It is plotted. Examine this feature story by Doris Wolf of the *Finger Lakes Times* in Geneva, N.Y.[2] Note how she uses description and environmental markers to put the reader in the story. As you read this story, you will be in the vestibule of a clerk's office, walk through large glass doors, sit in someone's kitchen over breakfast, witness the sale of a farm. You will feel the sadness. The headline writer avoided the typical subject-verb approach and instead put a title on the story: "The death of a family farm." That adds to its specialness.

> STANLEY — They'd been on life support for years before the plug was pulled. And even now, they hoped. The death of a family farm is slow and agonizing.
>
> For Stanley and Elizabeth Senack of Number Nine Road, hope flickered and died at about 10:30 Wednesday morning in the small vestibule outside the Ontario County clerk's office in Canandaigua when their 235-acre farm was auctioned off.
>
> No casket, no flowers, no organ music eased the passage — just men in white shirts and neckties, carrying briefcases, and farmers wearing plaid woolen workshirts who came to pray, "There but for the Grace of God go I."
>
> In the vestibule, Senack, 44, stood with his back to the wall, looking down at his scuffed and worn brown work boots, his green cap squarely on his head, his middle fingers in the pocket of his dirty jeans with the

---

[2]Doris Wolf, "The Death of a Family Farm," *Finger Lakes Times* (December 9, 1988). Copyright 1989 by *Finger Lakes Times*, Geneva, NY. All rights reserved.

small holes in the front.

His son, Stanley Jr., 18, who was to be the fourth generation to live in the older brown house and farm on the windswept hill, stood behind Senack. So alike, his feet placed the same, the fingers in the jeans pockets a mirror of his dad's — yet different with his black leather jacket and his white silk aviator-like scarf, his bright blond hair and unlined face.

Young Stanley has dreams, too, of becoming a car salesman. "I want money," he said. But he shares his father's love of the farm, postponing his dream to help scratch out a living cultivating cabbages and grain on the land. For him, the sale is hard, too, but it's liberating. Now he can follow his dream.

Elizabeth Senack was outside, sitting in the pickup truck their son drove to take them to the foreclosure sale. She had walked quickly out through the large glass doors, unable to hold back the tears any longer, as Kathleen Curran, court-appointed referee, began to read from the seven-page document that explained the terms of the auction and described the farm.

Cold and impersonal, the reading continued. An occasional blast of winter air rushed in to chill the vestibule as the door opened to admit strangers, carrying license plates or registration forms, frowning with curiosity as they walked quickly through the group to the Department of Motor Vehicles office.

Earlier that morning, the lingering smell of bacon and coffee had been warm and comforting as Senack sat at his kitchen table, staring at the documents spread in front of him.

After a county sheriff's deputy delivered the official papers with the blue cover last July from the Federal Land Bank of Springfield, Senack spent a frantic four months trying to find a way to save his home.

"When the foreclosure notice came, I went right to the bank," Senack said. "They told me they'd be willing to lend me money if I could catch up what I owed. If I could have done that, I wouldn't have needed to borrow money."

Senack owed more than $296,000 — $165,166 to the Federal Land Bank, $75,000 to the Farmers Home Administration and $55,144 to Production Credit Association, a national lending association for farmers.

He pleaded with the FmHA to exercise its second mortgage, to allow him a chance to restructure. Late Tuesday night, FmHA manager Gerald Killigrew telephoned Senack to tell him that wouldn't be possible.

Senack contacted his neighbors, hoping to find one who would buy the farm and let him rent for a few years, with a buy-back option, so they could keep the house.

"I like being here, the people around me," he replied when asked what was the best part of farming. "Every day when I get up, I thank God for being here."

About 9:30 a.m., time to go. Senack joked about taking his beat-up green Dodge pickup, of driving it through the sale, to stop it. "You'll go in my truck," his son said, as he walked toward the shiny black Ford with the white cap.

"When do you start to cry?" Senack was asked. "Right now," he replied, his eyes filling behind his flyspecked glasses.

Senack brightened when he saw Donny Jensen sitting in the pickup in the parking lot in front of the low tan brick building.

"I might be interested," Senack's across-the-swamp neighbor said cautiously when asked if he intended to bid.

"You'll never get a farm any cheaper than you will today," Senack said encouragingly.

Other neighbors filed into the tiny vestibule as though at a wake. They shook Senack's hand, lips pressed tightly together, and quickly looked away as they moved to places near the bright red, white and blue Pepsi machine, or leaned against the window, back to the others, looking out.

Joe Keyser of the Federal Land Bank and his attorney Mark Fandrich stood next to Curran at the front of the room as she read in a monotonous voice, a priest reciting the liturgy at a funeral.

To their left, John Karszes, 26, of Clifton Springs, and his wife, Kelly, a teacher in Gorham, waited nervously. They own a small 90-acre farm in Phelps, Karszes explained, and want to move up to a larger operation. They'd been to Senack's — it might be the right place to follow their dream.

"I've met them," Senack said. "They're nice people."

"We are now open for bids," Curran finally said.

"The Federal Land Bank will bid $196,350," Fandrich said.

"I'd like to bid $196,400," said Karszes hopefully. Senack swallowed hard and stared at the floor, lips clamped together tightly.

"I'll go $200,000," said Jensen, as a flicker of hope flashed in Senack's eyes.

"Does anyone want to make a higher bid?" Curran asked. Karszes looked at a small white notebook he held cupped in his right hand. His wife looked up at him questioningly. He bid $202,000. Jensen raised the ante to $205; Karszes whispered with his wife and bid to $210. Jensen talked to his partner, a builder. "I'd like to go $215," he said.

Pointing with his thumb to the bottom line in his notebook, Karszes bid $218. Jensen went to $219. After a long pause, Karszes swallowed and raised the bid to $220.

Senack glanced back at Jensen for the first time — a plea — then looked back at the floor and shook his head slightly.

"Do I hear more bids?" Curran asked. "Are there more bids? Anyone? Sold!"

"I'm sorry, Stan," Jensen said, walking over and shaking his neighbor's hand. "I hoped maybe we could have worked something out."

But I had my number and that was it."

"You've got to watch the numbers or you'll end up like me," Senack called after him as Jensen walked quickly away.

"Why wouldn't they buy it from me, so I could have kept the house? I hate to see it go this way," Senack said, his voice choking with emotions, tears welling in his eyes. "I tried, I tried."

Shoulders slumping, Senack walked across the parking lot to tell his wife. Awkwardly, his son reached up to pat his dad's back.

The family sat for a long time in the cab of the truck, Senack shaking his head, tears coming now unchecked. Elizabeth sat between the men, her hands over her face. Stanley Jr. leaned against the door, facing sideways toward his parents, crying, too. Then he wiped his eyes with the back of his hand, turned front and reached for the ignition key.

Slowly, the truck began to drive away, over the familiar back roads, to the home that was no longer theirs.

Some feature stories open more slowly. In this case, Wolf establishes within the first two paragraphs what the story is about and pegs it to an event that occurred two days earlier. The story is rich in detail. One of Wolf's virtues as a writer is her ability to say a lot with few words. The fourth paragraph is but one of many examples of this when she not only tells what Stanley Senack looks like but also conveys his mood.

Wolf is a good observer — unobtrusive, a fly on the wall. She went to the Senacks' home at breakfast instead of meeting them at the auction. That enabled her to provide scenes of the family in more than one setting and to get some background from the Senacks.

Wolf is specific. The clerk's office doesn't have a soda machine; it has a "bright red, white and blue Pepsi machine" and some people stand near it. And once she introduces the players in the story, a form of foreshadowing, she spins out a mini-story about the auction. The reader must stay with her to find out who buys the farm.

PROFILES

Whereas a feature story may focus on the people in an event and also reveal something about the event, a profile focuses on a person and its purpose is to tell readers about the person. Some profiles have the overlay of deadline reporting to them, because they are assigned when someone new appears in the news.

But profiles can also be about people who are well known. Then the journalist is aiming to tell something new, to explore a side of the person unknown to the public. "If the person is unknown," Shirley Biagi says, "you completely sketch the person's character."[3]

A good way of approaching a profile is to answer one question: Why is this person worth knowing? That question becomes the frame on which the profile is constructed. The answer becomes the theme of the story.

If a profile is written on deadline, most likely the writer will get information from clips, from the subject of the profile, and perhaps from an acquaintance or two. Deadline profiles tend to be more biographical than human.

But when a journalist has the opportunity to do a longer profile, he has several reporting methods at his disposal. One of those, of course, is the interview. At least two interviews are necessary. The best profiles come from journalists who know their subject.

Observation is another method, one vastly underused in profiles. Go back and read Doris Wolf's feature. She was at the Senack's home at breakfast; she was at the auction; she was there when the Senack family broke down in tears outside the clerk's office after the sale of their farm.

Observation allows a reporter not only to see the person in action but to get a chance to describe the person. And description is not limited to how the person looks, but also how a person behaves. For example, in a profile on a librarian, one beginning journalist included this paragraph:

> She said she knows people who have gone on sabbaticals. But she cannot do that. "The library is my life. It's crazy." She laughs. She laughs when she says something revealing or personal.

The journalist noticed that trait only after a second interview and through observation. The preceding paragraph appeared early in the profile and established a base for subsequent references to her laughing.

A great deal of research can be done on people, depending on who they are. Some people have written articles and books or have had public careers. They're fairly easy to do research on. For less public people, talk to their friends (and enemies). They can be sources of anecdotes, which are usually enjoyable to the reader. If anyone says something critical, give the subject of the profile an opportunity to rebut. In fact, the subject of a profile should be asked for his self-assessment. Also ask what other career he or she may have wanted to pursue. Perhaps the Shakespeare scholar is a stone mason on the side.

Build the story on facts so the readers can draw their own

---

[3]Shirley Biagi, *Interviews That Work: A Practical Guide for Journalists* (Belmont, CA: Wadsworth, 1986), p. 4.

conclusions. The best profiles speak for themselves. Here is a student's attempt of one such profile.[4]

> Jeff Ganaposki discovered his life's calling in a discount bin at K-mart.
>
> Partly by coincidence, partly by fate, a $2.75 paperback book titled "The Big Tax Lie" altered his life. Author William Kilpatrick traced all the nation's problems to income tax and its partner-in-crime — inflation.
>
> After reading the book in February of 1989, Ganaposki drafted an amendment to the U.S. Constitution that would abolish federal income tax and replace it with a fairer national sales tax. Now all the Boalsburg resident needs to do is convince a nation.
>
> Ganaposki immediately mailed an outline of his proposal to President Bush and several members of Pennsylvania's legislature. He also sent materials to some of the country's leading television talk-show hosts. Response has been minimal.
>
> "In a nation of 250 million people, for one person to make a difference when he doesn't have any connection to powerful people or the media seems an impossible task," he said. In fact, at times "I feel like Don Quixote."
>
> In October, he formed a group to increase the number of voices asking for changes to the tax laws. His first meeting of the "Committee for Truth in Taxes," of which he is chairman and currently the only member, was a disaster.
>
> On the night of the meeting, Ganaposki's was the only coat to hang in the entrance to Schlow Memorial Library's meeting room. Inside, he methodically arranged spreadsheets, complex computer printouts, charts and bar graphs detailing his findings. Tax information from foreign nations, which he had requested through the mail, was interspersed among his own documents. Finally, Ganaposki sat down behind the information-laden table and waited ... and waited. A flow chart on which nothing was written during his two-hour wait stood in the corner. A stack of 50 or more chairs leaned patiently against a far wall, but they were not to be disturbed this night. When asked[5] where the Committee for Truth in Taxes was meeting, a library aide snickered.
>
> "It slowed me down, but I just took it in stride," Ganaposki said. "I can't expect the whole world to come beating down my door. If the solution to our tax problem was that easy, someone else would have

---

[4]Mark Jones, written as an assignment for the author's reporting methods class during the fall semester of 1989 and used with the author's permission.

[5]In most situations where a sentence starts with "When asked ... ," the word "When" can be deleted and the sentence can just begin with "Asked ... . " The word "When" is superfluous.

thought of it by now."

Ganaposki's constitutional amendment would place the burden of taxes on the consumers when they purchase a product or service rather than taxing individuals' income — before they have the opportunity to spend the money.

"Under income tax there is no way you can stop inflation without crippling the economy," Ganaposki said. He later added: "We've been taxing ourselves backwards."

A more unlikely looking savior for the American working-class man would be hard to find. In his living room, a plaid-covered easy chair swallows his body — a body resembling that of Santa Claus. The beard and mustache that he sports are flecked with spots of gray, but he continues to wear a long, brown pony tail to the small of his back. When he speaks, his hands are folded over his stomach, which periodically escapes from between a faded yellow "Uni-Lube" T-shirt and gray sweatpants.

"I'm not so much an idealist as a technologist," Ganaposki said. "I'm looking for a technique that harnesses the natural financial human urges for profit and the easy way of doing things. And then make it so the goal or result is much better."

Ganaposki lives in a mortgaged single-story home located in a development of similar houses, surrounded by a tidy yard with newly planted shrubs. A single foreign-made car sits in the gravel driveway. He and his wife, Linnette, have three children.

Crayon drawings carefully crafted by children's hands hang in the picture window. The street outside is not heavily traveled. A sign warns drivers to watch for children. Temporarily riderless bicycles and abandoned big wheels litter the front yards of many of the homes. Ganaposki works 8 to 5 in Boalsburg as a hardware designer at Seven Mountains Scientific, Inc.

In many ways, he is a common man. Yet he is a common man with uncommon ideas.

"The fastest growing group of millionaires are lottery winners," he says as he sinks back into the easy chair. "That just goes to show you, in our system we create poverty. And the only way you can get out is not by hard work but by luck, speculation and gambling."

Ganaposki was a victim of that system. He grew up in the hard-coal mining region of Wilkes-Barre, nurtured by a mother who periodically relied on welfare to raise her two children. As a teenager, he counseled some of his peers at Malabar Drug Rehabilitation Center.

"Drugs were a thrill and a distraction from the pain of their lives," he said.

As a young adult, Ganaposki said he found "anything that was counter to the current way of authority or means of doing things was very attractive." He spent time between high school and college as a stand-up comic, a "professional panhandler," and a street musician. As an electric bass player, he said, "I had delusions of grandeur. An ego the size of a planet."

Like many youth in the 60s, he said, "I used to hitch-hike a lot. One year I racked up 13,000 miles in six months." Those miles were practically all covered on trips from Wilkes-Barre to Butler to see his fiancée.

For a short time he paid $20 a month to share a cabin in the mountains with "a bunch of guys from Philadelphia." The primitive get-back-to-nature setting came complete with outhouses and no running water.

"We were pretty much Bohemians," he said.

Through the assistance of state financial aid institutions, he was able to attend Luzerne County Community College. Later, while holding a part-time job at IBM, he attended the State University of New York at Binghamton.

"To this day, I think a lot of government grants to education are bad because they don't take into consideration the motivation of the student," the former college dropout and financial aid recipient said. The first time he entered college, Ganaposki said he lacked the fortitude and the motivation to handle the coursework.

In 1984 he left IBM and started graduate work at Penn State toward a degree in computer science. Lack of money and poor advising forced him to quit and consider suing the University.

"I was firmly convinced it was the University's fault," he said. "But when I tried to sue, the lawyers dissuaded me. Any educational establishment can claim a myriad of reasons why you failed and not that they failed."

After a brief stint as an employee in Penn State's department of computer design services, Ganaposki took his present job at Seven Mountains Scientific, Inc. Co-owner and fellow employee Josephine Chesworth said Ganaposki often bounce new ideas off other employees.

"The last thing he did was to pass around a petition to have the congressmen impeached after giving themselves a raise," she said.

Although Ganaposki's ideas may seem radical, his rebellious lifestyle has slowed somewhat over the years. Other than the pony tail he sports, the only visible reminder of his "hang loose" years is a huge collection of old 45s in the livingroom, and even they are surrounded on his bookshelves by encyclopedias and thought-provoking novels.

Now at age 34, Ganaposki said his life is moving in the direction of becoming a full-time tax advocate.

In January, he will address the Pennsylvania League of Taxpayers at Clearfield. He recently accepted that agency's request for him to be Centre County's regional director. He said with the help of massive petitioning by the 42,000 members of this group, he hopes to begin appearing on national television talk shows.

Currently, he is taking his message to local radio programmers and editors of area newspapers. WRSC featured Ganaposki several times during its radio call-in shows that focused on tax reform. He says that other members of the news media refused to talk to him or belittled his proposal.

As the year draws to a close, it appears Ganaposki will not have achieved his goal of eliminating income tax in the 1980s. However, he has no intention of ending the crusade.

"My biggest hope now is to see how much support I receive from the Pennsylvania League of Taxpayers," he said. "If I can get pre-paid orders, I'll be able to self-publish my book."

The book, still in the writing stage and yet to be edited by his wife, will provide a detailed explanation of how Ganaposki's proposed tax system works. It will appear in "fine book stores" and K-marts everywhere.

The challenge for the author, Mark Jones, was to profile a person who had a different idea. Since our society frowns on people who are different, it is easy for journalists to dismiss them. So Jones' challenge was to profile this person in a way that the readers could make up their own minds. He was sympathetic and fair to his subject, yet leaves no doubt that the person is outside the mainstream.

The next story is a cross between a feature and a profile. I wrote it shortly after retiring as a journalism professor and moving to New Mexico. This story is different from the usual story a beginner would write because I use the first person, which most journalists don't use. But as you can see, I know the subject well and first person was the only way I could write it.[6]

'FIRST BLOOD' AUTHOR OFFERS TIPS FOR THE WORKING WRITER[7]

SANTA FE, N.M. — As I handed David Morrell a copy of the *Centre Daily Times* that contained a very positive review of his latest book, *The Protector*, he said: "Oh, you must be the fellow from Pennsylvania." We had corresponded via the Internet several times and he knew I was going to show up for his one-day workshop on fiction writing. I was late and unable to introduce myself until the first break of the day.

But I was never late for Morrell's 8 o'clock class in short-story writing at Penn State. I took the course in the winter term of 1970 as

---

[6] I like to say that journalists aren't allowed to use the first person until they are 50.

[7] R. Thomas Berner, "'First Blood' Author Offers Tips For the Working Writer," *Centre Daily Times*, State College, PA (Aug. 31, 2003).

Morrell was completing his Ph.D. in English. In the summer, he would head off for a job at the University of Iowa, the manuscript of his first novel, *First Blood*, tucked away with his belongings. And 33-plus years later at age 59, I was back in his class, only it wasn't in the basement of Willard Building but in a private residence in Santa Fe.

Twenty-four adults have paid $125 for the six-hour workshop (seven if you count lunch) and five of them have published fiction or nonfiction books already. One woman heard Morrell talk in California and when she learned about the workshop here, she and her husband planned their vacation around it. Another participant had read nearly all of Morrell's 18 novels and was seeking a "catalyst to get me beyond thinking about creative writing to actually doing it." Yet another, the author of three local nonfiction books, was seeking inspiration to help her with a novel in progress.

The person who has traveled the greatest distance is Chris Viola of Clinton, N.Y., a Pittsburgh native and Carnegie Mellon University graduate who has read Morrell's *Lifetime of Writing: A Novelist Looks at His Craft* and who was urged by a mutual friend to attend the workshop. He spent eights hours on planes and in airports to get here. Morrell, 60, is wearing a green T-shirt with a pocket, tan shorts and tan tennis shoes. He wears glasses, which he occasionally removes. He uses a flipchart to list his points and he quickly cuts to the chase: No one should want to write for fame or fortune. He passes around a copy of the Myers-Briggs personality test and then tells the audience how he tested.

"I'm an introvert," he says, hoping that everyone will understand that the writing life is not filled with heady wine-and-cheese receptions and book signings attended by adoring fans, but is rather monastic. "You have to love being alone," he tells the group. "It is draining for me to be with a lot of people." Still, he mingles freely throughout the day and gladly discusses writing during breaks and lunch.

The flipchart already lists three of the five points he wants to make during the day: 1. Ability to tell a story, 2. Craft, 3. Discipline, and then he adds perhaps the most difficult of all, 4. Luck. He explains the long path that *First Blood* took, conceived and written while he was a graduate student and instructor at Penn State. And how Sylvester Stallone's movie version in 1982 gave the book the publicity it deserved. The film provided a much larger audience than the publisher's first printing and even the Literary Guild, which offered it as an alternate selection. Morrell's talk is part pedagogical, part psychological, part practical, part autobiographical. His life's story is an oft-told tale because he has written so often about his inspirations, his mentors, his ups and downs, including his decision to give up his tenured position at the University of Iowa to write full time in 1986 and the death of his son, Matthew, from cancer at the age of 15 in 1987.

Morrell credits retired Penn State English professor Phillip Klass for working with him diligently until he finally produced a good short story.

Klass, Morrell tells his audience, urged him to write about fear, and after many attempts the story that finally worked for Klass and became the motivation for Morrell was "The Plinker."

Memories

Morrell has many happy memories of Happy Valley. He and his wife, Donna, and their 2-month-old daughter, Sarie, arrived in June 1966, most of their possessions stashed in a Volkswagen Beetle, and spent the first couple of nights in their apartment in Graduate Circle in sleeping bags on hard floors. On top of that, the thermostat was broken and the heat was on, a not uncommon situation for buildings at Penn State unless it is the middle of winter — then the air conditioning runs full tilt.

Morrell was entering the master's degree program in English. He became attracted to Penn State because he had read a book by English professor Philip Young (*Ernest Hemingway: A Reconsideration*) and knew he wanted to study under Young. In fact, he reread the book upon arrival "and the magic was there twice over."

Morrell remembers his time at Penn State as "a really positive academic experience" and one in which everyone was civil. He recalls being greeted in the mailroom by professors he had not met. As it turned out, because he was Canadian, he added an international flavor to the student body, which seemed, Morrell recalls, to please everyone. Far from finding professors distant, Morrell considered them warm and welcoming. As part of his Ph.D. work, he had to take a course in Middle English from Robert Frank, later to become head of the department. Because only three or four students were in the class, Frank invited them to his house instead of meeting in a room on campus. Frank's wife, Gladys, served cake and coffee, creating an atmosphere that Morrell today says was "very pleasantly British."

Morrell was also captivated by the mountains. "Having lived in southern Ontario for all of my then-23 years," he wrote in an e-mail message, "I had never seen mountains. I can't describe how overwhelmed I was to drive into the Alleghenies and follow them to Happy Valley where gorgeous crests surrounded me, especially Mount Nittany. I've never forgotten how reassuring the dramatic scenery was, given my anxiety at having chucked my past to come to this brave new world. I've been attracted to mountains ever since."

And he was attracted to The Barrens in Patton Township, which became the setting for "The Plinker," the story of a person who goes into the woods to target practice, that is, to "plink," only to become hunted by someone with a rifle. Eventually, the wounded plinker kills the sniper, but then must crawl out of the woods to safety, hoping he does not encounter any snakes. It is all about fear. It is Morrell's leitmotif.

IN YOUR DREAMS

"If the worst-case scenario is being thrust upon you," Morrell tells his workshop students, "you've got a story." He explains that his novels are basically about a hostile world, bad things happening to the characters, the characters responding. He repeatedly makes the point that the more inner turmoil people have, the more fodder they have for fiction. "Fiction is friction," he says. For a writer, "Nightmares are a visit from Santa Claus." Although Morrell is lecturing without notes, he relies frequently on *Lessons from a Lifetime of Writing*, which he likens to a hymnbook, and it serves as his outline. Several participants have purchased the book at the door or, like Chris Viola (and me), have read it already. When Morrell reads from the book, someone in the audience asks for a page number so she can follow along — chapter and verse.

Despite his Ph.D. in English, Morrell likes to say: "This isn't Shakespeare. I'm just a working writer." But a worshipful reviewer on Amazon.com called him "a genre writer with a poet's soul." Morrell disdains those who make the distinction between high brow and low brow, and he mixes his talk with examples ranging from Stephen Crane to Stephen King, from Dante to Hemingway. After the workshop, one participant says she appreciated that Morrell's talk was grounded in American literature. By e-mail a couple of days later another participant raved about "the depth and amount of information imparted."

Morrell draws on Hemingway, the subject of his master's thesis, to make the point about good writing. Use concrete words to create images in the reader's mind; minimize the use of adverbs and adjectives. He cites John Barth, the subject of his Ph.D. dissertation, to make the point that writing is either stained glass or Windex. Morrell advocates windows cleaned with Windex.

"I write action," Morrell says, and advises his audience "to keep the story moving," which is reminiscent of what he told us those many years ago: "Get the reader into the story." On this last point, he contrasts films and highly descriptive and verbose Victorian novels and praises films for getting audiences into and out of scenes quickly. Morrell tells me later that the longest scene he writes is no more than six double-spaced typewritten pages, about 1,500 words, which keeps the reader reading rather than putting the book on the nightstand for another day. (I read *The Protector* in two afternoons.)

DIGRESSIONS AND ALLUSIONS

In 1992, David and Donna Morrell purchased a house here that had once been owned by Edward T. Hall, the well known cultural anthropologist. They converted the garage into a television room. Morrell feels at ease in the room and sat for an interview there shortly after the workshop. The room includes bookshelves, movie posters (both Morrell and non-Morrell) and photographs of Morrell with Stallone and with David Morse, who starred in the television version of Morrell's novel *The Brotherhood of the Rose*.

The house came with a detached office, where Morrell does all of his writing. As he tells the workshop participants, he has a writing desk and a reading desk, and he does not mix the two. Even though the writing desk holds a computer, it is a relic he keeps just in case he needs to access old files. He always reads on paper rather than a computer screen and will change fonts so he doesn't glide over his words.

At the workshop he doesn't always glide either, sometimes digressing and losing his place. When he is talking about his writing and reading protocols and forgets what he wants to say next, he lists out loud the topics he has just covered: "computers," "font," "first drafts."

"First drafts" is his next topic.

His digressions are literary or historical. He makes a point about showing, rather than telling, which leads him to talk about radio plays and then radio shows he listened to as a child. He then asks participants to name the voice of Matt Dillon on the radio show "Gunsmoke." But before anyone answers, he does. It was the late William Conrad, the rotund actor who later starred in several television series.

For the most part, he holds the audience's attention. At 3 p.m. with an hour left, it is an above-average 95 degrees on the shadowed patio outside the workshop room. At the airport 12 miles away, the National Weather Service has logged the temperature as 93. The room is cooled only by electric fans and the occasional breeze that comes in through the opened windows. Most of the participants have a bottle of water with them. It will thunder toward the end of the workshop and threaten to rain, but the rain won't arrive for another 12 hours, and it won't last long.

With 45 minutes to go, Morrell wonders aloud if the participants aren't ready to go home. They aren't, and he turns to one of the workshop's co-directors and, quoting from Shakespeare's Henry V, says to her, "Once more unto the breach," and then turns to his audience and keeps talking.

When he runs overtime, he acknowledges the restlessness of the participants, forgets the point he was making and says: "Ask me a question and maybe I'll remember it." Someone does and he remembers. What faculty member hasn't used that mnemonic device countless times?

EVALUATION

Class is over and the students get a chance to evaluate the instructor. Of the five participants who responded to my request for comments, only one was dissatisfied, in part because he thought the workshop was not as advertised. He expected a wider range of fiction and more hands-on activities and told me he had shared his unhappiness with the workshop's organizers. The others were happy.

The woman with a novel in progress said Morrell's comments helped her "sharpen up certain 'fuzzy' passages" and that his discussion on dialogue was valuable. "I 'fixed' passages," she told me, "in which my characters didn't really say what they really meant."

Another appreciated Morrell's advice about grabbing the reader from the start and making time to write every day. Although familiar with both concepts, hearing them reinforced the lesson.

And Chris Viola, now back in Clinton, N.Y., said he looks at his work and asks himself: "What would David do?" I sense that several participants will be asking that question in the years ahead.

STORY IDEAS

Morrell has told me in an e-mail that an idea for a novel "has kicked in." As one of the many who saw himself someday writing The Great American Novel, this is the lesson I want: Where do you get ideas? Journalism is easy; you write down what people say or what you see and make a story out of it. But ideas. How do you stoke your imagination?

Actually, Morrell has already answered that question in a collection of short stories titled *Black Evening*. The stories had been published individually before, but in this collection, he prefaced each one with a short explanation of how the idea for the story came about. For example, he once wrote a short story "The Storm" after his house in Iowa had been hit by lightning three times in one night. Another story, "Mumbo Jumbo," was inspired by a newspaper story about an Iowa football team that conducted a controversial ritual before each game. And so on.

As I had anticipated, he would not tell me what the idea was. Some writers, for their own good reasons, won't talk about an idea or a book until all is signed, sealed and delivered. Suffice it to say, it will be a sequel to *The Protector*, the first sequel Morrell has written. Morrell also has in mind a novel about the "blade culture," that is, people who are infatuated with knives.

WHERE'S "THE PLINKER"?

Although Morrell cites "The Plinker" often, it has never been published. Morrell sent it off to *Argosy* magazine, where it was mislaid. When the magazine went out of business, an editor belatedly found the manuscript and apologetically returned it, saying it was worthy of publication. Morrell then sent the story to *Playboy*, which rejected it, and shortly after that read it to his fiction-writing class, the one I was taking. By then, though, James Dickey had published *Deliverance* and "The

Plinker" appeared to imitate it, so Morrell has never tried to publish the story.

But he does make the point in the workshop that writers should not imitate other writers or attempt to write a novel that imitates a trend — trends in publishing having a maximum shelf life of three years. "Don't be a so-so imitation of another writer," he says. "Be a first-class version of yourself." Morrell has adopted that as a principle and it has served him well in his career "as just a working writer."

As you read back through the story, several things should be apparent and should guide you in writing similar stories. Obviously, the reporter was present. Note the description, from how Morrell is dressed to the temperature in the room. Since I could not get a reading at the time, I did the next best thing and checked the records at the Santa Fe Airport. Also note not just interviews with others, but their names and hometowns. Note specific times — how much time is left until the workshop ends. I tried very much to put the reader into the story so they could sense what the workshop was like. I wanted the reader to be there.

OBITUARIES

Obituaries — that is, accounts of people's deaths — run the range from short items on a specified page inside the newspaper and provided through a funeral director to lengthy stories that recount a person's life much the way a profile might, except it's retrospective rather than current.[8] I call myself a necrological groupie because I will read anyone's obituary in any newspaper. In fact, wherever I travel, I buy the local newspaper and I read the obituaries.

Why?

Obituaries tell you something about people, sometimes in ways a regular story never would. For example, there's the obituary of a man that said "he was a loving father, a great storyteller, and was particularly fond of his pet mule, 'Jack.'" It then listed his survivors. Here was a man whose mule was listed before his survivors — and his survivors wrote the obituary. A World War II veteran's survivors included this sentence in his obituary: "Charlie (also known as Donnie to his family) served in the Army Corps of Engineers during WW II, landing on Anzio, serving under Patton and going AWOL with a lovely Italian woman (or was she

---

[8]In fact, the *Albuquerque Journal* refers to its news obituaries about people in its circulation area as "local obituary profiles."

French?)." Those are the morsels of life that one can find in an obituary.

Death may be the great equalizer, but newspapers had tended to focus their news obituaries on the rich and famous. That is no longer the case and it is not unusual to find a news obituary about more common people in smaller newspapers. One news obituary that comes to mind was about a man who for decades walked the main street of a small college town and waved to every passer-by. He made people feel good. The newspaper had written a feature story about him at one point and a decade later relied on that and additional reporting to write the news obituary. Many people are worthy of a news obituary, not just the famous.

One person who has written about obituaries is Marilyn Johnson.[9] She calls obituaries "life stories," which is consistent with the way obituary writers generally see their work — writing about how people lived, not so much how they died. Among the parts of an obituary Johnson enumerates are the "tombstone" (opening paragraph), "bad news" (cause of death), and then probably the best section, "the song and dance." That's the part of the obituary that makes the person unique. It's something the person did, be it racing from a bunk in boxer shorts at Pearl Harbor to firing anti-aircraft guns on Dec. 7, 1941, or having a sex-change operation and becoming a professional whistler (after having served in Hitler's Wehrmacht as a man).

The labels are not as important as the content. What a journalist has to be ready to do — sometimes on deadline — is gather the information for a news obituary. Of course, a funeral director will supply detail provided by the family — name, age, where born, where educated, occupation, and so on. But only through interviews with the people who knew the deceased will the subject of a news obituary, ah, come alive.

Start with the family. The best way to approach a grieving family is through the funeral director, but if that person declines to cooperate, then the journalist must go to the family's home and ring the doorbell. Profess sympathy, apologize, then explain what you want to do. Many families actually want to talk about the deceased; it is their way of honoring and memorializing the person (and in some cases venting).

Ask what made the person special or unique. What were his quirks? (Maybe he had a passion for reading obituaries.) No one is perfect, and so

---

[9] Marilyn Johnson, *The Dead Beat* (New York: HarperCollins Publishers, 2006). I met Johnson at the Eighth Great Obituary Writers' International Conference in Las Vegas, New Mexico, in 2006 and made sure I got her autograph on my copy of her book.

you might ask what were his less-than-perfect attributes? You want a rounded story, not an application for sainthood. Explain that to the family. Always ask if there's anything they might want to add and always ask for a list of names of other people who knew the deceased well enough to comment.

As you might in a feature story or profile, ask for anecdotes that exemplify something about the person. Anecdotes are something all readers understand. Here is one of many examples of a news obituary.[10]

OLD WESTERN MAINSTAY GEORGE DEMARTINI DIES

By Larken Bradley

Longtime West Marin resident George DeMartini, a retired Point Reyes National Seashore employee and habitué of the Western Saloon, who sat in the bar window swatting flies while downing Olympian quantities of bourbon and water, died Jan. 17, after several years of declining health. He was 83.

His passion for eliminating flies from the Point Reyes Station watering hole was so ingrained that its owner kept a flyswatter close to his customary perch for him to use.

"He was a great old man," said Western Saloon bartender Helen Skinner. "We called him 'The Old Fart,' and he loved it," said Skinner. "He was insulted if you didn't call him that."

Mr. DeMartini became so attached to his moniker that friends gave him a matching ensemble of a hat, socks and coffee mug, all emblazoned with the 'Old Fart' insignia.

SEASHORE FOREMAN

Added hunting partner Al Crivelli, "my favorite nickname for George was 'Ornery'," he said with a chuckle.

Mr. DeMartini was one of the first employees hired by the Point Reyes National Seashore. He retired from the park service as foreman of the roads and trails crew.

Born in San Francisco on Feb. 22, 1922, young George learned many life lessons in the school of hard knocks. By all accounts, his mother was a barroom floozy, and he never knew his father. He had several half sisters, and his lineage included Cherokee, Portuguese and Italian blood. He was raised in foster homes and in a boys' residential facility.

---

[10]Reprinted with permission of the author from the *Port Reyes Light*, California (Feb. 23, 2006).

Rodeo Rider

Mr. DeMartini's formal education ended after the eighth grade. He went straight to work on a Sonoma County horse ranch. Short and wiry, he rode bulls and horses in rodeos, and had dreams of becoming a jockey.

During World War II he was drafted into the U.S. Army. While serving in Alaska on a gun crew, he sustained[11] injuries to his eyes and ears when a shell exploded, sending shrapnel flying.

After his discharge he went to work at the old Bear Valley Ranch in Olema, where he met his future wife, Ida Silveira, a housekeeper at the homestead. The couple married in Nevada.

Cork in the Bottle

This week his daughter Ronalda DeMartini recalled growing up on the ranch. The family home, she reminisced, was loaded with a choice of potential playrooms. "I loved that house," she said.

Mr. DeMartini worked hard, and he drank hard. As a younger man, his dipsomania led to barroom brawls, but five years ago, after suffering a massive seizure, he plugged a cork in the bottle and switched to Coca-Cola.

He enjoyed dancing and cut the rug on the Western Saloon dance floor with the ladies at the bar — and also with his daughter Ronalda.

His favorite pastime was deer hunting. "He was a good shot," said Al Crivelli.

Volunteered at Halleck Creek

In his retirement years he worked as a janitor at his second home, the Western Saloon. He also volunteered at the Halleck Creek Riding Club.

In 1978 his wife died of cancer. Some 15 years later he married JoAnne Damato. Their marriage ended in divorce in the late 90s.

In addition to his wife, Ida Silveira DeMartini, he was predeceased by his daughter Lenora DeMartini and by a stillborn son.

He is survived by his daughter Ronalda DeMartini and her partner, Joe DeLima of Point Reyes Station.

Burial was in Olema Cemetery beside his wife and daughter.

Mr. DeMartini's daughter suggests that any memorial contributions be made to Halleck Creek Riding Club or to West Marin Senior Services.

---

[11]The correct word, according to AP style, should be "suffered." Buildings and objects *sustain* damage, people *suffer* injuries.

One style quirk here. While many newspapers do not use Mr., Ms., Mrs. and Miss in second references in news stories, some make an exception in obituaries.

IN-DEPTH ARTICLES

Despite its primary focus on what occurs daily, good journalism also steps back to examine the larger picture — to put daily events into a bigger context of trends or patterns. This is achieved through comprehensive reporting of an issue that results in an in-depth article or articles. The in-depth article provides deeper and broader coverage. It is analytical and evaluative but not opinionated. Good in-depth reporting is rigorous and current. It can cover where the issue has been or where it is going.

In-depth reporting examines a variety of sources and blends them into a comprehensive account. It is not merely a series of interviews. A reader unhappy with a *New York Times* article complained in a letter to the editor that most of the sources came from one bar in an industrial town in Pennsylvania and were not representative of the workers of that community. The complaining reader referred to the writer as a "shot and beer journalist." Don't be a shot-and-beer journalist. Seek out experts and seek out people who disagree with them.

When going after experts, make sure you get the right ones. If you're doing a story on declining enrollment at your university, a good person to talk to is the official in charge of admissions. That person should certainly know more than, say, a junior professor, although the junior professor might have some ideas for good questions to raise.

Where do ideas for in-depth articles come from? One obvious place is the reporter's beat. A reporter might notice an issue dancing around the edges of the many meetings he or she covers and decide to write about it. Another place is through listening to others' shop talk. Good reporters are good listeners. They're also avid readers. Specialized journals are another source of ideas. Ask yourself: What do readers need to know?

Every in-depth project has a hypothesis. A hypothesis is, in effect, the focusing point of the story. It provides the reporter with a guide during the research. A hypothesis can be something as simple as "The new nuclear family does the job" or "A ban on hazing will improve the fraternity system" or "Local governments need to look to regional governments to solve many of the problems facing communities today." One qualification: A hypothesis is a guide, not a dogma. The reporter may find that the hypothesis does not hold up. That's OK. You can disprove your hypothesis and still write a good in-depth article. But you still need

a hypothesis from the beginning of the reporting process, because it functions as a navigational aid through the maze of information you gather.

Here's an example of a in-depth story that was triggered by the death of someone in a driving under the influence accident. It follows that accident story by one week. It aims to give the bigger picture. Note that the story provides comparative data, comparing the current year's DUI arrests to other years, that it relies on authoritative sources, especially the district attorney and police, but also the county probation office.[12]

DUI ARRESTS RISE IN CENTRE COUNTY
DUIs on Record Pace in State College

By Pete Bosak

A week after a 21-year-old was killed by a driver who police say was drunk, State College officers say they're on track to arrest a record number of DUI offenders in 2006.

Indeed, the number of DUI arrests throughout Centre County are expected to easily eclipse last year's numbers.

"I'm taken aback again and again by the sheer volume of DUIs," said Centre County District Attorney Michael Madeira. "It seems a third of what we do are DUI cases."

In 2005, Centre County prosecuted 744 DUI offenders. As of Oct. 31, with two months to go, Madeira's office had handled 708 DUIs. Last week, as Madeira was assigning cases to his assistant prosecutors, five of nine new cases on his desk were DUIs.

State College police officers also are on pace to at least tie the record of 462 DUI arrests in 2003. Borough officers have arrested more than 375 people as of the end of October. A normal weekend typically yields more than a dozen such arrests.

"Our officers don't have difficulty finding DUIs," State College Police Chief Thomas King said.

An arrest of one motorist suspected of driving drunk last weekend didn't come soon enough.

One pedestrian died and another was critically injured when a car driven by Anthony S. Torsell, 20, of State College slammed into them at 2:30 a.m. Oct. 28 at South Atherton Street and Beaver Avenue, police said.

---

[12]Pete Bosak, "DUI Arrests Rise in Centre County; DUIs on Record Pace in State College," *Centre Daily Times*, State College, PA. (Nov. 5, 2006).

Police say Torsell was driving with a blood alcohol content of .242 percent, three times the legal limit for an adult. Witnesses said the car was traveling at 50 to 60 mph when it struck Richard A. Smith, 21, of Conshohocken and Penn State student Aaron C. Stidd.

Smith died; Stidd remains in critical condition at Geisinger Medical Center in Danville.

DUI forever changes the lives of victims and their families, and should haunt offenders, Madeira said.

"You're going to have to live with that because, for the rest of your life, you're going to have to realize you took someone's life because you thought you were OK to drive," Madeira said.

UNEXPLAINED INCREASE

Authorities are uncertain whether the increase in arrests is a reflection of more drunks on the road or increased efforts to get officers on the street looking for them.

In 1997, State College police arrested 377 people for drunken driving. In 2003, that number climbed to a record 462, according to State College Police Sgt. Chris Fishel. That year, State College police Cpl. Bill Muse set the mark for police officers statewide by making 121 arrests by himself.

The numbers fell during the next two years, holding steady at 325 arrests, Fishel said.

But police have already nabbed more than 375 offenders this year, with two months to go.

"They're right on line with 2003," Fishel said. "Our department has increased our manpower during the times we know DUI is prevalent. This is consistent with our policy of assertive enforcement of alcohol-related offenses."

Patton Township officers arrested 69 people for DUI last year. They have arrested 65 as of the end of October.

"I can't really explain why (arrests have increased)," King said. "But we want people to know we take DUI very seriously. As we all too well know from what happened (last Saturday), getting behind the wheel can cost someone their life."

"I don't have an answer," Madeira said, about the reason for the increase. "But we have to keep pushing this. I support police in their effort to stop DUI."

BAC RISING, TOO

Police are also disturbed by the high blood alcohol contents they're seeing among offenders. Rarely is someone arrested for DUI even close to the 0.08 percent that is the limit for driving legally in Pennsylvania, police said.

"They're coming in much higher," King said.

Mike Watson deals with DUI offenders every day as Centre County's DUI coordinator in the probation office. He, too, sees a rising number of DUIs. He attributes the increase to enforcement efforts.

"I think the same amount of people are out there," Watson said. "I think police officers are more aggressive in stopping these people. Police are geared toward this. They have regular (DUI) patrols. They are out there looking for DUIs. Probably 60 to 70 percent of the DUIs are between midnight and 4 a.m. And that's when police are looking for DUIs."

He said he hears the same mantra repeated by most DUI offenders.

"They really didn't think it was going to happen to them," Watson said. "They read about it in the paper, they hear about it, but they just didn't think it would happen to them. But it does."

Watson also pointed to Smith's death last weekend as evidence of the dangers of drinking and driving.

"Your life can change in a split second," Watson said.

PRICE OF PENALTIES

Stiff penalties can be another consequence of driving drunk.

Some DUI offenders, if they have never been in trouble with the law before, may be eligible for ARD, or Accelerated Rehabilitative Disposition. In this program, the DUI charge eventually can be dismissed if the accused attends alcohol and safe-driving courses, pays a fine and completes any other requirements imposed by the court.

There are three tiers of DUI in the eyes of the justice system. The first tier would be an arrest with a blood alcohol content of 0.08 percent to 0.099 percent — something police say rarely happens. The second tier are people with BACs of 0.10 percent to 0.16 percent. The third is a BAC of 0.16 percent and up.

If ARD is not available, a first-time offender with a blood alcohol content of, for example, 0.12 percent, faces a mandatory 48 hours in jail and a one-year driver's license suspension. A "third tier" offender faces a mandatory 72 hours in jail and a year without a driver's license.

With repeat offenses come stiffer penalties.

For example, if a DUI offender is arrested a second time with a blood alcohol content of 0.12, he or she is off to jail for at least 30 days. Offenders in this category will lose their licenses for one year and, when they get it back, they will have to pay for an ignition interlock system for their vehicles, Madeira said.

This in-depth article was followed by an editorial. Such editorials usually call for action and try to unite the community behind a solution.

For examples of other in-depth stories, go to the Pulitzer Prize Web site and look under the category Explanatory Reporting.[13]

---

[13]http://www.pulitzer.org/

Chapter 7

NARRATIVE NONFICTION

Journalists use a variety of writing approaches to provide news and information to their readers. One such approach is narrative nonfiction, also known as literary journalism.[1]

WHAT IS NARRATIVE NONFICTION?

Although it may sound circular and confounding, the easiest definition of narrative nonfiction is that it is a story. All humans are familiar with stories because they tell them or listen to them every day, from each other or from mass media like television shows or movies. How many times have you approached a friend and said: "Have I got a story for you!"

But for someone who wants to write narrative nonfiction, saying it is a story doesn't help much. A story has a beginning, a middle and an end, but so does an editorial. An editorial, which is an essay, is a combination of fact and opinion meant to make a specific point, often to persuade readers to adopt a certain position on an issue.

You may recall from an English course that a story has rising action and falling action. Or that a story is the tale of a conflict and its resolution. Because of those elements, we say a story has tension, but it would be wrong to infer from words such as conflict and tension that in order to have a story you must have, say, a gang war or police chasing and capturing criminals.

Many years ago Associated Press reporter Max Hall described the tension-resolution model this way:

---

[1] I really don't like the word *literary* because it conjures up thoughts of fiction, which is not what is meant here. Nevertheless, I confess to having written a book titled *Writing Literary Features* when I was young and didn't know any better.

Suppose a baseball game is broken up by a home run in the ninth inning. The writer reports that fact in his lead — the top-heavy treatment. But somewhere in the body of the story, he makes a detailed narrative out of the events in the ninth inning leading up to the climax. And if he handles it well, there is a certain suspense about it. It is not the "whodunit" kind of suspense which would exist if the reader were in the dark as to the outcome. It is the kind of suspense that has been aptly called "waiting for the expected."[2]

One of my favorite examples is Shakespeare's *Taming of the Shrew*. We know from the title what the story is about, but we watch the play to see how it comes about — how the shrew is tamed. Thus, narrative nonfiction has the virtue of having higher reader attention and greater readership. It involves the reader because the reader sees the story unfold.

Narrative nonfiction has a long history, but for our purposes I will use the mid-1900s as a good take-off point. Then the public enjoyed such writers as John Hersey, Walter Lord, Lillian Ross, Truman Capote and Tom Wolfe, whom some credit with the rise of new journalism, although Wolfe is quick to point to Hersey as one of the progenitors.

Hersey is most famous for *Hiroshima*, a nonfiction account of the immediate aftermath of the dropping of the atomic bomb on the Japanese city of Hiroshima. Lord is famous for *A Night to Remember*, the story of the sinking of the Titantic, and *Day of Infamy*, the story of the Japanese attack on Pearl Harbor.[3]

Those books were reconstructions. That is, the information was gathered after the fact through interviews and documents rather than first-hand reporting. One of the trailblazers in first-hand reporting was Lillian Ross, who produced for *The New Yorker* such classics as "Picture" and "Portrait of Hemingway." For "Picture," an account of the making of the movie "The Red Badge of Courage," Ross spent a year living in Hollywood and attending script meetings, shootings and even parties. For the Hemingway article, she followed the author around for one day while he was in New York City. The type of reporting Ross did is called "fly on the wall"; that is, she was able to see and hear everything without being obtrusive or intrusive.

Truman Capote picked up on Ross' approach and successfully

---

[2]Max Hall, in L. M. Lyons (ed.), *Reporting the News: Selections from Nieman Reports* (Cambrdge, MA: The Belknap Press of Harvard University, 1965).

[3]Lord wrote several very compelling narrative nonfiction books about World War II.

applied it to *In Cold Blood*, the story of the murder of a family of four in Kansas and the capture, trials and execution of their two murderers. Like Ross, Capote was on hand for most of the story (except the murders) and told the story as it happened. Both Hersey, Ross and Capote published their work first in *The New Yorker* before it was issued in book form.

Inspired by this work and Wolfe's, newspaper journalists began to write narrative nonfiction, and in 1979 the Pulitzer Prize committee issued the first award for feature writing, which went to Jon Franklin of the *Baltimore Evening Sun* for his story about brain surgery.[4] Franklin followed up with a book titled *Writing for Story* in which he makes the case for narrative nonfiction in newspapers. Twenty-five years later many journalists were meeting at conferences to talk about narrative nonfiction, and they belonged to listservs devoted to the subject and routinely checked into Web sites where such stories were posted for all to read.[5]

ELEMENTS AND TECHNIQUES OF NARRATIVE NONFICTION

Hersey once wrote that "Journalism allows its readers to witness history; fiction gives the readers an opportunity to live it."[6] Put those together in narrative nonfiction, and the reader becomes a living witness.

The elements and techniques of narrative nonfiction are many and not all are necessary in order for a story to be narrative nonfiction. Here are some: narrative, point of view, scene and summary, verb tense, relevant detail, dialogue, foreshadowing and flashback.

Narrative, of course, means story. Confusion might arise between narrative and anecdote. An anecdote is a very brief story that might illuminate a point, but it is not the entire story. Anecdotes appear frequently as leads in feature stories. But, as noted earlier, a narrative needs a beginning, middle, and ending; conflict/tension and resolution, rising action and falling action.

Point of view means whose angle the story will be told from. Getting the right point of view for a story is a critical decision to make. If the wrong point of view is chosen, the story could collapse. If you wanted to write a story about illegal aliens, you need to decide whose point of view

---

[4]Franklin won a second under the category explanatory journalism in 1985.
[5]Check out the Nieman Narrative Digest at www.nieman.harvard.edu/narrative/digest/.
[6]John Hersey, "The Novel of Contemporary History," *Atlantic Monthly* (November 1949).

to tell the story from: an illegal alien, a member of the Border Patrol, the family left behind. Of course, all three can appear in the story, but one needs to dominate. That person is the one who has a conflict that needs to be resolved.

Scene and summary play off each other and go hand in hand. Scenes are wonderful ways to show action in narrative nonfiction. They advance a story by showing the process of something happening and by showing how the characters in the story change and evolve (or not). Scenes involve the reader. Here is the opening scene in a story about two men who dig graves by hand, something not done that often:

> The early-morning sun had barely cleared the top of the San Bruno mountains as John Fitzpatrick and Maurice Hickey trudged across the wet, well-manicured law of Holy Cross Cemetery, carrying shovels and spades.
>
> Fitzpatrick paused, took a folded yellow slip of paper from the pocket of his faded blue overalls and glanced at the name of the marble headstone.[7]

Anyone reading that is probably blinking as the sun hits him in the face and stepping gingerly on the wet grass. The reader sees the two men — not walking, but trudging — then they pause. Again, the reader sees one of them take a piece of paper from his overalls. No, a *yellow* slip of paper from the pocket of his *faded blue* overalls. So even if you might have been with the two men, you may not have noticed everything that the author Paul Shinoff noticed, but because he did and put the information in the story, you do see it. It's a lesson first mentioned in Chapter 6 under feature writing: Use all of your senses and write everything down: what you see, smell, taste, feel, hear.

Not everything in a story, however, needs to be shown in a scene or, for that matter, can be shown in a scene. Then the writer turns to summary, as in this story about stem cell research:[8]

> With the November elections over, the Republican Party was in elephantine glory. The GOP had added seats in both houses of Congress. President Bush was safely ensconced for a second term.
>
> Evangelicals were being credited with delivering his re-election,

---

[7] Paul Shinoff, "A Job Where Nobody Complains," San Francisco *Examiner* (Sept. 27, 1981).

[8] Wes Allison, "Republican vs. Republican: A Cellular Division," *St. Petersburg Times* (Aug. 13, 2006).

and the news was dominated by talk of the conservative agenda to come: restructure Social Security, cut taxes and entitlement spending, ban gay marriage.

But the mood was hardly heady for the moderates, who often felt as welcome by their party as Democrats.

They believed that centrist voters - their voters - were the backbone of the GOP but feared that Republican leaders were steering the party too far right. The moderates in the basement called themselves the Tuesday Group (and met, naturally, on Wednesdays). They half-heartedly had tried to push back against their party on abortion restrictions, environmental protection, funding for education and social services. They were used to losing.

On stem cells, they vowed, things would be different.

Verbs are central to all writing, but in most news stories, the most used verbs are in the past tense. In narrative nonfiction, however, the writer has a greater array of tenses to choose from, beginning with present tense then present perfect, past tense and past perfect. With four tenses on which to build a story, the writer has more options than she would in the traditional news story. Now the story can be told in four zones instead of two.

Present tense helps make a scene more immediate, as this rewrite of an earlier lead demonstrates:

> The early-morning sun has barely cleared the top of the San Bruno mountains as John Fitzpatrick and Maurice Hickey trudge across the wet, well-manicured law of Holy Cross Cemetery, carrying shovels and spades.
>
> Fitzpatrick pauses, takes a folded yellow slip of paper from the pocket of his faded blue overalls and glances at the name of the marble headstone.[9]

Present tense should be used for the main time of a story. Scenes that occurred before the main time of the story need to be in past and even past perfect time. Preserving the main time of the story in present tense enables the reader follows the storyline more easily.

Just back up a few paragraphs and look over the detail in Shinoff's lead. Rising sun, wet lawn, yellow slip of paper, faded blue overalls, marble headstone. Together they helped build a picture of the place and

---

[9]Paul Shinoff, "A Job Where Nobody Complains," San Francisco *Examiner* (Sept. 27, 1981).

the people — a picture the reader can see. Here's another example of detail from a feature story I wrote about a writer giving a talk on writing:[10]

> Morrell, 60, is wearing a green T-shirt with a pocket, tan shorts and tan tennis shoes. He wears glasses, which he occasionally removes. He uses a flipchart to list his points and he quickly cuts to the chase: No one should want to write for fame or fortune. He passes around a copy of the Myers-Briggs personality test and then tells the audience how he tested.

A good narrative nonfiction writer not only captures detail, but he listens to what people say. How people talk to each other says a lot about their relationship. A person uses a different tone of voice talking to the boss than to a subordinate or an equal or a lover. Dialogue between the same two people could differ depending on the environment. Colleagues might be formal at the office, but casual — even profane — when playing poker.

Dialogue moves a story along. Here is some dialogue between two brothers who are independent coal miners and a reporter regarding the records the miners must keep.

> "If we filled all of these books out complete, we wouldn't have any time left to go mining," Nathan concludes.
> "Only half of these reports are even needed," adds Jesse.
> "How do you manage?" the brothers are asked.
> "Let's just say we are practicing some civil disobedience," Nathan says with a faint smile. The brothers laugh, sharing their private joke on the federal regulators, and then the smoky room fails quiet again.
> "When I fought in the war (World War II under General George Patton) I believed I was fighting to make this country free," Nathan, the first to speak again, says thoughtfully. "Now I see that wasn't so. You're never really free, not even in this country."[11]

Just that little bit of dialogue provides good insight into two of the characters in the story.

Readers like to have an idea where a story is headed. Writers tell them by foreshadowing events. Give the reader hints. In the prologue of a story about a man who attempted to assassinate President Ronald

---

[10]The full story appears in Chapter 6.
[11]Gilbert M. Gaul, "A Fire on the Mountain: The Story of the Kintzel Brothers," *The Pottsville* (Pennsylvania) *Republican* (March 20, 1981).

Reagan, Donald C. Drake foreshadowed the assassination attempt in one sentence:

> He carried with him a suitcase, a $47 handgun and a letter describing how he intended to assassinate the President of the United States.[12]

Altogether, Drake's story covered more than two full pages of his newspaper, and it was not until the last two paragraphs that he got back to the assassination attempt. By then, though, the reader knew everything there was to know about the shooter. And part of that was learned in flashbacks. For as Drake wove his story, which breaks down into 14 scenes/summary, he took the reader back into the early life the shooter. They are flashbacks and appear just when the reader needs background to understand the main story. As the reader accumulates information through flashbacks, the tension mounts.

BEGINNING, MIDDLE AND END

The beginning of any narrative nonfiction story must attract the reader immediately. It cannot meander; it cannot be digressive; it cannot focus on a minor character in the story. Consider:

> Inside a limousine parked on the airport tarmac, Katherine Cathey looked out at the clear night sky and felt a kick.
> "He's moving," she said. "Come feel him. He's moving."
> Her two best friends leaned forward on the soft leather seats and put their hands on her stomach.
> "I felt it," one of them said. "I felt it."
> Outside, the whine of jet engines swelled.
> "Oh, sweetie," her friend said. "I think this is his plane."

That is the lead on "Final Salute" by Jim Sheeler of the *Rocky Mountain News*.[13] It engages the reader in the first sentence and as the scene unfolds the reader wonders more and more what is going on. The reader is first

---

[12] Donald C. Drake, "The Suspect: From a Lonely Childhood to a D.C. Jail," *The Philadelphia Inquirer* (April 2, 1981).

[13] Jim Sheeler, "Final Salute," *Rocky Mountain News* (Nov. 9, 2005). The entire story can be found at http://denver.rockymountainnews.com/news/finalSalute/. A good discussion on the story can be found at the *Nieman Narrative Digest* at www.nieman.harvard.edu/narrative/ digest/index.html. Search for Sheeler.

introduced by name only to Katherine Cathey. Who is she? Who's moving? By the third paragraph, you know she is pregnant and that it is her baby moving in her stomach. Each sentence adds more information and builds the story.

Guess what? The story is not about Katherine Cathey, but Marine Maj. Steve Beck, whose duties include notifying families when a relative is killed in war. Sheeler and photographer Todd Heisler spent a year with Beck and the families he notified compiling "Final Salute," which won both writer and photographer[14] a Pulitzer Prize. As a widow of someone killed in war, Katherine Cathey represents the situations Beck and his men encounter, from notifying families to maintaining watch over the body at the funeral home to helping conduct graveside services, finally removing the U.S. flag from the coffin, folding it precisely, and handing it to the widow.

This is how Mary Schmich of the *Chicago Tribune* began at profile on Judge Joan Lefkow:[15]

> A few days ago, Joan Lefkow was walking down a Chicago street flanked by federal marshals when a panhandler walked up to her and said, "God bless you, Judge Lefkow."
>
> It has been nine months since U.S. District Judge Joan Humphrey Lefkow's name and face made relentless news, but what happened to her the night of Feb. 28 still haunts her days and stirs the souls of strangers.
>
> On that winter evening, Lefkow came home from a day in the federal courthouse to find her husband and mother murdered in her basement. In Chicago and beyond, millions felt her loss and terror.

Again, the reader is immediately pulled into the story, this time by the juxtaposition of a person *Tribune* readers would know by name, federal marshals and a panhandler with a quote. Recall the lead by Donald C. Drake that you first read in Chapter 2:

> Dawn was just beginning to brighten the eastern sky. It was a sunrise that went unnoticed by the man asleep on the steam grate opposite Rittenhouse Square, folded up between a concrete trash

---

[14]He subsequently joined the staff of the *New York Times*.
[15]Mary Schmich, "The Journey of Judge Joan Lefkow," *Chicago Tribune* (Nov. 20, 2005). The *Tribune* provides a great selection of stories at www.chicagotribune.com/news/specials/.

receptacle and a newspaper vending machine.

An electric digital display in a nearby bank window gave the time: 5:54.

The sleeping man was wearing baggy corduroy pants, a wool hat, a shirt and a dirty blanket worn over his shoulders like a shawl.

His eyes still closed, the man reached into his open shirt to scratch at the lice, as he had been doing all night. A bread truck roared by on Walnut Street, followed a few minutes later by a milk truck. Then it was quiet again.

The sidewalk, which in two hours would be crowded with people hurrying to their jobs, was deserted now. The only signs of life were the man and a lone car that waited obediently at an empty intersection for the light to change.

The man started to stir and, still without opening his eyes, pushed himself up to a sitting position, leaning back against the concrete trash receptacle. Joggers began to appear across the street, resolutely circling the park, too intent on their exercise to notice the solitary man.

It took a long time, maybe 15 or 20 minutes, for the man to wake up fully, but by 6:15 his eyes were open wide, staring down the elegant street that had been his home for three years. At first he did nothing but sit, stare and scratch.

Another day was beginning for Jim Logue Crawford, 69, former mental hospital patient.[16]

All three leads share one attribute — the reporters witnessed what had happened. The more a reporter can witness events, the better the story. Use Lillian Ross's fly-on-the-wall approach whenever possible. When that cannot be done, the reporter must draw from sources detail after detail as Hersey and Lord did. Interviewing for a regular news account and interviewing for narrative nonfiction are two different processes. In the former, one asks for facts and opinion; in interviewing for story, one asks for details (again, the five senses).

All of that detail then enables the writer to construct a story, and how well the writer interviewed is revealed in middle of the story. The middle of the story shows the fruits of the reporting effort. The middle is where the story unfolds — and that can go in different ways. The Drake story about the assassination attempt on President Reagan can be broken into 14 sections, some scenes and some summary/flashback. Sheeler's piece is broken into 12 parts; Schmich comes in 11 parts.

How well a story ends is an indication of how well the journalist

---

[16]Donald C. Drake, "The Forsaken: How America Has Abandoned Thousands in the Name of Social Progress," *The Philadelphia Inquirer* (July 18, 1982).

gathered relevant material and how well the writer controlled the material and understood the narrative process.

Finally, appropriately, the ending. I've counted many labels for endings — tie-back, link, echo, direct quote, future — but all can be summed up this way: The best endings stay with the reader long after the reader has turned the page. The best endings endure. This is how Schmich ended her profile on Judge Lefkow:

> Michael Lefkow once asked his wife, "Even if there is no God and even if evil prevails, would you live your life differently?"
> She told him no. She still thinks no.
> "I have some core value that searching for the good and the honorable is the way to live," she says. "God is the spirit of good in the world. God is the spirit of love in the world. That belief is so engrained in me that even if someone proved point by point that it wasn't true, I'd still believe it."

That's a strong ending for several reasons. For one, the story ends with the same person the story began with, so the reader sees a link or tie-back. And it's a powerful quote. This woman's husband (Michael) and mother have been murdered and she could have expressed bitterness. Instead, she talks about love. The ending will endure. Readers will think about the ending days after reading the story.

Drake's ending on the assassination story is equally strong and hits the reader very hard.

> He fired.

Recall that in his lead Drake foreshadowed this so he doesn't have to go into any detail. The story has provided all of the detail on the shooter's life and there's nothing left to be said.

Narrative nonfiction is fact-based story-telling. Such stories are honored because editors know the readers will read them. After all, story-telling is as old as the human race.

Chapter 8

EDITORS

Many editors are involved in producing a newspaper and its related Web site. Key among them are copy editors, who edit copy and write headlines and photo captions and make sure libel is excised from stories.[1]

THE ROLE OF COPY EDITORS

Copy editors are in great demand. Wherever editors gather, eventually the talk turns to finding a way to woo young people into considering a career as a copy editor. No editor can publish a newspaper without copy editors. Reporters can come and go, get laid off or fired, but even in the most perilous of economic times, newspapers need copy editors.

Unlike some editors whose jobs have been immortalized by Hollywood and Broadway, the copy editor remains anonymous. The public image of the intrepid reporter or the barking editor belies the reality of newspapering, for it is the unglamorous copy editor who puts the paper together day in and day out. The fearless investigative reporter can uncover a scandal of national import and the editor can issue directions on how the story is played, but it is the copy editor who polishes the reporter's words and turns the editor's directions into reality. Without the copy editor (or deskperson, as the job-holder is sometimes known), the newspaper would be a ragged resemblance of good intention, and good intention does not result in good newspapers.

The copy editor assumed a greater role when newspapers entered the electronic age. Once thought of as the last person who could catch a mistake, the copy editor of old actually enjoyed superb backstopping from printers and proofreaders who were often as skillful as the copy editor.

---

[1] Before reading this chapter, you might find it useful to refresh yourself on news and reread the Introduction and Chapter 3.

But today those reserves are gone — victims of automation and modernization.

The copy editor now bears responsibility once divided among three or four people. As Robert H. Williams of *The Washington Post* explained the work of the copy editor:

> Copy editors come to be the institutional memory of a newspaper, the ones who know where bodies are buried inside the organization and outside of it, the ones who know when the last near-fatal policy errors were made and what they cost. Copy editors know that World War II came before the Korean War and that it wasn't David who went into the lion's den, but Daniel, and they are forever amending such bizarre mistakes in reporters' stories. Copy editors become terribly proficient in the industrial science of producing a newspaper and in the art of making words work together.[2]

Benefits come from all of that. The copy editor is generally better paid than a reporter and at most newspapers no one usually rises through the ranks without doing some desk work. Newsroom promotions from the middle to the top level usually come from the desk, not the reporting staff.

An old advertisement for *The New York Times Manual of Style and Usage* proclaimed: "As a writer you're judged by your consistency and accuracy of style and usage." It could also say: "As a copy editor you are judged by your ability to catch a writer's inconsistent and inaccurate style and usage." Writers up against a deadline make mistakes that in more casual circumstances they would not make. Deadline aside, every writer's copy needs an editor's eye to smooth the pace of words and parade of facts for the reader.

The copy editor must know not only how to use language well but also how to fix a writer's story without destroying the writer's style. A copy editor must spot errors lesser mortals would never see, must see that the story's unasked questions are answered immediately, must write accurately and with sparkle (a favorite word in copy editor job descriptions). The copy editor must select stories with unerring regard for reader interests, must design an attractive page around the selection, see that the tone, style and flavor of the newspaper are maintained, and must write headlines and photo captions that (again) sparkle.

---

[2]Robert H. Williams, "Giving Copy Editors Their Due," *presstime* (December 1988), pp. 34-35.

In evaluating copy editors, one newspaper examines their ability to identify important story elements, to organize stories, edit copy tightly, see when legal and fairness issues arise, meet deadline, identify the best headline angle and write headlines with flair. (*Flair* is a substitute for *sparkle*.) Copy editors must have a healthy skepticism about everything they edit. They should ask questions and ensure the story answers them — or get the writer to answer them.

For that, copy editors, who do not get bylines, take their gratification internally. They are secure in the knowledge that they have helped produce a first-rate newspaper. They know that their sharp eye may have saved the publisher millions in libel damages. They are, above all, humble.

The copy editor serves as a professional reader for the good of a very special client, the reader of the newspaper. Even when reading about a favorite subject, the copy editor, despite being well read and knowledgeable, employs ignorance to ensure that the final story is clear to the reader.

The copy editor respects the reporter; in fact, mutual respect for high standards serves the reader because the copy editors and reporters see themselves as working together. Decades ago a beginning reporter praised a column written weekly by his city editor. "It would be a lot better if I had a copy editor," the city editor replied. Then there is the story of the late Peter Kihss of *The New York Times*. Kihss was highly regarded for his accurate reporting and quit three times when editors introduced errors into his copy. Good copy editors respect reporters like Peter Kihss. Good copy editors engender rapport with reporters. To that end, they do not make changes in copy for the sake of change. "I'd write it differently" is no reason for a copy editor to change a reporter's story. A copy editor remembers that a change can just as easily make a story inaccurate as accurate. Copy editors are not infallible.

Those who aspire to the copy desk should know that, unlike previous times in journalism, today's newspapers hire copy editors directly out of college instead of making them serve an apprenticeship as a reporter. The copy desk today is not a place where worn-out reporters are tossed. Would-be copy editors must prove their potential, often by taking a series of tests that show not only the person's ability with the language but also the person's instinct to sense errors. Told to edit a story, one journalism graduate on a job interview asked: "Where's the city directory?" He knew some of the tools of the trade. He went on to pass the tests and get the job. Within four months he was news editor; within two years, managing editor. His assistant, who during college served a Newspaper Fund internship on the desk of the *Boston Globe*, moved on to become a copy editor for *Advertising Age* within a year of graduating from college. The closed door to early advancement has been removed from its hinges.

Copy editors need not feel cut off from writing opportunities either, for though they seldom get a chance to cover hard news, they do have time to produce work hard-pressed reporters don't. Copy editors bent on doing some writing find pleasure in writing editorials, columns, reviews or features for Sunday use.

A VARIETY OF EDITORS AND THEIR DUTIES

Copy editors are but one type of editor. Given the number of editors any one newspaper might have, an outsider would get the impression of too many bosses and no workers. In newspapers, though, the tendency is to put someone in charge of something and then call that person an editor. Thus, the person who writes play reviews might be called the Arts Editor or the Culture Editor on the basis that the person is a specialist and deserves to be so tagged. A copy editor might also have responsibility for selecting travel stories for the Sunday edition and thus be called the Travel Editor — and receive extra compensation for the work. And despite the notion that some news executives give subordinates titles rather than pay raises, many newspaper editors perform necessary functions in the day-to-day operation of the paper.

Editors make things happen. Editors generate ideas. Editors lead by example. The person responsible for the news and opinion content of a newspaper is the executive editor or editor.[3] Under that person can be found the editor responsible for overseeing the daily operation, the managing editor. Depending on the newspaper's size, the managing editor usually has more contact with reporters than the editor or executive editor, who must also deal with corporate responsibilities and long-range planning.

At some newspapers the person holding the title of editor is the editor of the editorial page only. If the paper is large enough and has an op-ed (for opposite-editorial) page, that page has an appropriately titled editor. Top editors have associates and assistants, listed under those titles or called by different titles such as news editor, city editor, metro (for

---

[3]This will depends on the newspaper's size. At larger newspapers, the editor of the editorial page reports to the publisher. But at smaller newspapers, that isn't always the case, so it's difficult to claim that one description fits all. I'm trying to convey an expansive view of the newsroom.

metropolitan) editor, national, foreign, sports, feature. Newspapers in nonmetropolitan areas often have county editors who are responsible for seeing that news in the less populated sections of the newspaper's circulation area gets covered. Give a newspaper a specialty, and an editor will be named to oversee it. A printer at a small-town daily I worked for once quipped that if he walked into the newsroom at his newspaper and said, "I need an editor out back," everyone in the newsroom would follow him to the shop.

More and more women and minorities are filling positions of responsibility in newsrooms of all media as publishers and station managers discover that a person's sex or race does not correlate with a person's abilities. Some gains by women and minorities have not come without lawsuits, and future editors would do well to ensure that today's gains are not lost tomorrow.

The advancement of women and minorities is good for the news media. What they bring to newspapers and broadcast outlets are new points of view so necessary to ensure that the news media understand their audiences. How can the news media report thoroughly and sensitively on, say, women's issues without women editors and reporters? They can't. Some female journalists believe that day care issues get better coverage in the news media because women journalists have helped their male counterparts understand the issue from a woman's point of view.

If the top editors of all news media have failed in any field, it is in the skillful handling of their subordinates. Time and time again journalism school graduates will complain that on their first job "Nobody tells me how I'm doing" or "Nobody edits my copy." One of the long-standing problems of journalism is that in a field predicated on communication, some of its practitioners cannot talk to each other. No matter what the level, editors must participate in the communication process.

One breakdown occurs in the hiring process in which the news executive fails to clearly explain what the company expects of a person in a job. The result is that after a person is hired or promoted, the executive says, "Oh, by the way, I also want you to do such-and-such," tasks the person has no interest in doing or for which the person is not qualified. Had the executive defined the job clearly, the problem could have been avoided. Instead, the reporter felt deceived and it affected his work.[4]

---

[4]In mid-2006 I counseled a former student to whom this had happened. She quit the newspaper and left journalism entirely. My advice to job interviewees is to ask what else the job entails.

The good editor recognizes that the newspaper's success depends on the staff. The good editor hires people who are not only bright but who are brighter than the editor. If editors who are weak writers hired only those people who wrote at the editor's level, the newspaper would surely fail. Editors who hire shouldn't feel threatened by talented people, and, in fact, should heavily recruit the best.

Once a talented staff is assembled, the good editor primes it for success. In such a newsroom, no recent journalism graduate can whine about not being told how he or she is doing because the good editor sees that the top editors routinely, albeit sometimes informally, meet with reporters to explain what they're doing wrong, and right. On a daily basis, copy editors ensure high morale by explaining to reporters why stories had to be cut or held. Nobody's left in the dark. By the same token, reporters should talk to editors and not wait for them to initiate every discussion. At some newspapers, in fact, reporters have initiated their own writing workshops as a way of improving each other's writing. Editors encourage such initiatives.

The editor continues staff training beyond that first day when the new reporter received a copy of the newspaper style guide and a list of office personnel and their telephone extension numbers. Formal and informal training sessions, including in-house critiques, continue throughout the reporter's career, and at larger newspapers, reporters are sent back to school for updating or to workshops to pick up information on a specialty.

Good editors pay attention to the development of their staffs. Good editors strive to involve staff members in decisions. After all, sub-editors and reporters are really middle managers and should be involved in making decisions that affect them. Good editors encourage staff members to improve their professional skills and to pursue other interests that will help round out the staff members.

In the training process, the good news executive is looking for managerial talent, people who not only possess qualities of leadership but who also want to lead. Not every person of leadership talent wants the promotion, and not every person who wants the promotion should get it. The classic example of poor management repeats itself time and time again when a very good reporter is transferred to the copy desk, there to fail because the reporter's interests lie in reporting. If kept too long, the reporter suffers the stigma of being a loser and the editor finds it more difficult to solve the problem. Making the copy editor a reporter again appears to be a demotion, even in the reporter's eyes.

When not functioning as executives, the many editors in newspapers perform a variety of duties not always foretold in their titles. The managing editor at a small newspaper might unlock the door in the morning, clear the wire, edit copy, write headlines, lay out Page One, hire and fire staff — and make coffee. In large newspapers, the managing editor ensures that the newsroom budget includes money to buy coffee.

At some newspapers, the city editor, often portrayed as a gruff-talking person, has final responsibility for all local copy. He or she might also be the assignment editor, telling reporters throughout the day which breaking news stories to cover or which stories to follow up. The city editor might check each story for content and then assign it an assistant for editing and headline writing, or the editor might process the story on the spot.

Other people working with the city editor are the wire editor, who at some newspapers is responsible for the state, national and international news sent by the wire services; the news editor, who might be in charge of dummying Page One; the photo editor, who may be a photographer in charge of the photo department or who may be responsible for the cropping and sizing of all photographs, and the copy editor, who edits and headlines stories under the direction of a chief copy editor or the city editor.

THE NEWSROOM HIERARCHY

All of the editors just mentioned and others must fit into a hierarchy. The following briefly describes the hierarchy of a composite medium-sized daily (75,000 circulation) that also publishes a Sunday edition.

At the top is the editor, who sits as an equal with other newspaper department heads, such as the advertising director and the circulation manager. The editor answers to the publisher. (On a larger newspaper, the executive editor would fill the role.) The editor, while exercising overall control, does not sit on the desk or edit copy. The editor assures overall quality by coordinating the work of the many assistants through the chief assistant, the managing editor.

Working under the managing editor are five assistants, who in some newspapers might carry titles, such as chief copy editor, state editor, news editor, wire editor, local or city editor. In this composite daily, these people are assistant managing editors.

The primary concern of the first assistant is the quality of headlines and copy editing. This assistant managing editor not only supervises the universal copy desk (explained presently), but also evaluates the writing in the paper and works with individual reporters who are having writing problems. One of this editor's duties is frequently compiling and writing a critique of the newspaper. (One of the best known critiques is "Winners & Sinners," which the late Theodore M. Bernstein wrote for the *New York Times*.)

The second assistant managing editor oversees coverage of state news — that is, news that occurs in the state but outside the paper's immediate circulation area. This editor also oversees the newspaper's bureau in the state capital and any other bureaus the paper may have within the state. All correspondents work under this editor, who also oversees the production of the paper's state edition.

The third assistant managing editor coordinates special projects, overseeing, for example, all election coverage. In such a case, this editor would work with the state editor to avoid conflicts, overlaps and duplication and to produce a smooth election package of preview stories and results. The third assistant also oversees the newspaper's special investigative reporting team. The virtue of having an editor oversee investigative reporting cannot be stressed enough. Some newspapers with investigative reporters forget that the editing of such work needs as much care as the reporting. Some newspapers fail to free an editor to coordinate investigative reporting and the result is that some harried editor with too much to do must take on the additional work of checking the investigative report. Not having been in on the story from the start, the harried editor begins work in ignorance. Pressed because daily work awaits, this harried editor rushes through the investigative work and misses holes. A special editor works with the team from the start and avoids those problems

The fourth assistant managing editor oversees all news received via the wire services. This job is more than just sign on, read and route. This editor must make sure that stories are distributed to the right desks and that updates and corrections get to the right editors. Automatic sorting systems do not replace this editor. They help the editor do a better job. At some dailies this editor is responsible for designing Page One.

The fifth assistant managing editor assigns stories within the newspaper's circulation area. Although the managing editor can generate story ideas, it is this assistant who sees that a reporter gets the assignment and the time to do the assignment.

Subordinate editors on this composite newspaper include graphics (responsible for overall appearance of the paper, but she or he does not lay out each page), photo, sports, business, lifestyle/leisure, presentation (a combination graphics and photo editor, but not a design editor). Where appropriate, these editors select which stories go on their pages and then design the pages within the framework established by the graphics editor. Some newspapers have an operations desk that is responsible for laying out the local and wire news sections of the paper.

One other editor oversees the Sunday edition, making sure that the content for the special sections gets in type throughout the week instead of at the last minute. News and sports sections in the Sunday edition fall outside this editor's purview; they are usually the responsibility of the editors mentioned before.

Yet another editor is responsible for the newspaper's Web site, for making sure stories are uploaded and presented in a timely fashion. This is a job that varies from newspaper to newspaper. An independent newspaper might have a publisher, editor and ad salesperson for the Web site; a newspaper owned by a chain might feed all copy to a central location where web-oriented workers (rather than journalism-oriented people) slot the stories into templates by sections. In those circumstances, each newspaper's Web site looks like the other, distinguished only by the content.

Depending on the newspaper, copy is edited on a universal desk or at individual department desks. In a universal system, all copy, with the exception of sports, is edited by the copy editors at that desk. A universal desk ensures consistency of writing and style much better than individual departments can. In newspapers where individual departments edit their own copy, minor stylistic and editing differences explode into newsroom warfare and the main purpose of the newspaper is forgotten as the lifestyle editor and the business editor feud over, say, the use of last names in second references. As silly as it may sound, such internecine debates can stymie quality work.

While it is often said that too many cooks spoil the broth, in the newsroom a lot of editors work to ensure that the daily newspaper is one of high quality day in and day out.

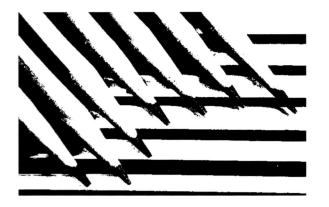

Chapter 9

THE EDITING FUNCTION I

Copy editors are responsible for all manner of things during the editing of a story. At small newspapers, copy editors not only edit copy, they also write the headlines, photo captions and design the pages.[1] At really small newspapers, copy editors also can be called upon to take stories over the phone when no reporter is available.

DO NO HARM

Copy editing can be broken into micro and macro editing. In micro editing, the copy editor is checking the parts of the story, while in macro editing the copy editor ensures that the parts fit together. Copy editors must consider copy flow and deadlines, writing style and tone. They must look for holes in stories and challenge stories that seem airtight. Libel is also a major concern. So, too, are matters of fairness and balance. Copy editors must ensure that words are used correctly and that the arithmetic adds up. They also need to ensure that copy does not disparage someone because of sex, race or ethnic background.

The copy desk is no place for the indecisive. Copy editors are expected to make quick — and correct — decisions. They must also know how to say "no" firmly when "yes" would be easier. Finally, some practical advice for copy editors. For one, many errors tend to be repetitive, and the better copy editors learn that early in their careers. Knowing the typical error created by a certain situation, the copy editor can quickly fix the mistake and spend more time seeking out the atypical. In fact, copy editors need to be sure that they don't spend all their time looking at the parts of the story and fail to notice if the parts make a whole story. As an unidentified editor once said at an American Press Institute seminar: "A good editor approaches copy as though it is a proposal

---

[1]Given the rise of design/graphics courses, I've chosen to forgo a discussion on design.

worthy of consideration, but guarantees no more than that. Too many stories get published just because they get written."

Second, a copy editor should read each story three times. In the first reading, the copy editor reads for the sense of the story, doing no editing other than fixing a misspelled word or taking out an extra comma. The copy editor makes sure the story develops as promised in the lead, that it contains no unanswered questions, that the transitions work. On the second reading, the copy editor edits. The third time, the copy editor makes sure no mistakes were edited into the story. The minimum time for completing the process is one minute per inch.

Beginning copy editors should remember the advice given to doctors: Do no harm. Unfortunately, when copy editors do harm, they can't bury their mistakes. Instead, the mistakes appear in print for all the world to see. Here are some of the duties of the copy editor.

MAINTAIN COPY FLOW

The copy editor is a primary mover behind the story. The copy editor fits into a chain usually started when the city editor assigns a story to a reporter. At that point the city editor might record in an electronic diary to whom the story was assigned and when the reporter is expected to turn it in.

The reporter, of course, gathers the information and writes the story, sometimes consulting first with the city editor if problems develop. In other cases, the city editor may have to prod the reporter to write the story. That happens not because the reporter is lazy but because the reporter may be checking out one last fact.

At the time the city editor expects the story, he or she checks the reporter's file to see if the story is ready. The city editor may check over the story, although not edit it, then assign it to the chief copy editor who assigns it to a copy editor for editing. Before assigning it, the city editor may decide which page the story will appear on and what size headline the story will get. Those instructions are placed at the beginning of the story.

All copy editors know they can find work in a special file in the newspaper's computer system, and once finished with one story and its headline the copy editors automatically check that file to see what other stories remain to be edited. When finished, the copy editor may assign the story to a second file or may return the story to the same file where a second copy editor will retrieve it for a final reading. All copy editors know which stories to read first because the city editor has told them which pages will be set in type early and which pages will go late. If Page 4 is an early page and Page 6 is a late page, copy editors will read all Page 4 copy before proceeding to stories for Page 6. If no other copy exists, Page 6 copy is read. A copy editor doesn't forgo editing a story just because it is for a late page or a later edition. Work cleared early in the shift eases the pressure before deadline.

Meet Deadlines

Everyone who has a deadline in a news operation needs to meet that deadline to produce an orderly product. Newspapers and newscasts put together at the last minute because someone missed a deadline announce their roughness to the impatient and easily dissatisfied readers and listeners. Although a newspaper's arrival in the home is not as precise as the beginning of a broadcast medium's news program, readers still expect their newspaper to arrive around the same time every day. Given that readers spend so little time with the product, a later newspaper may mean that day's issue goes unread because the time normally reserved for reading the paper has passed.

Copy editors need to worry about cash flow as well as copy flow. Missing deadlines has economic implications. Many people on a newspaper have certain jobs to do at certain times, and they report to work at times beneficial to printing and distributing the newspaper. The people who drive the circulation trucks begin work about the time the newsroom is closing. Those people are paid from a certain starting time, even if the newspaper isn't off the presses. It is not productive to pay people not to work. Eventually, missed deadlines that set back production result in overtime pay, which, in excessive amounts, could create financial problems for the publisher. It is incumbent on every employee of the newspaper to work for the economic well-being of the newspaper, lest the newspaper fold and jobs are lost.

Frequent overtime is not only hard on corporate profits, but also on people's morale. The people who must work overtime grow tired of their jobs and aren't as sharp. As a result, they don't produce a sharp product.

Meeting a deadline is more than turning in all of the assigned work at the deadline. Reporters and editors should strive to avoid peaks and valleys in workloads by working steadily. Copy editors who sit around chatting when work exists create their own pressure when the work piles up. The city editor and copy editors can also avoid peaks and valleys by assigning equitable workloads and by staying on top of the news flow. If some reporters are dealing with late-breaking stories, the copy desk should advise other reporters on routine stories to get them in sooner.

Most of the time a copy editor works in an almost pressure-free environment. Sure, there's work to be done, but if the pace is steady, the pressure is less. Pressure does mount toward deadline, which should not be used as an excuse to do poor work. The best copy editors shrug off the maddening pressure, do their finest work and still meet deadlines.

DEFLATE POMPOSITY

A reporter will not always realize that he or she is quoting the gobbledygook of bureaucrats or the empty sentences of politicians or the big words of academicians. The phrase sounded good at the time and the reporter didn't bother to analyze it. But now the story sits before the copy editor and analysis begins.

Pomposity defies clear-cut rules, but generally it appears in direct quotations that the copy editor should paraphrase into something clear. For example, an academic report says: "First, many respondents indicated the desirability of understanding the relationship between the level of tuition and its impact on enrollment." That means: The report said it was important to understand how a tuition increase affected enrollment. Regrettably, the sentence still does not make clear who has to do the understanding.

Politicians are notoriously pompous, often because they want to sound as though they're saying something when they're trying extremely hard not to commit themselves to anything. Thus, this sentence:

> The senator said his proposed new infusion of assistance is needed "to offset the erosion in the value of aid caused by our inflation over the past two years."

Note how the reporter got caught up in the fog of pomposity by using "infusion of assistance." What the sentence means, and the desk should create through rewriting, is:

> The senator said his proposed aid is needed to offset what inflation has done to the value of aid in the past two years.

A bureaucrat once proposed that the best way to get the public's opinion on a proposed rate increase was to schedule "public input sessions," whatever that means. The desk should question such inane phrases.

A copy editor may also find that many pompous sentences are better deleted than rewritten. But when rewriting is the answer, the copy editor should show the rewrite to the writer to ensure accuracy.

PUT LIFE INTO BREATHLESS PROSE

Newspapers are no longer written for, as an editor once put it, "people who move their lips when they read." But that observation doesn't excuse this 57-word sentence:

> One department spokesperson who was asked about the figures that showed Americans had to work longer to eat last year than in 1974, while the average in other countries declined, said that "no doubt inflation rates were higher in the other countries last year" and speculated that wages probably rose higher than food prices in other countries.

The reader who finishes such a sentence is no doubt left breathless. The copy editor who let the sentence into print could have avoided cramping the reader's breathing by creating two sentences, such as:

> One department spokesperson was asked about the figures that showed Americans had to work longer to eat last year than in 1974 while the average in other countries declined. The spokesperson said that "no doubt inflation rates were higher in the other countries last year" and speculated that wages probably rose higher than food prices in other countries.

The resulting two 29-word sentences still make no sense, meaning the copy editor must query the reporter for an explanation. Some long sentences, though, repair easily.

> A government spokesman said the departure had been delayed but would not say why, and unofficial sources said authorities were awaiting assurances from Libya, the eventual destination, that the hijackers would be granted asylum before dispatching the aircraft carrying the hostages.

Broken in two:

> A government spokesman said the departure had been delayed but would not say why. Unofficial sources said authorities were awaiting assurances from Libya, the eventual destination, that the hijackers would be granted asylum before dispatching the aircraft carrying the hostages.

For quick reading, the best sentences are on average 17 to 20 words long, but a copy editor should not automatically divide every long sentence into shorter ones. A good sentence derives its beauty from the rhythm of the words, not the number.

FILL IN THE HOLES

As a copy editor reads a story, questions arise. If the story does not provide the answers, back it goes to the reporter. And if the reporter is not available, the copy editor must turn into a reporter and get the answers.

Some of the questions are obvious. In a story about the suspensions of a police officer for one day without pay, one question is: How much pay did the officer forfeit? Other questions might not be as obvious. A story reporting that city council has raised property taxes should include an explanation of what the action means to the typical homeowner in dollars and cents.

Filling in for the reader, a copy editor examines a story about a legislator calling for a law that would require engaged couples to wait six months before getting married. The story appears complete, but several questions arise in the mind of the copy editor. What is the legislator's marital status? More important, what is the constitutionality of such a law? The copy editor returns the story to the reporter to track down the legislator and ask the questions. But if the reporter is unavailable, then the copy editor should call the legislator and ask. And if the legislator is unavailable, the copy editor should call some legal expert for an opinion.

The day after a general election, the Associated Press filed a story with this lead: "U.S. Rep. Tom Foglietta, in a race to keep his congressional seat Tuesday, also found himself in a race to apprehend a purse-snatcher." The next six paragraphs of the seven-paragraph story detail how the congressman witnessed a purse-snatching and chased two youths. They were not caught, but they did drop the purse. The story also gives the name and age of the victim. But one thing the reader does not learn is whether Foglietta kept his congressional seat. Even though a wire service copy editor missed the hole, the local editor shouldn't have.

And there's the story about the man who became the founder and president of a frog collectors club (honest). The lead says:

> It all began when his girlfriend, who later became his wife, purchased an orange, yellow and green shower curtain. To coordinate, she picked up a toothbrush holder, soap dish and hand towels — all displaying frogs with bright orange and yellow eyes.

Two paragraphs later:

> Twelve years later, he added, "I still have the frogs but not the wife."

In the six paragraphs that complete the story, the reader never learns what happened to the wife. Divorce? Death? Did she croak? (Sorry.) Did she leave him? What happened? The desk needs to ask.

And here is the first paragraph of a two-paragraph obituary:

> Molly Price, the author of "The Iris Book," generally considered the definitive work on the subject, died of a cerebral hemorrhage Friday at Good Samaritan Hospital in Suffern, N.Y. She was 81 years old and lived in New City, N.Y.

The other paragraph details her survivors. Meanwhile, what's the subject of the book? The eye? Flowers? The desk needs to ask.

Other holes in stories often result from carelessness. An address given only as "Meadow Lane" needs a number with it: Check the telephone book. A story contains a name with "nmi" (no middle initial): Check the city directory or some other source. A suspect's age is missing: Call the police. A direct quotation does not match the speaker's previous stance: Call the source to clarify the quote. Then there's the story announcing that the city is hiring a new public works director — what happened to the former director? Whatever the story's shortcomings, the copy editor sees that they are corrected.

QUESTION FACTS

It is not unfair to expect copy editors to know when the facts aren't facts. Copy editors are often thought of as trivia experts and knowledgeable in many fields, not just the humanities in which they are usually bred.[2] One legendary editor found an error in a complicated equation done by Albert Einstein.

Internal clues should tip the copy editor to a factual error. For example, the obituary of a man who died in 1981 says he was a 1940 graduate of the University of Notre Dame. The obituary also says the man was 54. Assuming that the man was 21 when he graduated in 1940, in

---

[2]Two of the creators of the board game Trivial Pursuit were Canadian journalists.

1981, 41 years later, he would be 62. Since the story doesn't say the man was a child prodigy, you can't account for the eight-year discrepancy by saying he graduated when he was 13.

In 1981, the *New York Times Magazine* published an article that the author later admitted was in part plagiarized from a novel. Daniel Burstein, then a freelance writer, raised some questions about how the story got by *Times'* editors. He noted that in one sentence, the author claimed to have seen someone on a distant hillside through binoculars and that "the eyes in his head looked dead and stony." In the next sentence, Burstein notes that the author says: "I could not make him out in any detail." As Burstein observed, no one had to be an expert on the subject to see the contradiction and ask questions.

Another story with internal clues comes from the society pages, where a bride is described as having received a certificate in dental assisting and being employed as "an orthopedic assistant." She worked for an orthodontist, as in teeth, not in bones, which is what an orthopedist does.

Then there is the example of the reporter who wrote that the date of the next general election was Nov. 10. But since the general election always falls on the first Tuesday after the first Monday, the latest a general election can occur is Nov. 8.

Sometimes, though, the error is not so clear-cut. What is the error of fact in a story saying that a state's Supreme Court ruled that the state police may not reveal a suspect's prior record? Although the case involved an action by the state police, the decision really applied to all police in the state, not just the state police. Realizing that, a copy editor called the wire service that produced the story and shortly after received a correction.

Such fussiness not only gives the reader a better product, it also serves historians who frequently rely on newspapers as a starting point for research. A historian can lose precious time chasing a false start provided by a newspaper. Corrections often don't help because they usually receive less prominent display than the error. Of course, if the historian is conducting research in a newspaper's database, the correction is usually affixed to the story, which helps.

GET THE FACTS STRAIGHT

The suspicious minds that edit newspapers do not know everything, but they know enough to recognize their limitations. Good copy editors are smart enough to know what they don't know.

A story that says a jury ordered testimony stricken from the record should raise the eyebrows of a high school student in a civics class and should move a copy editor to change "jury" to "judge," who is the only person in a trial with authority to order testimony stricken. The same copy editor knows that referring to the senators who represent the 50 states in Congress as "state senators" confuses them with the senators who convene in state capitols. A senator in Washington is a "U.S. senator." Similarly, the copy editor knows that the headline "Russian ambassador appointed" suggests someone from Russia, not the U.S. ambassador the story is about.

Eyebrows go up again when a reporter turns in a crime roundup story and writes in one paragraph that someone forged the name of "Irene Zepanski" on a check and three paragraphs later that someone damaged a bicycle owned by "Irene Zepanski." Either it's a lightning-strikes-twice story that needs a new lead, or it's a case of reporter carelessness. The copy editor must ask. (It was reporter carelessness.)

In that category of suspicious editing is the story about the columnist who referred to wasps, hornets and yellow jackets as "bugs." Checking with a dictionary and an entomologist, the newspaper's in-house critic learned that wasps belong to the superfamilies *Vespoidea* and *Sphecoidea*; yellow jackets are small wasps and belong to the family *Vespidae*; hornets belong to the genera *Vespa* and *Vespula*. Bugs, on the other hand, belong to the order *Hemiptera*, which is none of the preceding. Unfortunately, the abuse appeared in print because a copy editor decided to make a guess rather than check it. Said the entomologist: "All bugs are insects but not all insects are bugs." He said nothing about copy editors.

WATCH FOR NEW WORDS MADE BY "TYPOS"

Many typographical errors leap out at copy editors when they're reading the newspaper, which is the wrong time. The more serious errors are those that create new words, usually turning an otherwise serious story into a funny one. For example, when Gerald R. Ford was president in the mid-1970s, this headline appeared: "110 refugees hit by Ford poisoning." (The story was about food poisoning.) The headline writer either was making a political statement or not thinking. And from time to time, the birth announcements have listed the birth of a male child, "the sin of Mr. and Mrs. ... ." And occasionally a newspaper will announce a "pubic meeting," which may be where the "sin" came from in the first place, instead of a "public meeting."

Countless other "typos" (as typographical errors are called) include the infamous "not" of "not guilty" being turned into "now." Less serious errors include those that refer to "closet friends" (which we could all use) or "closest fiends" (which we don't need). Then there's the bluegrass music columnist whose reference to a "mandolin picker" came out "pecker." With the copy editor now the only backstop between reporter and reader, vigilance to catch errors must be tripled. Computers don't proofread stories.

GANG UP ON DOUBLE ENTENDRES

It has been said that if anyone on a newspaper staff needs a dirty mind, it is the copy editor, who must watch for two-faced sentences. One of the double meanings is usually salacious, and that's usually the meaning the reader remembers. These headlines — "Prostitutes appeal to pope" and "Police can't stop gambling" — may get by, but a reporter who writes about a police officer who "relied on intuitive judgment when he exposed himself to an armed suspect" invites smirks and maybe an angry telephone call or two.

Copy editors must be alert for the reporter who writes "the climax of the meeting arrived with a bang when a spectator's chair broke and the person fell to the floor," because the reporter is obviously trying for the double entendre. The columnist who began his essay on turkey callers with this quotation knew he would raise eyebrows: "'Put it in your mouth and blow,' he said as he handed the little moon-shaped object to me." The reporter who wrote "Idi Amin is holed up in Libya with his two wives and a concubine" may have missed the subtle double meaning, but, then again, so did the newscaster who read the sentence over the air.

Many double entendres are not only salacious but also sexist. From a wire story on the Mummer's parade, a New Year's Day tradition in Philadelphia: "Women first cracked the all male Mummers ranks about five years ago." A copy editor changed the verb to "entered." A photo caption of a boat crew composed of a female coxswain and seven male rowers reported, "It was the first time both universities were coxed by women." While "coxed" is the correct verb, one wonders if it is the appropriate one. The caption writer could have easily stated that it was the first time both crews had female coxswains. Then there are these sentences from a newspaper story:

> She said the man sat on the bench in only his boxer shorts for about five minutes and exposed himself.
> "It wasn't long, but it was long enough," she said.

Since the direct quotation adds nothing to the story, delete it. If it had contained worthwhile information, it could have been paraphrased.

Challenge Profanity

Profanity should not be used unless it is part of a direct quotation and then only if necessary to tell the story. Otherwise, remove profanity from a story.

One of those necessary times for printing profanity arose when the Watergate tapes of the mid-1970s were released. The profanities showed a mentality impossible to depict without publishing the foul words of a president and his aides. The wire services marked the stories so newspapers and readers knew the stories contained profanities. Television newscasters blipped the foul words, but as they read a direct quotation, all the words, even the ones not spoken, appeared on the screen. Those were unusual times and called for unusual approaches.

In its entry on "obscenities, profanities, vulgarities," *The Associated Press Stylebook* advises:

> In reporting profanity that normally would use the words damn or god, lowercase god and use the following forms: damn, damn it, goddamn it. Do not, however, change the offending words to euphemisms. Do not, for example, change damn it to darn it.

Put Precision into Sentences

Sentences constructed with misused words and phrases quickly fall apart, leaving behind a rubble of imprecision. The copy editor who allows contradictions such as "about 26.5 percent" or "some 17 people" creates ambiguous situations that becloud a sentence's intent. Generalities don't convey information the way specifics do. Faced with this sentence — "Acting on a tide of amendments at the special two-day meeting, the bishops have consistently strengthened injunctions against ... " — a copy editor reached deeper in the story to find the number of amendments proposed and inserted it, giving the reader something closer to precision with "Acting on a tide of nearly 100 amendments, the bishops ..."

The reporter who refers to the U.S. House of Representatives as "Congress" and the copy editor who does not fix it both need civics lessons.[3] "Tossle-capped children" may conjure up for the reporter an

---

[3] This mistake is commonly made, even by members of the Congress. However, the U.S. Congress is made up of the House of Representatives and the Senate. Members are congressmen and congresswomen. Those in the House are representatives; in the Senate, senators.

image of children frolicking in the snow, but the reader sees nothing because "tossle" is not a word. (The writer meant "tassel.")

To say that "Tom O'Hara had both hands amputated at City Hospital" suggests he intended to inflict the amputation. Who knows what kind of action is taking place in this example: "The governor said he spent hours trying to smooth over conflicts but concluded the constant clashes were hampering government operations." At first it suggests that the governor ended the clashes, but what he really did was "conclude that the constant clashes were hampering government operations," which is an entirely different ending. Watch out for the oxymoronic, the contradictory, as in this sentence: "The test was ended because one student did not want to be forced to take an optional swimming test." If it's optional, how can it be required?

Given a public not as skilled with the language as journalists are supposed to be, letters to the editor can present challenges for the desk. A letter writer angry that she had missed a deadline for paying a traffic ticket complained about the delay of "receiving a traffic violation in the mail." What she got in the mail was a "ticket for a traffic violation," because traffic violations are hard to mail. Finally, what of the reporter who wrote that "the controversy erupted last week when the chairperson requested her to respond to published reports about her absences in writing"? How is one absent in writing? The sentence should say: "The controversy erupted last week when the chairperson requested her to respond in writing to published reports about her absences." Those and other examples throughout this book build a case for precise reporting and writing and thorough copy editing.

Do the Arithmetic

Journalists like to joke that they went into journalism because they were no good at math. But math is as much a part of journalism as words are.

Any time numbers appear in a story, the copy editor should do the arithmetic. A reporter once claimed that a litigant in a small claims case had stopped payment at $600 on a job that totaled $1,344.67 because he felt the $810 labor charge was too high. But if you add $600 and $810, you get $1,410. How do you account for the $65.33 difference between $1,410 and $1,344.67? Likewise, another reporter explained how 35,000 square feet of office space was going to be used: all purpose room, 1,400 square feet; kitchen, 200; restrooms, 300; activity room, 850; game room, 600; office, 150. That totals 3,500 square feet, not 35,000 square feet. the reporter mistyped the total square footage. The copy desk caught the error because a copy editor did the arithmetic.

One of the seldom thought-of basic tools of copy editing is the calculator, which allows a copy editor to easily check a reporter's arithmetic. If a story says snow removal costs are up 5 percent over last winter, the copy editor should do the arithmetic to make sure.

If the unemployment rate last month was 10 percent and this month it is 5 percent, the decline is 50 percent or 5 percentage points but not 5 percent. On top of that, the 50 percent figure says so much more than the 5 percentage points and is the preferred way to express employment statistics. Only with interest rates does an increase or decline expressed in percentage points mean more to the reader, since interest points can be translated into dollar amounts. As for the stock market, percentage declines mean more than point declines, as the *New York Times* once reported. When President Eisenhower had a heart attack, the market declined 31.89 points or 6.54%. Thirty years later, the market declined 86.61 points, or 4.61%. It's all relative, which is what percentages show better than points on the stock market. The desk should be alert for any story in which the insertion of percentages will make the story clearer. Election returns expressed in whole numbers alone are not always as meaningful as when they are accompanied (not substituted) by percentages.

When a story says five people were arrested, a copy editor should count the names listed. A reporter can easily forget to list a name or two. Also, the desk should check reporters on how they have come up with unusual figures. One editor tells about the reporter who claimed that thousands of people had entered a new store in one hour. "How did you arrive at that figure?" a copy editor asked. "Well," the reporter said with pride, "I counted the number of people who went through the door in one minute and multiplied by 60." But, of course, that was no guarantee that the minute the reporter selected was representative of the traffic during the hour. After all, the number of newcomers probably diminished after the initial surge. Needless to say, the reporter's figures were not used.

In general, the desk should check any use of numbers. For example, a news release from a county office included this paragraph:

> According to population figures, Abington Township has taken over the top spot as the most populous municipality in Montgomery County, with a population of 58,624, some 4,200 less than 1970 when the township was the second most populated municipality in the county with 63,625.

The copy editor who automatically checks the arithmetic will find a discrepancy of 801. Even if the copy editor must call someone at home at night to clarify the arithmetic, the copy editor should not hesitate. The county officer who made the mistake appreciates the backstopping, and the newspaper, by not publishing the error, saves its credibility from another beating.

VERIFY NAMES

A radio news reporter who was terrible at remembering people's names would greet a familiar face but forgotten name with, "Hi, how are you?" and then slyly add: "By the way, just how do you spell your last name?" The ploy fell apart one day when a person haughtily responded: "S-m-i-t-h." The news reporter, though, should not have been embarrassed, because some "Smiths" spell their names "Smyth" and others spell it "Smythe," and all pronounce it the same way.

The failure to correctly spell a person's name when compounded with the failure to correctly identify the person through age and street address could result in a lawsuit. The reporter who heard a court official say "Robin Shoemaker of Pilsdon was arrested on sodomy charges" has created a problem when it was not the 22-year-old Robin Shoemaker at 136 Bath Ave., but the 53-year-old Robin Shoonmaker at 211 S. l0th St.

"Francis" sounds the same no matter if it's a man or a woman's name, but the person's sex does determine the spelling (*is* for men; *es* for women). Is that person's name John R. Nichols or John S. Nichols? The telephone book, the newspaper's files or the city directory can provide the detail. The ultimate source, of course, is the person in the story, who can be queried by telephone. As a matter of policy, a copy editor should check every name in a story even if a reporter swears the check was already made.

VERIFY DATES

Some would argue that the best degree for a copy editor is a history degree. Although journalism tends to focus on current events, current events come with a history.

In writing the obituary of a local politician in 1987, a reporter talked about a meeting in 1944 between the local politician and Harry S Truman, then vice president of the United States. After recounting some dialogue between the local politician and Truman, the obituary writer said: "Two weeks later FDR was dead and Truman became president." Nope. FDR died on April 12, 1945. Someone on the desk should have checked.

USE FOREIGN WORDS CORRECTLY

Someone once complained that the English language does not follow the rules, especially when it comes to spelling. Well, that person is wrong. Anyone who knows the root of a particular English word should know how to spell it.

The plural of the Latin *alumnus* is *alumni*. Something done in memory of someone is *In memoriam*, not *In memorium*. The plural of *criterion* is not *criterions* but *criteria*.

Spanish causes problems for some copy editors. One copy editor headlined a story about Col. Sigifredo Ochoa Perez with "El Salvador shuts off rebel Perez." In Spanish, the surname is usually not the last name, which is the mother's name, but is the middle name, which is the father's name. The correct second reference is *Ochoa*, although that's not consistent. For example, Colombian novelist and journalist Gabriel García Márquez is referred to on second reference as García Márquez, not Garcia.

A good copy editor also needs to know — or have a sense of — other languages. For example, in editing this sentence, someone inserted the italicized article: "When they dominated the National League in the late 1960s, they were known as The El Birdos." In Spanish, *el* is *the*. Drop *the* in this use. It's redundant, and any copy editor who has taken at least one foreign language should detect that, especially when the language is one of the Romance languages, which are consistent in having short articles.

One foreign language that has changed in English is the Chinese language. Starting in 1979, the Chinese government changed the system it used to translate stories into English, converting from the Wade-Giles spelling system to Pinyin, meaning "transcription." Thus, Peking, the capital city, became Beijing[4] and Mao Tse-tung, the legendary leader of China, became Mao Zedong. Another conversion was Szechwan into Sichuan and Honan into Henan, although some American restaurants, when boasting of their regional Chinese cooking, advertise it as Szechuan and Hunan.

Spanish names are not the only ones that do not follow English style.

---

[4] I've seen letterhead and business cards from Beijing University that still call it Peking University. And people in Beijing still order Peking Duck, although some call it Beijing Duck.

Asian names are also different and not consistent from one country to another. In China, a person's name consists of a family name followed by a personal name. Thus, Li Xiguang's surname is Li and his first name is Xiguang. However, ethnic Chinese outside the People's Republic of China generally use the Wade-Giles system of spelling, which also uses hyphens. Korean names are similar to Chinese names, meaning that a second reference to former South Korean President Park Chung Hee was Park not Hee.

In some Asian countries, married women adopt their husband's name, except in the People's Republic of China. The good reporter, when dealing with people of a nonwestern culture, will ask what their preference is, rather than imposing the western preference.

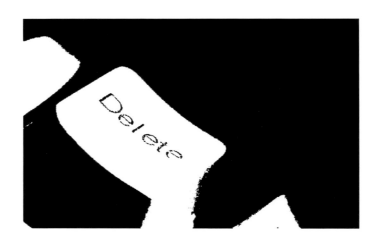

Chapter 10

THE EDITING FUNCTION II

It is to every copy editor's advantage to know the frailties of each reporter. One reporter overwrites every story because he sees a Pulitzer Prize at the end of the daily press run; another is too lazy to check names; so-and-so fancies herself an expert and knows more about the subject than her sources (she never makes mistakes; her sources do); another turns in sloppy copy; still another begins every story with a direct quotation, despite the general injunction against that practice; finally, another is mischievous. He filed this story:

> City police estimate damage of $150 in an incident of criminal mischief at Memorial Park yesterday.
> Police said a 1,750-pound gravestone was reportedly moved from its place over a grave. Memorial Park attendant Caesar Romane said he was asleep at the time it occurred. When he went on his early morning rounds he said he noticed the incident in the "J" section of the cemetery.

A sleepy copy editor forgot the reporter's mischievous nature and didn't realize that the story was turned in on Good Friday. The next day's paper reported that the story was fictitious and had not been intended for publication. Neither the copy editor (who removed a direct quote: "Lo, the stone was rolled away.") nor the reporter was fired, but both could have been.

Less spectacular, but every bit as much an error, is the story about a man who donated 14 gallons of blood to a bloodmobile during one visit. Eventually the story reveals that the man began contributing blood in 1953 and then the reader realizes that the 14 gallons weren't given in one visit.

There's the story quoting an athletic director as saying he has devised a scheme for crowd control at the local football stadium — a scheme that will eliminate the panic and pressure at the stadium's "portholes." Unfortunately, the word appeared four times. The athletic director knew the difference between windows in a ship (portholes) and entranceways in a stadium (portals), but the reporter and copy editor didn't.

And a beer columnist once wrote a column about German beer, noting that German law permitted only four ingredients in beer — barley malt, hops, yeast and water. But a typist turned the ingredients into "barley, malt, hops, yeast and water" and the copy editor changed the number "four" to "five" rather than checking.

Despite the initial tone of this section, future copy editors should not assume that reporters are nothing but a bunch of error-prone, carefree, pompous egotists who care not one whit about quality. While all humans (copy editors included) have their shortcomings, many reporters are dedicated to their craft and become upset with themselves when they make mistakes and unhappy with copy editors who don't catch the errors. Rapport between reporters and copy editors makes for a better newspaper, and both would be remiss to view the relationship as "us vs. them." Reporters and copy editors are not separate camps; in fact, they cannot function as separate camps.

DON'T TRUST THE WIRES

The editors of wire services advise that their work should not go into any newspaper without first being checked by a copy editor at that newspaper. The wire services make mistakes, sometimes attributable to humans working in haste but other times attributable to electronic machines malfunctioning.

The human errors show up in such examples as the story that starts out saying four women were sterilized and then refers to one in an attribution tag as "one of the five women sterilized."

Wirephoto captions tend to be more error-prone than wire copy. In part that occurs because the person writing the caption is seldom the person who wrote the story. Information in captions can get superseded by additional information, making the initial caption wrong. Thus, it is the responsibility of the copy editor to check the wirephoto caption against the most recent story.

Finally, a copy editor should immediately report to the responsible wire service bureau any error in a wire service story so the wire service can issue a correction.

KEEP STYLE CONSISTENT

"Style," a beginning copy editor once said, "is like a pica. Every editor works with it, but there's always an aura of mystery over the concept."[1] The editor was complaining because she felt her co-workers did not appreciate the need for a consistent style. "You cannot have as many styles as you have reporters and copy editors," she said. "Style is not just a needless, antiquated detail, but a way of keeping the consistency and thus the credibility of the paper alive." Consistency, she might have added, establishes order, which aids clarity.

The reader who sees a reference to "110 E. Foster Ave." in one story and to "110 East Foster Avenue" in another must wonder about the reliability of the people reporting the news. The reader affixes that doubt to the newspaper, whose credibility suffers not only on Page One, but in every department. A newspaper that lacks credibility speaks with a muted editorial voice. Copy editors should not only keep the stylebook by their side, they should also refer to it frequently. The best copy editors, however, learn their paper's style to avoid spending too much time reading the stylebook when they should be editing copy.

PROTECT AGAINST LIBEL[2]

One restaurant reviewer said a restaurant offered "rock-hard Italian bread, pricey steaks and indifferent cooking." That remark cost his newspaper $23,000 in libel damages. Another reviewer at another paper said of a different restaurant: "My steak, listed as 10 ounces, seemed smaller. It appeared to have been cooked in a blast furnace, which may have accounted for its scrawny look." The reviewer also said that the prime rib his spouse ordered had "a strange, unpleasant flavor." The restaurant sued and lost.

If you were an editor in Florida and you looked to those court decisions to figure what is libelous and what is not, you'd have a hard time deciding. Both decisions were made in Florida.

No editor can be certain what a judge will find libelous and what a judge will say represents truth, qualified privilege, or fair comment and criticism — all defenses against libel. But a copy editor has to have a good working knowledge of libel law.

Generally, libel is anything published that besmirches or defames a person's good name; that is, a person's reputation. Libel comes from printed or prepared material (scripts from television or radio broadcasts apply here). Slander is defamation that is spoken, which generally applies

---

[1] Personal note to the author.
[2] See Chapter 14 for more details about libel.

to broadcasted material that is not scripted (i.e., ad-lib comments).

It does not matter if the libel appears in a letter to the editor, an advertisement, a Web site, a blog or a comic strip, the newspaper can be sued, which is an expensive proposition even before a court hearing begins. (Radio and television stations are not responsible for libel committed in a live broadcast, but the person making the defamatory comments is.) In the heat of a good story, a copy editor should remember that waiting 24 hours before printing a charge against someone is better than damning a person to an onslaught of innuendo brought on by an erroneous newspaper story. When a person's reputation is being maligned, proceed cautiously.

Calling someone charged with a murder a "suspected murderer" means the person is a murderer suspected of having murdered again. The safest approach: Say the person has been charged in connection with murder. That's a fact. "Allegedly" won't save the newspaper. A sentence saying someone was "allegedly" involved in a check-forging scheme makes the scheme a fact before a court has found anyone guilty. Thus, even a person "allegedly involved" is tainted by association. To allege is to assert without proof. Say what the person has been charged with rather than alleging a criminal act.

Ascribing any criminal intent to someone invites libel lawyers by the dozens. In a strike, the president of a union was quoted in a newspaper as saying one of his supervisors (and he was named) had sped through a picket line and hit a striker with his car. The story contained no confirmation from the police or the hospital, yet a crime had been claimed (it is illegal to hit someone with a car). Lacking some confirmation from authorities, the newspaper's best bet was to use the item without names and add a sentence saying the newspaper could not confirm the incident. The major point behind that example is that even though the newspaper quoted someone as making the charge, the newspaper can still be sued. So can the person making the charge, of course, but the newspaper has more money. Quoting someone accurately does not absolve the newspaper of responsibility in a defamation action.

One day, for example, a college senior complained in his college newspaper that he had bit into a nail in the pizza he was eating at a local (and he named it) restaurant. The senior went on to condemn the manager for not giving her a refund and then closed by saying her letter should serve as "a warning to unsuspecting pizza-eating college students. Beware of nails!" In this case, the newspaper was lucky: The article generated only an angry complaint from the restaurant's owner.

Libel appears most frequently in crime news, sports stories, restaurant and art reviews (that go beyond the bounds of fair comment and criticism), cartoons (such as caricatures), local government reports and editorials and commentaries (such as satire). Stories from the police beat need careful attention. More important, police reporters need to make sure they do follow-ups. In one instance, a newspaper reported that a teenager had been arrested in a rape investigation. Later, the police changed the direction of their investigation and the person was never charged. This incident took place in a state where an arrest and a charge are separate actions and public information. The newspaper, failing to do a follow-up story, missed this, and the man won a $1 million libel suit. The jury said the newspaper had published false information, even though it was correct at the time, and had failed to exercise reasonable care. In fact, the teenager waited a year before suing (the statute of limitations varies widely among the 50 states; see Chapter 14).

At the end of a court case, a judge sentenced a convicted woman to 60 days in jail for cruelty to her child. The newspaper ran an account of the trial and a photograph of the convicted woman, only it was a photograph of the official court reporter, not the convicted child abuser. The court reporter had a good case, but graciously let the matter drop after the newspaper published a correction.

But even corrections don't always help. In 1998 in Pennsylvania, a jury awarded a man $100,000 and his wife $50,000 after his local newspaper published his photograph instead of his indicted cousin's. The jury ignored the newspaper's prompt and prominent correction. More recently, a photograph meant to illustrate a story on the sexuality and promiscuity of teenagers led to a defamation suit because the teenagers in the photograph could be identified — and were not the promiscuous ones.

All stories, of course, are prone to providing material for a libel suit, and, as Florida restaurant reviewers can attest, a valid defense in one court may not work in another. Is the story balanced and fair? The test a copy editor should try: "How would I feel if this story was about me?"

Copy editors are not lawyers and should not be the last word when doubt exists about a potentially libelous story. Nevertheless, copy editors can do their best to protect the newspaper by ensuring that

- all sides of a story are given;
- potentially libelous material is backed up by more than one source;
- when criminal activity is alleged the accused person be given an opportunity to comment;
- that headline and story agree (in fact, headlines lack the qualified privilege some stories get; see Chapter 14);

- that identification of people in a photograph is accurate;
- in exceptional cases, copy editors should not be bashful about consulting a lawyer. Smart publishers keep one on retainer for just such a purpose.

RESPECT PRIVACY

When editors talk about respecting the privacy of individuals, they raise the issue beyond what a newspaper may legally publish and enter the realm of ethics: What should a newspaper properly publish? What is legal is not necessarily ethical, and what some people regard as an ethical issue, others do not.

One area where privacy issues arise frequently concerns rape victims. Some newspapers have been reluctant to publish the name of a rape victim, even when she testifies in open court. The assumption is that rape goes unreported because many victims cannot stand the perceived humiliation of being identified in public. In other words, they blame themselves for what clearly was a crime of aggression and violence against them.

In the mid-1980s, a 16-year-old girl in Mason County, Wash., was raped. She said later that she had been victimized three times — first by the rapist, second by testifying at the trial and third by the local newspaper's account of the trial in which she was identified. (Curiously, *The New York Times* wrote about the controversy and published her name and photograph. Perhaps she was victimized a fourth time.) The publisher of the local newspaper argued that the newspaper published the victim's name out of a longstanding policy that seeks to get rape out of the closet and force society to confront it and to do more to help its victims.

Part of the argument focuses on treating rape just as the newspaper would treat any other crime. Others argue that rape is not like any other crime. Journalism professor Carol Oukrop says that "no other crime is so privately, personally devastating." Oukrop has come up with guidelines for handling rape stories, guidelines that copy editors would have to enforce. Among her suggestions:[3]

- Publish a victim's name only in unusual circumstances (death of the victim or kidnapping);

---

[3] Carol Oukrop, "Is There a 'Right' Way to Cover Rape?" ASNE Bulletin (February 1983), p. 26-27.

- Don't specify the location of the crime, since this could help people identify the victim;
- Don't sensationalize or titillate.

Oukrop also advises reporters to check with police to make sure they believe a crime was committed. She suggests this because newspapers may not publish the name of the victim, but they will most likely publish the name of the accused. In fact, she urges that no story be published until formal charges are filed and then follow up throughout the process. When there's an acquittal, make sure the accused gets at least equal coverage.

Oukrop's advice may be applicable to more than just rape stories. For example, Louis W. Hodges, a professor of religion at Washington and Lee University in Lexington, Va., tells of the newspaper story about an accident in which four of six people died. The two survived in the submerged car by finding an air pocket. One of the four friends was trapped below the air pocket, and one survivor later told of the friend's hand "reaching up toward him from below the water level." The one survivor said he pulled on his friend's arm in an effort to save him, but he could not free him. The survivor said he knew his friend had drowned "when the air bubbled up."

Hodges described the story as a "splendid piece, the kind editors delight in, the kind readers devour. The details of the wreck, those things that preceded and perhaps caused it, were vividly told."

As Hodges noted, the mother of the boy who died last also learned about her son's final minutes. She told the newspaper that scene would haunt her for the rest of her life. "God," she wrote, "hasn't anyone got a heart anymore?" Hodges pointed out that some tragedies come with what he calls "innocent victims." As he puts it, "Tragedy struck them; they did nothing to cause it, and they usually could not have anticipated and prevented the bad thing that happened. They feel that they have been victimized by hostile forces beyond their control. They hurt." In effect, the vivid newspaper story invaded the mother's life. It is something for copy editors to think about, because situations such as this one will arise again, and it will fall to some copy editor to at least ask questions about how vivid the writing should be.[4]

Privacy issues arise elsewhere. Several years ago a woman who worked at a day care center in the Bronx, N.Y., was accused of molesting

---

[4] I'd recommend "Tragedies & Journalists: A Guide for More Effective Coverage," available from the Dart Center for Journalism and Trauma at www.dartcenter.org/.

young children. The Bronx district attorney brought charges against the woman, a 62-year-old grandmother, and she spent a night in a police station jail, where she was verbally abused by guards and prisoners. She was formally charged the next day. She passed a lie detector test. A few days later a grand jury refused to indict her.

By the time the case reached the grand jury, it had been sensationalized in some newspapers. They had a field day. The district attorney looked like a hero for a few days. But in the end, the newspapers had been used. They jumped on the story without questioning the district attorney closely. If they felt the competitive need to publish, they could have done it without naming the woman. After all, her name was in print before she was formally charged. Reporters need to realize that public officials, especially elected ones, are not necessarily the paragon of ethical behavior, and their word is no better than anyone else's. Copy editors need to serve as the conscience for reporters. (Five years later, the New York Court of Appeals overturned the conviction of the only teacher charged, saying that the indictment had not been sufficiently specific.)

The reporter who interviews a child who just witnessed a fatal shooting has not only invaded the child's privacy but has offered the child a model of insensitivity. The reporter who rings the doorbell of someone whose only child has been missing and asks, "How do you feel about the disappearance of your only child?" deserves the contemptuous stare that serves as a response. If, however, the parents step from their home and conduct a news conference, the right to privacy recedes (although it doesn't go away completely).

A person's privacy seems invaded when that person, as an innocent third party, reports a crime, such as rape, and that person's name appears in print while the name of the victim does not because the newspaper has a policy of not publishing the names of rape victims. Fearful that innocent parties may suffer retaliation, some news media wisely refrain from reporting the names of third parties. After all, the person reporting the crime is not the news.

It is also not fair to visit the sins of adult children upon the parents, which is what happens in this story:

> The son of a Pilsdon police lieutenant was in court yesterday[5] on several charges of theft, forgery and unlawful use of a credit card.
> Harrison K. Jones, 22, of Waverly waived his preliminary hearing

---

[5] AP style says use the day of the week except when the event happens on the same day (i.e., today or tonight is OK).

and was bound over for trial on charges filed by Pilsdon police. He is the son of Pilsdon police Lt. Percival Jones.

The charges involved a credit card allegedly taken from a family member in May and about $1,500 in charges made on the card.

Harrison Jones has been charged with burglary in the theft of two guns, which were later sold, and he was charged with several counts of theft and forgery involving stolen checks, which he later allegedly cashed.

No connection exists between the father's duty and the adult son's crimes. The newspaper was wrong to make one and publicly apologized a few days later.

Other privacy invasions include eavesdropping and publishing or broadcasting stories that intrude on someone's seclusion or that present an excess of publicity on a person's private life. A transsexual who had undergone a sex-change operation from male to female won a $775,000 libel award after an *Oakland Tribune* columnist called her a male. The plaintiff said the column was a "callous invasion of privacy." A *Tribune* lawyer argued that the transsexual, then president of the student body at a small college, was a "public figure," which would have made it more difficult to win the lawsuit. But the court disagreed.

Publishing the criminal record of someone who has paid the debt and lived a crime-free life since then may not legally invade that person's privacy, but it will certainly not win the newspaper any respect in the community. An exception most certainly would include anyone seeking a law enforcement position. The public has a right to know about such a candidate's past, because it could have bearing on how the candidate will enforce the law. Likewise, the history of a convicted child molester should not be ignored if that person is being hired for a job involving children.

REMEMBER YOUR AUDIENCE'S TASTES

Community standards — sometimes more than the law — dictate what a newspaper will publish. In many newspapers, four-letter words are taboo simply because editors believe that children will read the newspaper and learn the words. That's not how children learn four-letter words, but seeing them in print can serve as reinforcement that such words are all right.

Sex provides another area where community coyness may determine what a newspaper publishes. Some mental health experts suggest that society has sexual hang-ups and that perhaps news media that publish or broadcast stories on the subject have contributed to the hang-ups, an issue

I'm not going to tackle in this book.

A newspaper should avoid such tastelessness as exhibited in the headline on a story about two composers dying two days apart, "Composers dropping like flies," or the attempt at humor when Ray Kroc, then chairman of the board of McDonald's Corp., announced that he had entered an alcoholic treatment center and a columnist wrote: "I guess this means that Ray won't get Krocked anymore." Likewise, the headline on a story about U.S. Sen. Edward M. Kennedy seems oblivious to the assassination of two of his brothers: "Kennedy comes to town to do or die." On a story about a blind person, an insensitive headline-writer wrote: "Okay to be blind." Another headline writer, on a story about brain cancer among workers at a nuclear weapons plant, showed a lack of taste with "Brain cancer deaths spur thinking in weapons plant." A page editor, offered a feature photograph of a shrimp fisherman off the coast of Maine, declined to use the photograph because the fishermen was wearing a hat with this message on it: "LIQUOR IN THE FRONT POKER IN THE REAR."

In the graphic writing category, a reporter, in writing a story about a high school teacher charged with 113 counts of corruption of minors, 18 counts of indecent assault and four counts of criminal solicitation to commit perjury, reported that the teacher sometimes touched the penises of the boys who posed for him. Some of the six telephone complaints the reporter received suggested that he had been too graphic. As an alternative, some newspapers would have changed "penis" to "private area" to ward off offending anyone but still conveying what had been alleged.

Copy editors need to be sensitive to their readers. That doesn't mean they should automatically remove something they perceive to be graphic. But they should not let something questionable get by without a challenge.

COOL OFF COPY

One of the jobs of a copy editor is to step back and take an objective look at a story. Just because a reporter turns in a story doesn't mean it should be published at all, or at least that day. This sentence raises several questions and would be better without the italicized portion: "The only legal combatant defending the Illinois law is Eugene F. Diamond, a pediatrician who objects to abortion on moral grounds *and who has a daughter of child-bearing age.*" That phrase is unnecessary. It is inflammatory and suspect. One wonders whether the writer would have included that phrase if Diamond had had sons.

Here is a story that needs to be calmed down and cooled off.

CORAL GABLES — A man police suspect may be a drug user is being held tonight for the vehicular deaths of two members of a Little Havana family.

Orlando and Lourdes Alvarez were killed instantly when their car was sideswiped by another car whose driver police said may have been under the influence of drugs at the time of the accident.

Right there the red flags should rise to the top of the flagpole and start flapping loudly. As the story later says, "Charges of possession and use of a controlled substance are pending, following a blood test and lab report on approximately one ounce of white powder found wrapped in a plastic bag inside White's car." That sentence wasn't even attributed to anyone. The driver of the one car was charged with vehicular manslaughter. That's the story. If the tests show something else and the police file additional charges, then the newspaper has another story.

Less spectacular is the story about a fired government official showing up at a community Victorian-age Christmas celebration. This is the way the local newspaper covered his appearance.

> The two officers were joined by two others in modern dress. One of the officers said the added police presence was because of reports that the celebration might be disrupted by former Main Street Coordinator Thomas Williams. Williams was fired Oct. 6 by Historic Gibbsville Inc. for failing to follow directions.
>
> Police officials said that one other officer had been assigned to patrol the area because Williams had indicated that he might "take over the microphone to expand upon why he was fired."
>
> Williams showed up in top hat and cane at about 7:15 p.m. and mingled with those watching the carolers on the courthouse steps. The duty officers moved toward the steps as Williams moved closer to the steps. However, he departed as the singing finished. He could not be reached for comment.

The next day's paper devoted an entire story to explaining why the preceding information was wrong. The story included comments from several officials rightfully condemning the newspaper for poor reporting. It is the copy editor who challenges poor reporting and keeps the results from seeing print.

Test Sources

The reporter who swallowed her pride and wrote the follow-up correction to the last story in the preceding section informed readers that the only source for the fired official's planned disruption was "a citizen on the street" — someone police would not identify. The moral of the story: test sources.

The line most frequently used in a discussion like this is: "If your mother says she loves you, check it out." Copy editors, of course, don't always have the time to check sources. One chief copy editor has a policy of quizzing reporters about their sources just to make sure the reporters have good sources. The policy paid off one night when a reporter turned in a story saying that a man about to go on trial in a rape case was a suspect in 20 other rapes. "How do you know that?" the reporter was asked. "The D.A. told me," he replied. "Can we quote him?" "Oh, no," the reporter said, "he won't say it for the record."

One night a copy editor received a story stating that a woman accused in the mercy killing of her mother had apparently attempted suicide on the eve of her trial. The only source supporting that was someone in the district attorney's office. The hospital would not confirm the nature of the woman's illness.

A day later, the newspaper reported the woman's illness: She had a blood clot on her brain. And that came from the hospital. The moral of the story: Identify the primary source and then write the story according to that source. In a medical case, a medical person, not a legal person, seems to be the obvious source, and when the hospital refused comment, the reporter should have had doubts. She didn't, and neither did her back-up, the copy desk.

Bad sources turn up in obituaries and weddings. People will submit false information to a newspaper to play a joke on a friend or on the newspaper. One Pennsylvania newspaper once published the wedding of a couple that included ushers named Hugh G. Wrection and Amos Behavin. The children of the groom were named Zachariah and Malachi and the guests were entertained by "Shalome of the Middle East Dance Troupe, who performed a Syrian folk dance." Something there should have raised the eyebrows of a copy editor. The groom, by the way, was listed as the owner and operator of "Uncle Eyeball's Mountain Travelers' Emporium." He certainly pulled the wool over the copy editor's eyes. It never hurts to ask.

STRIVE FOR BALANCE

Good journalists are fair. When a story contains information that is critical of someone, good journalists seek comment from the person criticized. Some stories virtually cry out for a balancing comment or fact, and when a reporter fails to provide one, the copy editor must flag the story.

Once, in a gubernatorial campaign, a story appeared saying the incumbent held a 2-1 lead over his challenger, according to information released by the incumbent's committee. The story contains the incumbent's opinions on why he is so far ahead. But it does not contain comment from the challenger, nor does it explain how the poll was conducted. When a story is deficient, the copy editor raises questions. The methodology of any poll or survey should be included in a story reporting those results.

A group of county prisoners once raised some issues with their local editor about balanced coverage of their plight. They advised the editor on how he could improve coverage of the criminal justice system (and, no, they didn't suggest that the newspaper stopped reporting criminal activity). The prisoners said:

1. Before a trial, avoid publishing what evidence the police have, because not all evidence is admissible in court.
2. Publish only the charges and avoid much of the background. One prisoner noted that even his parents' occupations were included in a story about him.
3. Get the defense's version of events. Too much of the pre-trial publicity comes from the prosecution's side. Seek out the defense attorney.
4. Aim for uniform coverage. Acquittals deserve as much display as the original story.
5. Explain the procedure better. For example, in some states, someone accused of a crime appears before a minor judiciary official. This represents the formal filing of the charge. Some newspapers report this part of the process — usually called "arraignment" — as though it is part of the trial, when in fact, the defense does not even make a case at this point.

Newspapers may have policies urging balance in reporting, but it is the copy editors who must make sure the policy is carried out.

STAMP OUT STEREOTYPES

The time has long passed for the news media to cease reinforcing stereotyped views of females, veterans, the United States, people over 60, African-Americans, Jews and Asians (not Orientals) and any other ethnic group whose image is misleadingly preserved in a narrow wedge of description. This is a pitch against "isms" — sexism, ethnocentrism, ageism, racism — and phobias, including homophobia and xenophobia.

The issue is how news media portray the society they report on and the assumptions journalists make in their copy about, among other things, sex and race. And the issue gets discussed in an editing context because copy editors are the ones who ultimately must change stereotypical writing.

First, consider the portrayal of women. Frequently, that portrayal suggests that they are not the equal of men and that women gain their status only by their relationship with men as opposed to being individuals in their own right. This lead is a good example: "A Center City man and his wife have been arrested on warrants charging them with a variety of sex offenses, including corrupting the morals of a minor." In other words, the woman here is defined by her relationship to her husband. The lead should say couple or "A woman and man have been arrested ... ."

Here's another example from a caption showing siblings Marvin and Anna Gaye attending the funeral of their father, Marvin: "Marvin Gaye III and sister Anna attend the funeral services yesterday ... " Again, the female person gets her status from the male.

The preceding may be subtle to some, but the next example is blatantly sexist and racist. From a *New York Times* story: "'I have an unlimited supply of wisdom,' said Mr. Holmes, who was accompanied on his rounds by a striking young woman of Asian appearance." In the first place, avoid references to a person's physical attributes. Delete "striking woman" and "muscular man." Focus on substance.

Second, but just as important, avoid unnecessary references to race. Racial references appear frequently in crime news. One college newspaper, in a roundup of police news, reported in one paragraph that a man had complained "about an African-American male choking and punching him repeatedly in the face and back." Two paragraphs later, in an unrelated incident, was this: "Williams said he became involved in an angry dispute with a man who left in a vehicle bearing a New Jersey license plate." Why is race mentioned in one but not the other? Do we assume that African-Americans are violent but don't drive cars? Is race necessary in either? Should race be used as a description at all?

To that last question, some people would respond "yes." They argue that by publishing the race of a criminal suspect, the general populace can be on the alert and help police. So they would say that it is all right to publish a story about "an African-American male choking and punching him repeatedly in the face and back. The suspect was described as being 6 feet tall." Can you imagine the residents of a town out looking for all the 6-foot-tall African-American males?[6] Realistically, how many suspects are captured because some alert newspaper reader saw them and turned them in? Besides, eyewitnesses are notoriously inaccurate with verbal descriptions. What police have found best for descriptions is to create a composite that the eyewitness endorses and to publish the composite.

One exception to the no-race rule occurs when crimes are committed against people because of their race. If a person of Chinese ancestry is beaten to death because his killers thought he was Japanese, then race is an important element in the story. When five white police officers shoot a man after a high-speed chase and the man was an African-American with no criminal record, race could have something to do with the shooting, and it becomes a factor in the story.

Sometimes writers and their editors assume the point of view of a while male. In a newspaper essay on alcohol-dependent authors comes this racist paragraph:

> "I have a feeling that most writers write for one of three reasons — pain, fear or anger," said the playwright, who is black. "For me, it's been anger. When I was drinking, I'd collect grievances. I had this pile of news clippings from *The New York Times* that made me say, 'Isn't this sickening? Isn't this awful?' Alcoholics love to collect grudges and grievances. And alcohol helps ease the pain."

Is the playwright's race relevant?

The essay, by the way, contains a sexist reference a couple of paragraphs later. This is the essayist telling how he found subjects for the essay: "So a friend in A.A. arranged an informal seminar with three writers who are recovered alcoholics — a veteran screenwriter, a middle-aged playwright and a woman who writes children's books and suspense novels." Any doubt about the color and sex of the "veteran screenwriter"? Spurn the mentality of the reporter who always identified African-American criminal suspects as blacks but never whites as whites and who

---

[6] An African-American colleague opened my eyes to this problem with this example. The description fit her husband, then in law school.

passed off his ignorance with the line, "If they're not black, they must be white."

Ignorance also produced this lead on the story of an African-American man found guilty of murder:

> Jimmy Lee goin' to the Big House.
> Killed a man.
> Now he's going to pay — 37 1/2 years to life is what District Attorney Paul Carbonaro will ask.

The writer is mocking a speech pattern attributed to African-Americans who grow up in poor neighborhoods. That's racist, and the copy desk should have red flagged it.

Other forms of racism occur when an African-American might be described as well educated or a woman performing well in a job as capable. Such references suggest that these people are not the norm, which is another form of racism and sexism. The rule of thumb: If you wouldn't write it about a while male, don't write it at all.

African-Americans are not the only ones to suffer at the hands of stereotypical writing. Several years ago a police department reported to the local news media that someone had committed a robbery at a local convenience store. The suspect was described as a Native American. Suspicious, the local radio station newscaster called the police chief. "How do you know this?" the newscaster asked. "Because he had long hair," the chief of police replied.

Native Americans are portrayed as backward savages in the cowboy-and-Indian mode. Little effort is made to tell the entire story of Native Americans, the problems with unemployment and alcoholism, unless an inebriated Indian kills someone. As one Indian editor and publisher put it: "The mass media have not been kind to the American Indian. We are either the noble savage or the falling down drunk. They have left us little ground." In reality, as with any ethnic group, there are many Native Americans who are quite successful and are leaders not just in the Indian community, but the broader community.

Asians suffer, particularly in editorial page cartoons in which Asians are shown as having slanted eyes. This leads to the racial slur "slant" or "slant-eye." Another stereotype is the image of the Asian woman as exotic and submissive. References to "China doll" and "dragon lady" reinforce that notion. Racial slurs that may not be self-evident include "Chinaman" and "Jap." Use *Chinese* and *Japanese*.

One time a sports columnist was writing a story about foreign gymnasts on his local university's team. Among the foreign gymnasts, he said, was Mario Lopez, a native of Puerto Rico. Puerto Rico is a commonwealth of the United States and people born in Puerto Rico have the same citizenship rights as people born elsewhere in the United States. So the columnist corrected himself, explaining first what he had said then adding: "Wrong. Puerto Ricans are accorded U.S. citizenship at birth." Wrong. Puerto Ricans are born citizens of the United States. Nobody does any "according." Keep in mind, too, that America is two continents and several islands large and is not confined to the United States. The wire service reporter who wrote that "Cuban president Fidel Castro came to America today ... " probably flunked geography. After all, Cuba is part of America and, as the sentence concludes, Castro knew where he was — "I'm glad to be in the United States."

Be sensitive to ethnic origins, unlike the writer of a caption on a photograph of an anti-Israel speaker. The editor began the caption with "Shalom," which is Hebrew for "peace." No anti-Israel speaker would use the word and pro-Israel people would be offended by its use in this situation.

Consider senior citizens. They, too, are the subject of stereotypical writing. This example, which also shows a dangling participle, will suffice: "Munching on homemade lemon cake and sipping coffee or tea, casual conversation is exchanged. By the loud laughter and jokes passed back and forth, perhaps with unconscious alterations, no one would expect a bunch of senior citizens to be so full of energy." Beware of demeaning and patronizing stereotypes: cute, sweet, dear, little, frowning, feeble, fragile, gray, doddering, eccentric, senile, fuddy-duddy, Geritol generation, golden agers. With life spans lengthening and the vitality of people lasting into their eighth and ninth decade, do not use terms that suggest people older than 60 are elderly or slow moving or senile.

Also suffering at the hands of insensitive writers is the handicapped person. The better description is a "person with a disability" and the better description for "disability" is "inconvenience," because it lacks a negative connotation. Furthermore, journalists should not refer to a person's inconvenience unless it is relevant to the story. So what if a person sits in a wheelchair while playing a violin; the action is playing the violin. Don't turn the achievements of persons with disabilities into superhuman efforts, which suggests they normally lack talent. Treat people the same rather than differently.

Journalists should challenge racist, sexist, homophobic language in their news medium. In fact, journalists should challenge any language that demeans anyone in our society. Copy editors, as the last line of defense, have to be doubly on their guard to keep demeaning language and demeaning stereotypes out of news copy. Apply a suggestion made earlier, How would I feel if this story were about me? Treat the subjects of stories as individuals, rather than as members of a race or a sex or an age group, and stereotypes can be avoided.

BE A SELF-CHECKER

Except on larger newspapers, a copy editor lacks a backstop — another copy editor to ensure that mistakes were not edited into a story or that a headline fits a story or that a caption is accurate. On the third read of a story, good copy editors check their work carefully and with prejudice. They do not say, "I did it, therefore it must be right." At all times they keep their limitations in mind. Did they make a change that creates another problem? A self-checker makes the time to do the job well and takes the time to check the job once it's completed.

Chapter 11

THE WRITTEN WORD

The copy editor plays a roll in making sure the newspaper is well written by removing infectious writing and protecting original and thoughtful prose.

THE NEED FOR GRACEFUL PROSE

Have you ever walked through a stream with a mucky bottom and your feet stuck with every step so that you had to jerk them to get them out of the mud and move on? Then you know how readers feel when they encounter sentences bogged down by wordiness or ambiguity or when they trip on points unrelated to the main thought. Smooth writing, in other words, equals smooth reading, which is an essential ingredient in any printed medium competing with television and radio (the "easy" media to consume). The television viewer merely sits before a moving picture enhanced with sound; that requires no effort. But reading a newspaper or magazine requires some energy on the reader's part, which means the writer must use good writing to reduce the reader's expenditure of energy.

The bridge between the writer and reader is the copy editor, who must carve — but not butcher — each story so that it runs smoothly through the reader's mind. The copy editor works harder for the reader to ensure easy reading by deleting clichés, extraneous words, jargon, ambiguities, nondescript adjectives and adverbs. How well the whole stands up, of course, is as important as its parts.

Does the story get right to the point? Is it accurate? Is the lead smooth or does it meander and puzzle? Does the second paragraph deliver on the promise made in the lead? Does the third paragraph continue the development implicit in the lead and second paragraph? Are the direct quotations worthwhile to the story? Are opinions attributed? Is the tone of the story appropriate for the subject matter? Do sentences flow one unto the other? Has the writer drawn the most out of the language?

Those and other questions should confront copy editors every time they edit a story. The errors copy editors fix vary as much as the personalities of the writers, but the principles of good writing and good editing remain unchanged, and it behooves each copy editor to answer to those principles time and time again with concern for the quality of the prose and the exactitude of the message.

The good copy editor does not suffer from itchy cursor, does not edit for the sake of editing, but instead carefully, yet quickly, studies the story to ensure that it performs, that it is the concert of words the writer intended for the reader to enjoy. A good copy editor does not automatically remove verbiage without reason. A mindless copy editor, intent on saving space, would have told President Lincoln to tighten the opening of the Gettysburg Address from "Four score and seven years ago ... " to "Eighty-seven years ago ... ," assuring brevity, but destroying rhythm.

A good copy editor knows that subjects and verbs function best when close together. Search through this example for the impact neutralized by too great a distance between the actor and the action:

> The Barbell Club, which also won't be able to use the facilities during the day even though it donated approximately $1,200 in equipment to the weight room last year, also had no say in the change.

Pity the reader who must stumble over word after word after word — words that don't link directly to the subject. Recognizing the muck at the bottom of such a sentence, the copy editor inverts the order, putting the verb and subject up front and close together, the better to make the point:

> Also given no say was the Barbell Club. It won't be able to use the facilities during the day, even though it donated about $1,200 in equipment to the weight room last year.

Comprehension advances a big step in the rewrite and transition is aided, almost by accident, because also leads off the sentence, thereby linking the previous thought to the new thought.

Points unrelated to the main thought of a sentence fall to the copy editor's cursor. A sentence contains one thought, the copy editor knows, and when a sentence wallows in several, the unrelated points become non sequiturs. "Born in Los Angeles," such a false sentence might begin, "the deceased was a member of the Barbell Club." The copy editor separates the nativity from the activity and reunites them with their appropriate relatives.

Words get special treatment, almost a fondling, among copy editors eager to oust gracelessness and inelegance from a story. Times have changed since copy editors lost a week's pay for letting into print one misused word, but the punishment might be worth restoring for those who perform slovenly at the terminal.

No copy editor sensitive to the difference between transitive and intransitive verbs would allow either of these headlines: "Girl in red bikini defects Russia" and "Scared Americans evacuate Iran." Russia and Iran can be objects of verbs, but the verbs must be transitive. In fact, *evacuate* has one transitive meaning that describes bodily functions, not bodily fears.

One wonders who the bigger fool is when sentences such as this see print, "Lubold was almost near perfect": the anonymous copy editor who was far from perfect or Lubold, who might as well be "almost nearsighted" or "a little bit pregnant" or "virtually unique." For the reader, the error besmirches the newspaper's credibility, while inside the newspaper, the desk, not the writer, bears the shame. The laughter born in "Former President Gerald Ford breakfasted on Capitol Hill today" does not hide the shortcoming of the copy editor who failed to see the double meaning. As the copy editor's editor later asked: "Isn't Capitol Hill nutritionally deficient?" The copy editor wisely did not respond.

THE NEWS STORY

In the news story, attention focuses on various related parts. Most obviously, the lead is central to the story. But the copy editor must also examine the remaining parts of the story to see how they fit with the lead. Even the ending of a news story bears examination. The copy editor must ensure that news style is followed and that the context of the story is clear. Does the story flow smoothly? And when the story is not the standard inverted pyramid, what should the copy editor be looking for? We begin with the lead.

LEADS

Although the inverted-pyramid formula for writing news has fewer and fewer adherents as newswriting styles change, its underlying concepts are still valid. No matter if the story begins with a who-what-why-when-where-how lead or with the subtlety of a novel, the principle remains the same: Does the lead work? The person who can best answer that is the copy editor, the first tester any story comes up against. The copy editor, although required to read the entire story, must decide if the reader, lacking the compulsion of a job, will do the same. If the lead fails, the copy editor must determine why and then return the story to its writer or apply the polish at the desk. The lead is an implied promise to the reader. The body of the story delivers on the promise.

Leads come up short or fail outright for any number of reasons. One guarantee of failure is the imprecise lead that waffles for 40 words and never settles down to tell the story. Such leads attempt to say too much and are best repaired through excision. Cut the facts not required to tell the story's main point and blend them as needed in subsequent paragraphs. In some cases, the excised facts might provide the information for a new paragraph.

Leads can present so much information that the reader feels overwhelmed rather than informed. This lead, for example, says too much; the reader is left gasping.

> FBI investigators poked through debris in a marble hallway outside the Senate chamber this morning, searching for the remnants of a bomb that exploded in the heart of the Capitol shortly before midnight, heavily damaging a congressional cloakroom and destroying priceless works of art.

That lead can be dismissed out of hand on length alone: It is 43 words. But length aside, count the number of verbs. The lead contains five verbs — *poked, searching, exploded, damaging, destroying* — which leaves the reader wondering what the action was. Verbs are the engines of sentences, and the good writer uses just enough power to pull the nouns along. In this particular example, a copy editor rewrote the lead into two paragraphs.

> FBI investigators poked through debris in a marble hallway outside the Senate chamber this morning, searching for the remnants of a bomb that exploded in the heart of the Capitol shortly before midnight.
> Although no one was hurt, a congressional cloakroom was heavily damaged and many priceless works of art were destroyed.

Badly written leads become parodies of themselves and sometimes sound like the summary of a soap opera. This lead suffers from that problem and from having too many verbs: "Relatives prayed at her bedside and her mother, the victim of a mistaken injection, lay comatose, as a premature girl took a turn for the worse and lost a 24-day fight for her life, the family's lawyer said." Simply put, the baby died.

Another parody lead: "Emergencies have been declared in two

northwest Washington counties hit hard by mudslides and flooding while a woman who was swept into a lake by a 4-foot wall of water escaped unharmed after a 20-minute swim." The writer is trying to convey too much in a sentence. The copy desk should rewrite the lead into two sentences.

Leads without news put readers to sleep. The story that begins "City Council convened Monday night to discuss next year's budget and last year's unresolved contract with union employees" only to later let out — and there's no more accurate description for such sleepers — that the City Council raised taxes and fired the unionized employees is certain to ensure an unread story. Operating with the news-eager reader in mind, the copy editor reorders the story, often by eliminating the discussion angle for one of precision. "City Council Monday night raised taxes an average of $20 to pay for hiring employees to replace those fired for not signing a contract." Now the story will probably be read, because it has consequences for the typical reader.

Cliché leads dampen reader interest because they display the writer's lack of concern for original prose and their lack of news. "I've read that before," the reader might think when the same old words appear. Consider the family-outing-ending-in-tragedy lead: "A family fishing outing ended in tragedy when a man and his 14-year-old son were swept off a breakwater by the highest surf in eight years Tuesday." A copy editor could remove the cliché with: "The highest surf in eight years swept a man and his 14-year-old son to their deaths from a breakwater where they had been fishing Tuesday." Removing the cliché makes the lead direct, appealing and more original.

Leads lacking comparative data leave readers suspended in a "So-what?" state, where they refuse to hang on long enough to see what the second paragraph says. A lead that reports the number of deaths from heart disease without comparing that number to the total number of deaths in the population leaves the reader without a yardstick to measure the information. For example: "Heart disease claimed 378 lives in Pilsdon last year, according to a recent report from a Heart Association official." Is 378 high? Low? How does it compare with total deaths? That information probably hides in the story's body whence (not *from whence*) the copy editor should dislodge it and place it up front: "Heart disease claimed 378 lives in Pilsdon last year — more than any other cause of death, a Heart Association officials says."

A lead piled high with statistics is likely to stupefy readers rather than enlighten them. A story beginning "Four Clive County residents ranging in ages from 17 to 75 died in three traffic accidents within a 12-hour period" suggests the clumsy hand of a sportswriter raised on stolen bases, runs batted in, walks, and, yes, strikeouts rather than the deft sense of a writer working for the reader.

Leads containing lists, a superficial check-off of major actions taken at some meeting, make the reader yearn for the lead that puts the most important action up front. A lead of lists delays the news and keeps the reader from finding out what happened. Here is a list lead from London: "Suspicious vans stacked with cages, 800 paws found on a rubbish dump and thousands of missing felines point to catnapping on a massive scale in England and Wales, a pet charity says." It is not until the second half of the sentence that the reader learns what the list is all about.

Dependent clauses at the start usually put leads into the read-me-again category because the clauses appear ahead of the main part of the sentence, the part the clause depends on to make sense. They begin: "Armed with a bat that was heavier than any he's ever handled before, Tiger star 'Slugger' Strongarm tapped in the winning run." Another: "Because of the high divorce rate, State Rep. Jonas A. Winston proposed Wednesday that the state require engaged couples to wait six months before getting married." In both, the beginning clauses bewilder the reader because the clauses lack context. "Why am I reading this?" the puzzled reader asks as he stops. Rewritten, the second lead might say: "State Rep. Jonas A. Winston has proposed making engaged couples wait six months before marrying as a way of curbing the state's high divorce rate." (Dependent clauses at the start of nonlead sentences usually cause none of the same problems.)

Leads that come up short can usually be repaired with information from the second paragraph of the story because that's where the news frequently lies. The writer failed to report first the most current important detail. For example: A person has been arrested and taken before a judge and the judge has set bail. The arrested person cannot post bail and has been jailed. The lead that misses the mark reports the arrest, but it should report the person being in jail in lieu of bail. The jailing of a person in lieu of bail usually subsumes the arrest, the appearance in court and the setting of bail, so provide that information in subsequent paragraphs in decreasing order of importance.

Direct quotation leads, especially in hard news (24 hours young or younger) should be paraphrased on the assumption that any writer can improve on the spoken word. To be allowed into print, a quotation lead must be compelling, must still meet the number one purpose of a lead — engage the reader. Quotation leads are also flawed because they lack context. The reader first meets quotation marks, not an attribution tag, and thus does not know who is speaking. Such leads make a reader go by twice (if the writer's lucky enough to get a second chance) in order to make sense out of the direct quotation.

Copy editors should be alert for cute leads. Oh, they may raise a smile, but the smile soon will be replaced with a question: What is this about? Consider this lead: "It's Fall, they're falling, the leaves are appalling." The story is about a board of township supervisors setting the schedule for leaf collection, hardly the stuff of rhymes.

On the other hand, when the tax collector appeared at the board of supervisors meeting to ask that all houses get street addresses so that he could reach people through the mail the first time, a reporter missed an opportunity to be bright. He turned in this yawner, "The Ferguson Township Board of Supervisors Wednesday night authorized a system of numbers for street addresses for Ferguson Township residents." A copy editor converted this into: "Ferguson Township supervisors want to make sure the taxman doesn't have to write twice." Even if you are not familiar with James M. Cain's *The Postman Always Rings Twice* and miss the literary allusion, you can still appreciate the sense of the story.

That does not happen with this lead. "Students wearing the single white glove and black-studded belt popularized by Michael Jackson told the school board that a high school rule barring them from honoring the superstar by mimicking his wardrobe is no thriller." Only if you know that Jackson had popularized a song titled "Thriller" would you get the allusion.

The good lead does more than recite a story; it advertises the story's best points. When two men being chased by a state police officer because they were speeding crashed their car, jumped out of their car, swam across a river and through the woods in an attempt to escape, Linda Koehler of the *Times-News* of Lehighton, Pa., penned this lead, which the copy desk wisely left untouched:

> They went over the river and through the woods. But odds are they weren't going to grandmother's house.

If the good lead isn't there, the copy desk needs to improve it. This lead was spurned by the chief copy editor one night, who commanded one of his rim people to brighten it: "Many businesses around the country have been affected by the baseball strike, although the Gillette Co. of Boston, the country's leading razor company, may suffer more because it has tied a promotion to the baseball All-Star game next month." Given that the story was going on the business page, a copy editor could assume that the readers would know who the Gillette company is. He produced this lead: "The Gillette Co. of Boston could be in for a close shave if the baseball strike continues until the All-Star game in July."

A time element can dull an otherwise good lead when placed out front. Newspapers usually do not report hard news older than 24 hours so no story needs a time element at the beginning. Given newspapers' trend toward feature leads on news, copy editors have to decide if the time element is necessary in the lead at all. Thus, an otherwise interesting lead should not be tampered with to fit in a time element not crucial to the major point of the story. This Thursday afternoon lead on a Wednesday morning story by Paula Maynard of United Press International ignores the time element and stresses the human element of a tragedy.

> Six-year-old Travis Crook, stabbed and bleeding, walked with his dog the one block to school with a message for his principal: The boy's mother and younger brother had been slain.

Editors call the preceding a second-day lead because it appears not necessarily in the second day after the news, but it is the second lead on the story, the first having been written for an earlier edition or by the competition. Faced with a competitive situation, Athelia Knight of *The Washington Post*, started a stabbing story this way:

> It was about 3 a.m. yesterday when D.C. City Councilman David A. Clarke left a sandwich shop at 18th Street and Columbia Road and began walking home. As he reached 16th and Harvard streets NW, he said he sensed someone behind and continued walking at a steady pace.
>
> Clarke said that when he reached the walkway to his home at 320 17th St. NW, three men jumped him from behind, punched him in the face and stabbed him twice in the back. Clarke suffered superficial wounds to his back and was in good condition late yesterday at the Washington Hospital Center.

Perhaps the example shows a case of having your hard news and featurizing it too, because the headline on Knight's story makes clear what the story is about: "City councilman is stabbed outside his Northwest home." That shouldn't detract from what Knight did. She told the story from the victim's point of view, and her approach makes for a more compelling beginning than this:

> A D.C. city councilman was in good condition late yesterday at the Washington Hospital Center, where he was taken after he was stabbed twice by three men near his home early yesterday morning.

That's what used to pass for a second-day lead at third-rate newspapers.

THE BODY OF THE STORY

Once the lead has taken shape, the development of the story concerns the copy editor next. One of the single biggest story organization problems stems from reporters who fail to follow their leads and, thus, their initial promise to the reader. They instead lapse into background in the second and third (and maybe fourth) paragraphs while the reader hangs around (and a writer should not assume that will happen) waiting for current information. A news story should play up the news, what happened within the past 24 hours, not what happened two days or three weeks ago. Save that for later in the story, or for history books. Here is a story in which history wrongly takes precedent over timeliness:

> WASHINGTON — John Newton Mitchell, the gruff former attorney general who went to prison for conspiring to cover up the Watergate scandal in his friend Richard Nixon's White House, is dead at 75 after collapsing on a Washington street.
>
> Mitchell was the highest ranking of the government officials who served time for the political scandal that brought about Nixon's resignation from the presidency in August 1974.
>
> "I considered John Mitchell to be one of my few closer personal friends," Nixon wrote in his memoirs. "I believed that I owed my election as president in 1968 largely to his strength as a counselor and his skill as a manager."
>
> An ambulance crew, alerted by a 10-year-old boy who was skateboarding, found Mitchell unconscious on a street in the Georgetown section of Washington in early evening Wednesday. Mitchell had suffered a heart attack.
>
> He stopped breathing as he was being taken to the hospital and died despite cardiopulmonary resuscitation.
>
> Mitchell was convicted on Jan. 1, 1975, of conspiring ...

The story should first focus on how the man died — that's what the lead promises — then provide background for people who need detail. This organization seems more suited to the facts:

> WASHINGTON — John Newton Mitchell, the gruff former attorney general who went to prison for conspiring to cover up the Watergate scandal in his friend Richard Nixon's White House, is dead at 75 after collapsing on a Washington street.

> An ambulance crew, alerted by a 10-year-old boy who was skateboarding, found Mitchell unconscious on a street in the Georgetown section of Washington in early evening Wednesday. Mitchell had suffered a heart attack.
> He stopped breathing as he was being taken to the hospital and died despite cardiopulmonary resuscitation.
> Mitchell was the highest ranking of the government officials who served time for the political scandal that brought about Nixon's resignation from the presidency in August 1974.
> "I considered John Mitchell to be one of my few closer personal friends," Nixon wrote in his memoirs. "I believed that I owed my election as president in 1968 largely to his strength as a counselor and his skill as a manager."
> Mitchell was convicted on Jan. 1, 1975, of conspiring ...

Another organizational problem develops with the multi-topic story, which begins on one issue then abandons the issue in the second paragraph for another issue. For example:

> Mayor William F. Shanahan says disciplinary action will be taken against police sergeants and lieutenants who, angry over unprecedented layoffs, called in sick or generally ignored prostitutes, gamblers and traffic violators.
> Meanwhile, members of Firefighters Local 69, whose ranks also are to be trimmed by job cuts, planned to set up informational picket lines today outside the fire administration building.
> Local President John Henry said on Wednesday that members of the Fraternal Order of Police, which represents much of the city's 8,000-member force, would join the firefighters and march to city hall for a joint informational picket.
> "We will do whatever is necessary to save the jobs of our members," Henry said.
> He noted that the membership had voted to authorize a strike but said no walkout was planned. Reilly said he would meet today with Shanahan.
> Shanahan's promise of disciplinary action followed a day in which officers in some districts refused to write tickets.

Four paragraphs intervene between the lead and the first paragraph that fills out the lead. The lead and the reader deserve better and the copy editor should make the appropriate changes by shifting paragraphs or creating a sidebar.

Endings

Not every story is written in the inverted pyramid style, that is, to peter out as the facts diminish in importance. Sometimes a story can have an ending, something that neatly ties the information together. The copy desk needs to be sensitive to the journalist who puts an ending on a story. Does the ending work? What might be done to make it better?

One word of advice: Don't end a story with an attribution tag. It is the direct quotation that makes the ending, not the attribution tag. Compare these final paragraphs and see which one ends the story better:

> "If I had to depend on men to buy romance books, I'd be broke," she said.

> "If I had to depend on men to buy romance books," she said, "I'd be broke."

The original ending on the story is the first paragraph. An alert copy editor improved it immensely merely by moving the attribution tag. Another copy editor improved the ending of an analytical story that moved the day Indira Ghandi, the prime minister of India, was assassinated. The story focused on the political dynasty of Mrs. Ghandi's family, beginning with her grandfather, an early political leader in the Indian independence movement, and then her father, Jawaharlal Nehru, the first prime minister of India. The original story ended this way:

> The following year, her first-born, Rajiv, yielded to mounting pressure and quit as an Indian Airlines pilot to become a member of Parliament. He too moved full time into the prime minister's residence to learn politics and power.

The copy editor realized that the ending wasn't enough, that it failed to fully exploit the theme of the story, which was the political dynasty. So she deleted the last sentence and substituted this one:

> Today, Rajiv was sworn in to succeed his mother as prime minister of India.

That sentence, provided by an alert copy editor, ties the story together. Copy editors need to be alert to every story's potential.

NEWS STYLE

Presenting news to readers who might want information quickly requires the news writer to avoid an episodic bent (and then ... and then ... and then ...) and to condense information as tightly as possible. Don't allow two sentences in backward order when one in news style order will do. "Hockton proposed that the trustees add a surcharge to the Spring Quarter bill instead of raising tuition." (*No news so far; the trustees' vote will be the news.*)

"The motion failed, 14-7." (*The news!*)

Regrettably, the reporter has forced the reader to hang on to learn the news, which is then poorly presented in a limp sentence that seems stuck on to the end of the paragraph as an afterthought. This rewrite rejects the episodic structure and condenses the information for a quick read. "The trustees rejected, 14-7, a motion by Hockton to place a $35 surcharge on Spring Quarter bills instead of raising tuition." The issue here is not sentence length but priority — of letting the reader know quickly what happened. The copy editor who turns episodic writing into news style serves the reader well.

CONTEXT

Context problems arise on different levels. At one level, a reporter fails to provide the context for a direct quotation. Reading through a story, the reader encounters: "We've asked for Timothy O'Hara's resignation." The next paragraph reveals that O'Hara is the county planning director but doesn't explain why his job is on the line. Three paragraphs later the reader learns it was O'Hara who hired the consulting firm that approved building a county park on chemical-infested land, a problem that should have been detected before the county purchased the land. But the reader doesn't learn that at the right moment. The copy editor, thus, must rearrange or rewrite the story to give the direct quotation context.

The larger context problem occurs when a writer assumes the reader knows the history of the story and fails to provide brief but appropriate background. The focus of a breaking news story is what happened within the past 12 to 24 hours. But many of these stories come with history — history that needs to appear somewhere in the story. The caution is that it not appear too soon as to intrude on the current angle.

VIEWPOINT

Point of view problems occur when the reporter forgets how the reader will receive what has been written. The reporter writes a story from his perspective rather than the larger perspective of the reader. When such errors appear, they should be removed from copy. The reporter who writes about "our weather" might confuse the reader who thinks "our" refers to the newspaper. Change "our" to the appropriate name for the area. Similarly, a reporter could unintentionally become part of a story by using the personal pronoun "I" outside direct quotations. Usually, the reporter failed to provide quotation marks, but the copy editor should ensure that the "I" doesn't refer to the reporter.

The writer of this headline also has a point of view problem, "Spring cold snap sends snow to Pa.," since the headline writer works for a Pennsylvania newspaper. The headline would work well in Ohio, but to reflect a Pennsylvania point of view, it should say: "Spring cold snap *brings* snow to Pa."

Fairness must be maintained, leaving it up to the copy editor to ensure the reporter is neither under- nor overplaying a story. Likewise, the copy editor must function as a goad when a reluctant reporter holds back because of the fear of offending some newspaper policy. Similarly, the copy editor should ensure that the reporter did not fashion the story to elicit undeserved display from a prejudiced editor. That often puts the copy editor in the middle, but if copy editors remember that they work for the reader, they'll maintain their balance.

ATTRIBUTION

Attribution tag placement rates special attention from the copy editor, who should make sure that all tags appear as unobtrusively as possible. Bury attribution tags so they're not hanging off the ends of paragraphs or not starting paragraphs in such as way as to disrupt the flow of the story. Within paragraphs, the best place is between two sentences, such as:

> "We've come to the end of the road," Herlocher said. "Nothing can go beyond March 1. That's the absolute final date."

A similar situation occurs in compound sentences, where the attribution tag fits best between the two sentences joined by a conjunction or a semicolon.

"Michael played a great game, but you shouldn't let one person beat you and that's what we did," Boston's Kevin McHale said.

Rearranged:

"Michael played a great game," Boston's Kevin McHale said, "but you shouldn't let one person beat you and that's what we did."

Within a sentence the attribution tag fits best at a natural break, as in this example:

> Officials earlier reported only six deaths. Eight of the deaths, they said, went unreported for a time and three people reported dead were found safe.

The preceding sentence also demonstrates a method of emphasizing a phrase by breaking the sentence with an attribution tag. By placing the attribution tag after "Eight of the deaths," the writer puts emphasis on that phrase. The tag could begin the sentence, but they might confuse the reader who momentarily links the plural pronoun to deaths rather than officials. Tucked inside the sentence, the tag remains out of the way yet still functions as intended.

An ill-placed attribution tag can disrupt the flow of a sentence. For example:

> "We were very pleased," Mitinger said, "very happy and very lucky. To win any golf tournament, you have to have a little luck."

Such placement of the attribution tag breaks the rhythm of the direct quote. The sentence sounds better if the attribution tag appears between the sentences.

> "We were very pleased, very happy and very lucky," Mitinger said. "To win any golf tournament, you have to have a little luck."

It is also essential that an attribution tag not be torn asunder. Speaker and verb should be close together, if not next to each other. This is an example of how not to write it:

> "I have a sore back and a stiff neck," Sampson, who has played in all 72 of Houston's games this season, said.

The writer of that sentence blindly followed the dictum that attribution tags should always appear in the subject-verb sequence. And that is good advice, most of the time. But sometimes a long modifying clause comes with the subject and the dictum doesn't hold up. In this case, an inverted attribution tag is the lesser of two evils.

> "I have a sore back and a stiff neck," said Sampson, who has played in all 72 of Houston's games this season.

For transition purposes, attribution tags need to begin paragraphs or appear early in the first sentence of a paragraph, when the story contains more than one speaker and the writer is shifting from one speaker to another.

Attribution tags are also sources of information for the reader. They must be placed correctly so the reader knows the source of information. This sentence suggests the source of information for not releasing someone's name is some detectives. Actually, the reporter is making the statement.

> The charges involved Platt's 11-year-old daughter, whose name was not released, detectives said.

The only way of making that clear is to begin the sentence with the attribution tag.

> Detectives said the charges involved Platt's 11-year-old daughter, whose name was not released.

Direct quotations provide another spot where a copy editor must maintain vigilance against error. The Iranian student who refers to the United States' acceptance of Iran's former shah as "an insultation to the Iranian revolution" doesn't know he has misused a word, but the copy editor does and should repair the damage. The issue, in that case, was political, not grammatical. Similar errors should be fixed rather than published to the embarrassment of the speaker and the newspaper. Intentional language errors should stand, especially when they are used by the speaker for effect or are typical of the speaker and are used by the writer for flavor.

However, the best way of fixing errors is not to clear up the mistake within quotation marks. That misleads the reader. One editor, for example, always shifts the word only in a direct quote because people usually place it incorrectly. But that is false, because spoken speech and written speech are not always the same. Thus, the editor who fixes direct quotations makes people sound stiff and formal. If the sentence contains a mistake, the editor should paraphrase the sentence. The virtue of a journalist is telling an accurate story. Direct quotations can be ambiguous or presented out of context. The journalist's first obligation is to accuracy, not a writing formula. There is no shame in paraphrasing.

When copy editors believe they can edit direct quotations, problems arise. One beginning copy editor, told to tighten sentences, deleted the italicized words from the following direct quotation:

> "He was an average student, an *average* wrestler on the freshman wrestling team and an *average* instrumentalist in the concert band," Hoose said.

Unfortunately, Hoose fell victim to a below-average copy editor. Hoose was making a point that the subject of the sentence was average. If the copy editor felt the quotation was wordy, paraphrasing it was the only recourse.

Hoose said he was average in all areas.

Of course, that loses the flavor of the quotation.

Finally, copy editors should ensure that tags not only appear in the right place but that they appear at all. Unattributed sentences in news stories read like opinion. But the newspaper wants only to cover the news as fairly as possible and to keep opinion out of the news columns. When anyone on the desk doubts the veracity of anything, senior editors should be consulted.

TONE

A copy editor should also oversee the tone and mood of a story. Keep irreverence from serious stories and confine flippancy to night club acts. Remove unintended slang and colloquialism. The following sentence from a caption on a photograph of people piling sandbags next to a threatening river strikes the wrong tone.

> Building sandcastles is fun, but these Tijuana volunteers are not having a good time.

Combining a fun idea with life-saving efforts does not come off well. This headline, about the fatal crash of a jet owned by the Kellogg company, should not have seen print: "Kellogg jet takes dive." The copy editor may laugh when seeing such absurdities, and that alone should flash the warning light that something's wrong.

Sentences and Paragraphs

Rules about sentences and paragraphs in the news media are based on utilitarian notions, not literary concepts. Journalists lean toward short sentences (an average of 17 to 20 words) because readability experts say that such sentences convey information easily. Still, don't count words in a sentence, but ask first how the sentence works. That's the test. It's a matter of quality, not quantity.

Here is a sentence that runs on and on because the writer tried to link too many facts.

> According to Jefferson, the latest fossils came from a site that was first discovered in 1972, when utility work crews accidentally cut into it, "but we hadn't expected it to be this size."

And nobody expected the sentence to be that long.

The most accursed sentences of the lot are the fragment and the run-on. The fragment usually lacks a subject or verb; the run-on, as the name implies, is a continuous gaggle of words that seem to never stop. Because so many thoughts make up a run-on sentence, clarity suffers; a run-on offers too much for the reader to digest.

The good copy editor, however, does not join a fragment to a whole or halt the run-on sentence without first ascertaining that the "error" impedes reading ease. Fragments can effectively make a point, especially in an editorial or a column. They are not as useful in straight news stories.

As for paragraphs, the best rule is to keep them short, say, two sentences, sometimes three, and then only if the sentences are short. An important reason for short paragraphs is the reader. Newspaper readers, research shows, have difficulty reading long paragraphs and their interest in reading will flag if they sense a long paragraph ahead. Also behind that rule was a desire to make stories easier to cut (computer typesetting has negated that reason) and to put white space among the gray columns of type.

Newspaper utility aside, one old paragraph rule retains its virtue: A paragraph is (at the least) a series of related sentences. If a copy editor reads three consecutive one-sentence paragraphs, the copy editor should evaluate them to see if they are related. If they are, they should be yoked into one paragraph. Paragraphs of related sentences make the story easier to read. Paragraphs of related sentences establish relations and make the information more understandable.

By the same token, if a paragraph takes three sentences, then the first cannot be about oil in Iran if the second is about a rebellion in Afghanistan and the third is about Muslims in Pakistan — unless the writer makes the relationship clear. If no relationship exists, the copy editor should depress the paragraph key at the end of each sentence to create three paragraphs. If a relationship exists, then the writer or the copy editor must show the relationship through transition.

TRANSITION

Transition is the lubricant of good writing. The lack of it makes the reader stumble and turn away from a story, because topics will change without warning. Abrupt shifts are avoidable, although a writer might slip when writing against deadline. Then the desk must provide transition, which can improve a story faster than rewriting because one word can perform well by making a lot of words make sense. In fact, journalistic writing avoids long or formal transitions because they delay the reader who is quickly seeking information. By the same token, a story should not come off as a disjointed gathering of paragraphs. The longer the story, the more formal the transition.

In the typical news story (l0 to 15 inches), the most effective transitional devices are short. A copy editor can readily change a topic on the strength of one word (e.g., but, however, and, meanwhile). A change in time or location can also be signaled easily later. Geographical references make effective transition. In a winter storm roundup written for a national audience, the change of location can be heralded with the name of a town. For example:

> A winter storm pounded the Middle West today, then headed toward the Atlantic Ocean ...

[two paragraphs later]

> In Des Moines, Iowa, schools closed as l0 inches of snow piled on top of 24 inches left by a storm a week ago.

[four paragraphs later]

Commuters in Chicago were kept home ...

[three paragraphs later]

By the time the storm reached Cleveland ...

Each stop along the way comes early enough to alert the reader to the change in location. The failure to provide transition can make for ambiguity beyond repair, as shown in this example:

> In Laramie, a 53-year-old man opened fire Tuesday with a shotgun and killed a youth after the youth threw snowballs at his house, according to police.
> Wyoming Gas Co. spokesperson William C. Freed ...

At first the reader may believe that Freed pulled the trigger, but what happened was the writer failed to use transition to advise the reader that the story was shifting from a slaying to a statement on thermostats. The copy desk failed for not catching the shortcoming and fixing it, perhaps by starting the new paragraph with elsewhere.

Starting paragraphs with titles instead of names is also effective transition. Imagine a story on Pentagon spending that begins by quoting some members of Congress but eventually shifts to get the Pentagon's version of events. If the shifting paragraph begins with a person's name, the readers won't realize that a shift has occurred. But if the shifting sentence begins, "The Pentagon's chief spokesman, Fred Hoffman, disclosed ... ," the reader knows a shift has occurred. That's good transition.

A good writer can also rely on topics to effect good transition. Here are two paragraphs from a story about a dangerous stretch of Interstate 24 in Tennessee. Note how the first paragraph ends and the second begins; note how the writer, Justin Catanoso of the *Knoxville Journal*, went from the general to the specific.

> In an effort to decrease the dangers of Monteagle, the state Public Service Commission is planning to pull over all trucks at the top of the mountain, inspect the vehicles and the drivers, and remind them that 35 mph is the downhill speed limit.
> Excessive speed was a contributing factor in more than 70 percent of the fatal accidents, according to records provided by the Tennessee Highway Patrol.

Repeating the word "speed" also aided transition. Repetition of key words is an effective transitional device. The journalist who won't use the same word twice but instead seeks out every synonym does not do justice to clarity. In such writing, a rainstorm becomes a torrent becomes a gusher and then a cloud emptier and so on. A copy editor can create good transition by repeating the word "rainstorm."

Avoid jarring the reader. Here are two paragraphs from a talk about suicide. After the speech, a student named Janet stood up and talked about the time she attempted suicide. One journalist covering the talk used the story of Janet as his lead and then switched to remarks by the speaker. But he did it clumsily, as this example shows:

> Janet did not succeed in ending her life, but she did discover that her problems could be solved and that living was the answer.
>
> Dr. Renae Grant, a clinical psychologist at the University's Center for Psychological Services, told the same audience that if people are aware of the warning signs of suicide, more people like Janet may receive help.

The change from Janet to Grant can be done more smoothly by rewriting the second paragraph. This is what a copy editor did:

> More people like Janet may receive help if people are aware of the warning signs of suicide, according to Dr. Renae Grant, a clinical psychologist at the University's Center for Psychological Services.

With the rewritten paragraph, the story's focus shifts smoothly from Janet to Grant.

Transition bridges thoughts, sentences and paragraphs, and copy editors need to be good bridge builders.

No Story Is a Formula

Unfortunately, some people have developed the attitude that a story for a newspaper or a broadcast can be written or edited only one way. Editors addicted to formulas count not only the number of words in sentences but the number of syllables in words. Four syllables and more and a word is out. No lead can be longer than 15 words. A 16-word lead? Rewrite it.

Those same editors insist that the inverted-pyramid style of newswriting be followed to the point of absurdity — absurdity being the turning of an interesting story into a dull one. The inverted pyramid is functional and utilitarian, but editors should recognize it as the basis for newswriting, not for the form all newswriting must take. The narrative approach to newswriting, especially with stories not of a breaking nature, may be the salvation of a print medium facing the appeal of television, Home Box Office, movie theatres, specialty magazines and the World Wide Web. Not only will some rules be broken, survival may dictate they be discarded.

Similarly, the advice given in this chapter — in fact, throughout this book — should be measured against common sense. Function should dictate form. If the inverted pyramid works best on a story, use it. By the same token, the narrative approach to story-telling may not work if the result is too long to engage the reader on the run. All rules require the copy editor to blend the practical and the theoretical with experience to learn.

Chapter 12

TIGHTENING COPY

Nobody enjoys listening to someone at a party tell a story in 10,000 words when the storyteller could have made the point in 250. Newspaper readers are like everyone else: They don't like their time taken up with word-inflated stories. Readers don't have time for verbosity. A journalist must get the most information into the least space or time and do it clearly. Every story, regardless of the news medium, should be written as tightly as possible. The goal should be: Leave not one extra word for the desk to remove.

SPARE THE READER

Good intentions aside, the copy editor prunes any word or detail or bulky phrase that would slow the reader or listener. The process of carefully removing extra words and reshaping sentences to condense the message is called "bleeding." It is a challenging job. But extra words mean fewer stories; fewer stories make the news package less interesting. The copy editor aims to produce the tightest, fullest package possible, whether it's a weekly newspaper or network news.

Here's a 39-word sentence that can be reduced by almost 50 percent.

> The bomb squad went to the scene and removed the grenades, placing them inside a bomb container and hauling them to the Philadelphia Police Academy in Northeast Philadelphia where they were temporarily put in a bomb pit, police said.

Let's make one pass with the cursor:

> The bomb squad removed the grenades, hauling them in a bomb container to the Philadelphia Police Academy in Northeast Philadelphia, where they were temporarily put in a bomb pit, police said.

That pass reduced the sentence to 31 words.[1] Another pass will get it to 25.

> The bomb squad removed the grenades to the Philadelphia Police Academy in Northeast Philadelphia, where they were temporarily put in a bomb pit, police said.

The final pass will reduce the sentence to 21 words.

> The bomb squad put the grenades temporarily in a bomb pit at the Philadelphia Police Academy in Northeast Philadelphia, police said.

The principle behind the editing of that sentence can help a copy editor in any situation. Simply put, the copy editor needs to ask what action (verb) subsumes all other actions. That verb then carries the sentence. Is it necessary to say that the bomb squad went to the scene? Must the reporter say that the squad placed the grenades into a container? Must the reporter say the squad hauled the container to a pit and dumped the grenades into the pit? All the writer needs to say is that the bomb squad put the grenades in a pit.

Here is another example:

> A college graduate, he went to Boston College, where he earned a B.A. degree in economics.

So much of that sentence is unnecessary. A rewrite:

> He earned a B.A. in economics from Boston College.

Subsumption is but one of many principles behind the tightening of copy. The remainder of this chapter explains how to identify and excise wordiness, make sentences direct, strengthen weak verbs, remove the passive voice where appropriate, eliminate redundancies, omit the obvious and reduce prepositional pile-up.[2]

---

[1] And if you remember your lessons from an earlier section, you would be counting the words in the sentence to make sure I am correct.

[2] A good exercise that I've used in my editing courses: Reduce "Death of a Family Farm" in Chapter 6 by 25 percent through bleeding.

REMOVE VERBOSITY

Unnecessary wordage plagues all members of the news team, from the political columnist to the sportswriter. It is even more evident in the broadcast media, whose anchorpersons and commentators work without scripts and lack an opportunity to edit their speech. The best, though, are skillful enough to speak tightly without a script.

Examples of verbosity include the phrase *on the grounds that*, which can be reduced to just one word, *because*. *In the intervening time* can be replaced with *since*. Related errors include verbs with unnecessary particles appended to them, such as *continue on, follow after, miss out, ponder over, slow down, slow up, cancel out, revert back, raise up, slim down, head up, check out*. They are better reduced to one word. Similarly, *take into consideration* equals *consider*. The problem also arises with modifiers. *Game-winning run* equals *winning run* and *three separate buildings* equals *three buildings*.

Make Sentences Direct

Indirect writing manifests itself in sentences beginning or containing it is/there is/there are. Those weak phrases can't always be eliminated, but not cutting them is the exception. In addition to reducing sentence length, the copy editor who cuts such phrases also strengthens the sentences, a virtue among readers who like their language in good shape.

> *There are 42 gallons per barrel* becomes *A barrel contains 42 gallons.*
>
> *As of this morning there had been only one artist cancel the trip* converts to *As of this morning, only one artist had canceled the trip.*
>
> *There is no tangible evidence to back up the account* is stronger as *No tangible evidence backs up the account.*
>
> *There is a possibility that the U.S. Customs Service may charge Harrison with smuggling* translates to *The U.S. Customs Service may charge Harrison with smuggling* because *may* means possibility.
>
> *It was the second such shooting incident in a little over a month* works better as *The shooting was the second in little over a month.*
>
> *There is no death penalty in Panama* gains force as *Panama has no death penalty.*

Copy editors will find plenty of indirectness because such sentences come easily under the pressure of writing against deadline. Despite the pressure of deadline, such sentences are easy to repair. The detached perspective copy editors have allows them to see most damage easier and to repair it faster.

Eliminate Conventional Information

Information that readers know simply because it is part of their culture can be deleted. Typically in accident and fire stories, reporters will write or say: "City police, who investigated the accident, said the driver fell asleep at the wheel" and "Ladder Company No. 6, which responded to the alarm, helped contain the blaze within a half-hour." If the police made the statement and if the firefighters fought the blaze, they had to have investigated or responded. It should go without saying.

Similarly, "The dentist cleaned out the cavity with a drill" and "Firefighters fought the blaze with water." When the dentist doesn't use a drill or firefighters don't use water (which can happen), then it might be newsworthy. Otherwise, the tools of most trades are fodder for the editor's cursor.

Strengthen Weak Verbs

Any time actionless verbs appear, a copy editor should see if they can be replaced with strong verbs. The lead that begins "Four people are dead as the result of automobile accidents ... " gains strength when changed to "Four people died in ... " To say "The city has no good water supplies" means "The city lacks good water supplies." "He said he had a poor start this year" means "He said he started poorly this year." With a strong verb, the preceding sentences shed their mealy-mouth image.

Oust the Passive Voice

The passive voice (any form of "to be" and a verb's past participle such as *mistakes were made*) represents one of the most anti-news constructions possible in the English language because passive voice hides the actor of a verb, who is the newsmaker. Consider this lead:

> The awarding of contracts to two firms for supplying furnishings for county-contracted services was delayed by the county administration Thursday until it is determined who will own the equipment.

In the first case, the passive voice buries the identification of the delayer, and in the second the passive voice enables the lazy journalist to avoid telling who will make the determination. Journalists should report the news, not hide it. Here is the active voice rewrite, which adds a fact and is still tighter than the original:

> The county administration Thursday delayed awarding contracts to two firms for supplying furnishings for county-contracted services until the county controller determines who will own the equipment.

The controller's role surfaced in the fourth paragraph of the story.

CUT WEAK PHRASES

The flexibility of the English language allows its users to say the same thing in different forms. The copy editor must decide if the form chosen best suits the pace. Often weak phrases can be converted into nouns, as in this: "Seven people who were at the party were treated at the hospital" becomes direct when recast as "Seven party-goers were treated at the hospital."

GET THE RIGHT WORD

Journalists cannot survive without words. And when they use the wrong words, they threaten their own survival and cheapen the coin of the realm. One day a wire service reporter wrote:

> The regime admits that 5,000 have been interred since martial law was imposed, but reports reaching the West say 10 times that number have been seized.

As the closing verb should reveal, the regime had not buried 5,000 but had interned them — that is, put them in jail. Putting quotation marks around a misuse of a word does not excuse the misuse.

> University police told the department that judging the degree of lighting depends on a person's frame of reference.
> "It's objective," said Bob McNichols, crime prevention supervisor.

Sorry, Bob. If you accept an individual's frame of reference, it's subjective.

Then there's the reporter who wrote about "the 'vanishing art' of telegraphy — sending messages over wires in Morse code." Unsure of herself, she even put "vanishing art" in quotation marks. Telegraphy is a skill, not an art.³

In a newspaper strike story, a journalist wrote:

> Teamsters drivers, topographers, the Newspaper Guild and the mailers who rejected the four-year pact last Friday plan to reconsider the contract today.

But let us hope they invite the *typographers*, which is the correct word for the people who set type, rather than the people who specialize in the surface of a region (*topographer*). Also the word "last" is unnecessary, since the past-tense verb makes the time element clear.

An Orlando, Fla., sportswriter once wrote:

> Johnston, marred in a recent slump which saw his average dip into the .230s, slapped four singles and knocked in three runs Wednesday as the Knoxville Blue Jays defeated the Orlando Twins, 9-3, in Southern League Baseball.

It must have been the Southern accent spoken into a Yankee ear, my correspondent suggests, that turned *mired* into *marred*. But nobody's accent misused *ironically* when Joe Namath did his first broadcast for ABC. "Ironically," a wire service reporter wrote, "Namath's first telecast for ABC was last summer on the day he was inducted into the Hall of Fame." Sorry. The events were coincidental, but hardly ironic.

Then there's the book reviewer who began a review with this hard-to-imagine transformation:

> Okay, let's get it right out in the open. I'm a very serious Robert Ludlum fan. Well, better make that fanatic.

Fan is merely a backformation of *fanatic*.

Journalists fracture words more than they should and the copy desk needs to pay attention. There was the journalist who wrote about *imminent domain* for *eminent domain*; another used *bacon soda* for *baking soda*; another decided that *duplicitous* meant *duplicative*; another described a *non-denominational* meeting as *non-dimensional*;⁴ still another decided that *cocking* was the word to use for *caulking*; an obituary writer at the same newspaper listed a dead person's final resting place as the "Sylvan

---

³Some years ago I was a Navy radio operator.
⁴In the 1990s, AP eliminated the hyphen when adding "non" as a prefix to most words. Exceptions include words that start with "n" and proper nouns.

Heights moslem" instead of *mausoleum*. Some writers confuse *either* (one or the other) with *each* (both).

Many editors frown on the use of the word *approximately*, since *about* says the same thing and is much shorter. Also, the word *around* should not be used as a substitute for *approximately* or *about*. Around refers to physical space (e.g.,His arms are around the ball.).

And finally there is the confusion between *eager* and *anxious*. Some journalists refuse to understand that eager brings with it a certain fever pitch — a desire, if you will — while *anxious* (think of anxiety) suggests concern. The easiest way to remember the difference is to memorize Berner's lament for middle-aged couples: "When you're no longer eager, it's time to get anxious."

WATCH FOR REDUNDANCIES

Reading a story written as follows would be tiring: "The *fiery* flames burned the *center* core of the building where vandals earlier this month had *intentionally* destroyed some offices." The italicized words are redundant because their meanings are inherent in other words — all flames are fiery, the center is the core, vandals act intentionally.

If a person has *sufficient enough time* that person can just as easily have *sufficient time* or *enough time*. Watch for the reporter who writes that a judge will hear oral arguments when the reporter could have written: The judge scheduled oral arguments. Obviously oral arguments are heard. Pay attention for sportswriters who say a football player quickly sprints. Until coaches develop slow sprinters, quick sprinters are all they have and all they really want. And be careful of the bank that offers *free gifts* for a large deposit; after all, if it isn't free, it isn't a gift. And if your editor offers you an added bonus, note that a bonus is something added. Remember, though, to collect first.

Journalists, writing on deadline, are not always looking at the finer edges of their work. That's where the desk comes in. When someone wrote "Previously, she has been a teacher, administrator and volunteer," the desk should have realized that the verb "has been" makes "previously" unnecessary.

Of course, deskpersons can make mistakes, too. A headline writer announced in 30 point bold: "A conference explodes some old myths." Perhaps, but *old* does seem unnecessary. And a caption writer once declared that a football player had been named to an All-American team for "the second straight year in a row." Either, it's "second year in a row" or "second straight year," but not both.

Finally, stay awake for those times when a seeming redundancy is needed. Referring to something as a "thousand square feet in size" is redundant but the same phrase can't be cut from this: "She's small in size but big in stature." In that sentence, in *size* balances with in *stature*.

COMPRESS WORDY PHRASES

Provided with a bountiful supply of nouns and verbs, some reporters will use a verb-noun construction in place of a verb. Stronger writing results when such constructions are turned into verbs. For example:

gave approval	approved
make a visit	visit
hold a meeting	meet
get in contact with	contact
get underway	begin, start
express different views	differ
made two attacks	attacked twice
caught many by surprise	surprised many
held a rally	rallied

These phrases and countless more like them appear in stories and should be compressed.

EVALUATE DETAIL WITH A CUTTING EYE

Detail serves an invaluable purpose in newswriting, especially when people can choose between the words of their newspaper and radio station and the pictures and words of their television station. Details enable print and radio journalists to compete against a television journalist who offers detail merely by focusing a camera on something. Despite the competition, print and radio journalists should recognize some detail for what it really is — filler — and delete it accordingly.

For example, the sentence, "The defendant stood before the judge and read the seven-page typewritten statement," can be pared several ways, depending on the circumstances. At the least, *typewritten* adds nothing. It doesn't matter if the statement is typed; in fact, given the increasing number of people who use typewriters and computers, reading from a handwritten statement would be more unusual. *Stood before the judge* — in court that's usually the way judges are addressed, so four more words of unnecessary detail can go. The kind of detail worth keeping would describe the defendant's mannerisms, delivery style, the judge, and so on.

OMIT THE OBVIOUS

A 3-year-old boy climbs into a washing machine and his sister closes the door, thereby activating the machine. The reporter, though, wants to make sure the reader understands the sister's presence and bogs down the story this way: "According to Todd's 7-year-old sister, Amy, *who was with the boy*, the washing machine started when she shut the door." Since she could not have done it by remote control, the italicized phrase adds nothing. Cut it.

Similarly: "The biology of sex, Biology 341, has been offered every winter for the past nine years and is continually filled *with students*." What else could fill a class?

Finally: "The cavern was flooded when a sudden rainstorm caused a stream to rise and seal the only exit." If it is the exit, it is the one and only, and *only* can go.

UNPILE PREPOSITIONAL PHRASES

Under "Oust the Passive Voice," you saw a lead containing four prepositional phrases. Here is the active voice rewrite with the prepositions in italics:

> The county administration Thursday delayed the awarding of contracts to two firms *for supplying furnishings for county-contracted services* until the county controller determines who will own the equipment.

Notice how the phrases pile one atop the other until it becomes difficult to figure which phrase modifies what. Carefully edit such writing to remove the ungainly mess.

> The county administration Thursday delayed awarding contracts to two firms that would supply furnishings for county-contracted services until the county controller determines who will own the equipment.

Converting prepositional phrases into possessive or modifier forms usually removes the problem, although be careful not to pile too many possessives or modifiers in a row lest you replace one problem with another. Here are two good conversions: *The battle appeared to be the most significant issue of the decade* becomes *The battle appeared to be the decade's most significant issue*; *Requirements for the certification of paramedics will be upgraded* converts to *Paramedic certification requirements will be upgraded*.

KNOCK DOWN STONE WALLS

A stone wall in any form of news reporting is a sentence or paragraph that does not advance the story by offering news. In this example, the second paragraph is the stone wall.

> Pilsdon City Council Tuesday night raised real estate taxes 1 mill in order to pay for a new street sweeper.
> The council met in its chambers at 8 p.m. and was called to order by Mayor Joseph Picciano.
> The city needs the sweeper, City Manager James T. Owens said, because an unusually high number of storms have left streets dirtier than in past years.

In some cases, rewriting may be necessary to blend some of the information in the second paragraph with news in the third.

EDIT ELLIPTICALLY

Sometimes the repetition of a word between sentences is unnecessary.

> The grant program receives the most federal funding; institutional programs receive the least.

Even though the second receive is plural, an editor can still safely delete it because the reader provides the correct form.

> The grant program receives the most federal funding; institutional programs the least.

The elliptical approach works well in lists:

> Guiser said strokes caused 67 deaths; hardening of the arteries, 17; rheumatic heart, 10; high blood pressure, 6.

Imagine how boring the sentence would be if caused and deaths were repeated in each grouping. Faulty elliptical usage causes problems. For example, this extract from a caption:

> Two youngsters passing a gasoline station are unconcerned with the near $2 price of premium. You can bet motorists are.

The caption writer meant: "You can bet the motorists are concerned." But because the reader supplies the missing word from the previous sentence, the caption really says: "You can bet motorists are unconcerned."

Related complications arise with names in possessive form in which the writer believes that the name will carry over to the second thought. For example, this headline: "Simeon's conviction upheld; will reappeal." That says the conviction will reappeal, although the headline writer thought it said Simeon will. It's a case of trying to make a modifier change to a noun elliptically. In that case, try this rewrite: "Simeon's conviction upheld; he'll reappeal."

DROP UNNECESSARY PRONOUNS

Part of elliptical editing is omitting some pronouns at the beginning of clauses. *The editor who is highest in my esteem edits all copy carefully* can be tightened to *The editor highest in my esteem edits all copy carefully* with the deletion of *who is*. Likewise, *that*, *which* and *where* sometimes can be deleted provided their omission does not create a cacophony as in *The fire chief said when the fire company arrived flames were spilling from all sides of the building*. The fire chief did not say that when the company arrived but after the fire. Insert *that* for clarity: *The fire chief said that when the fire company arrived flames were spilling from all sides of the building*.

A CLOSING NOTE

Every time someone puts words on paper, a copy editor needs to examine the writing for extraneous words. Remove them. Make copy as tight as possible without destroying meaning or rhythm.

Chapter 13

HEADLINES AND CAPTIONS

Both headlines and photo captions are important parts of the news package. They should be concise, accurate and well written.

HEADLINES: AID TO READERS

Shortly after Harry S. Truman was elected president of the United States, he was invited to speak to a convention of editorial writers. As the Democratic nominee for president, Truman did not enjoy the support of many editorial writers. Still, he won the election. As he addressed the editorial writers, he paid the usual homage one would to his hosts and then said, "Still, I'd rather have a good headline writer on my side."

What Truman knew has since been borne out in research. Readers form their impressions of the news — in fact, believe they are getting all of a story — from the headline. Headlines bear a heavy burden in communicating clearly what's in a newspaper. Whereas a writer might get 10 or 15 paragraphs to tell a story, the headline writer gets space to fit only five or six words.

The headline's most important function, then, is to tell the reader what the story is about. A good headline may also attract the reader to the story. One wonders how many well-written stories go unread because of a poor headline. When a sports editor won a prize for a column he had written, the headline writer took several bows, too. After all, he argued, who could resist this headline: "Hot dog vendor peddles inside dope."

The headline serves the reader in a number of ways beyond telling what the story is about and attracting attention. The size of a headline enables the reader to evaluate the importance of a story. When combined with story position on a page, a headline says to the reader: "In the opinion of the editors, this story is more important than that story but not as important as this other story." In this bigger-is-better world, the larger the headline the more important the story. That is why the lead story of the newspaper contains the largest headline on Page One and the most important story on any page has the largest headline. Some newspapers have rules that reserve a certain size headline for the lead story of the day only, and no other page editor may duplicate the size.

A Guide to Writing Headlines

A good headline is a straight line to the reader's mind. A good headline gets right to the point. It tells and sells the story to the reader. As editors have often said, a Pulitzer Prize story is not a prize unless it is read. Getting the reader to start reading is the job of the headline writer. Stories with poor headlines don't get read. In large cities, stories with good headlines can ensure extra street and newsstand sales for newspapers.

In general, headlines are sentences stripped of the frills. That means they usually have subjects and verbs and (if needed) objects. They are written in the present tense, active voice. The best way to write a headline is to put down in as few words as possible what you believe the headline should be. Fitting what you've written will require you to trim some words and collapse prepositional phrases into frontal modifiers. For example, you have a story about a group of U.S. veterans of the Vietnam war who have announced they are going to build a health clinic in Vietnam. You are assigned a two-line head. Your first effort might go like this:

> U.S. veterans of Vietnam war
> plan to build health clinic in Vietnam

What can you trim and still do justice to the story? Since you're writing a headline for a paper published in the United States, it is unnecessary to identify the veterans as "U.S." Furthermore, you can reduce "veterans of Vietnam war" to "Vietnam war veterans" or even "Vietnam veterans," because "Vietnam" when linked with "veterans" says "war." Likewise, it isn't necessary to say "in Vietnam," if the word appears elsewhere in the headline. That produces this:

> Vietnam veterans plan
> to build health clinic

As you read that over, you have second thoughts. The phrase "Vietnam veterans" could be taken as Vietnamese. So you try again.

> U.S. veterans plan to build
> health clinic in Vietnam

That headline does not fit within the limits assigned by the chief copy editor. How do you trim it? What can go and still be implied? The phrase "to build" seems implicit if not unnecessary. That results in:

> U.S. veterans plan
> health clinic in Vietnam

The bottom line is too long and you must shorten it. Then you realize that you have a prepositional phrase "in Vietnam," which can be converted into a frontal modifier. That results in:

> U.S. veterans plan
> Vietnam health clinic

The headline fits and the chief copy editor approves. You go on to your next story, which is about a woman who adopted a child and then demanded a maternity leave from her employer. She was turned down, so she went to court and a federal arbitrator ruled in her favor. The story reveals that the woman won the right to a one-year leave and that she is glad she fought. If you're not careful, you can miss the point of this story and produce something like this:

> Right to maternity leave
> makes Mom glad she fought

But that isn't really the point of the story. One critical missing element is the mother's adoptive status. Another element worth getting into the lead is the length of the leave. After all, a month-long maternity leave isn't much — a year is. You come up with this as your first effort at rewriting:

> Mother who adopted baby wins the right
> to a one-year maternity leave

The four-word phrase "Mother who adopted baby" can get reduced to two by making it "Adoptive mother."

> Adoptive mother wins the right
> to a one-year maternity leave

Neither "the" nor "a" is necessary.

> Adoptive mother wins right
> to one-year maternity leave

This is still outside the specifications. In trimming further, consider that the verb "wins" implies "right." Also, at some newspapers, the rule on numbers in copy (to spell out) is not followed in headlines. The result:

> Adoptive mother wins
> 1-year maternity leave

It passes muster. Next.

Now you're writing another two-line head; this one on the news story about the death of General Maxwell Taylor. He was 85 and a war hero. In your first try, you come up with:

> Celebrated war hero
> dead at the age of 85

A good part of the second line can go. If you say Taylor was 85, you don't have to say "age," and, as you know, most headlines don't include articles. But the headline really suffers because no one knows which "celebrated war hero" died. So in this case, his name is a critical element, and, as it will turn out, his age isn't. This is the final version:

> Celebrated war hero
> Maxwell Taylor dies

In fact, if this headline were on a page devoted to obituaries, the verb would be dropped, resulting in this:

> Celebrated war hero
> Maxwell Taylor, 85

Your next effort, on a story about an earthquake in Colombia,[1] produces an indirect headline.

> 60 dead, 300 injured
> as earthquake strikes

---

[1] Please remember that *Colombia* is the country and *Columbia* is the university.

That headline does not directly connect the dead and injured with the earthquake. It leaves the reader in doubt about what happened. So you rewrite to make the connection and leave nothing to chance for that reader on the run.

> Earthquake kills 60,
> hurts 300 in Colombia

That headline leaves no doubt about what the earthquake did and where it occurred. In a present tense, active verb, the headline puts the story out front. If the reader does nothing more than read those seven words, the reader will still know something about the story. That's the mark of a good headline.

The headline about the earthquake demonstrates the wisdom of writing headlines that contain one verb and one thought. On a story about the pope approving a church law that declares women the equal of men, you might create this two-verb, two-thought headline:

> Pope signs new law;
> women deemed equal

What is the real point of the story? It is not that the pope signed a law, but what the law says. That should be the thought that dominates the headline:

> Pope deems women
> equal in new law

A similar example comes from a story about 10 miners dying after some methane gas exploded. An early effort produced this:

> Mine explosion kills
> 10; worst in 4 years

But when written as one thought, a smoother headline results:

> Worst mine explosion
> in 4 years kills 10

A good headline emphasizes the main point of the story and is as specific as it can be. This headline, from a story about a fatal plane crash, emphasizes the crash over the deaths: "Soviet jetliner crashes in

Luxembourg, kills 12." To put the emphasis on the deaths, try this headline: "Soviet jetliner crash in Luxembourg kills 12."

Speaking of emphasis, this headline suffers from what might be known as a "good news" mentality: "Two live, 49 die in air crash." Specificity is missing in this headline: "Winds ground shuttle launch." How long? "Winds delay shuttle one day" tells all.

Another mark of a good headline is how well it relates to the lead. Occasionally, a headline writer will base the headline on information deep in the story, which confuses the reader because the headline and the lead don't match. If a headline writer believes the lead of the story is incorrect, the writer should inform the chief copy editor. Also, a headline on a feature story, which often builds to a climax, should not steal the punch line. The writer who spends three pages weaving a story will not appreciate the headline writer who gives the story away in three or four words.[2]

HEADLINE RULES

Headline writing follows a lot of practical rules intended to help the neophyte. Some rules, of course, bend better than others and some newspapers ignore them altogether, relying instead on intuition. The newspapers read that way, too. Intuition is best applied in unfamiliar situations, which is not the case confronting headline writers most of the time.

The best headlines are written in the present tense because the present tense provides the reader with a sense of immediacy. "President signs tax bill" involves the reader; "President signed tax bill" turns the reader away because it sounds like old news.

Frequently, present tense, active voice headlines count better — that is, allow extra room for the writer to say more. This passive voice headline, "Vienna's largest store destroyed in fire," is longer than its active voice counterpart, "Fire destroys Vienna's largest store."

Do not blindly follow the present-tense rule. Headlines containing time elements usually sound better in past tense. For example, "Personal income rises in October" would not make a lot of sense in November. Better to use past tense: "Personal income rose in October."

The headline sets the tone for the story and should be serious for

---

[2]*Nieman Narrative Digest* contains many good headlines that enhance a story without giving away the ending.

serious stories and light for light stories. When a U.S. diplomat named Richard Queen was freed after eight months as a hostage in Iran, one newspaper headlined the story: "Queen was not treated royally." The headline writer was trying to show off at the expense of someone.

Not every headline needs to have a subject and verb. Headlines on feature stories, in-depth articles, editorials and columns sometimes read better when written as titles. After a one-time New York gambling czar died in obscurity, *The New York Times* published a retrospective titled, "The Lonely Death of a Man Who Made a Scandal." That sounds like a short story.

Regardless of the approach, use only commonly understood abbreviations and, then, be careful. Is "Reps request inquiry" about Republicans or representatives? More common abbreviations include FBI, CIA, U.S. U.N. and compass points that are part of a name, as in "Rising crime adds to S. Africa's misery." Avoid regionalisms, such as CLUM, which stands for Civil Liberties Union of Massachusetts but which when used in a headline is clumsy. And what is the reader to make of "CLEP tests set for 2 dates"? Some readers may think the story is about a sexually transmitted diseases.

Headline writers are also very good at making a part stand for the whole. It is not uncommon, when referring to a country's government, to use the name of the capital city in a headline instead of the country's name. Thus, when there isn't room for South Korea, a headline writer will use Seoul. And in states with long names and short capitals, the capital city serves well in a headline.

The need for attribution in a headline parallels the need for attribution in a story. If, without attribution, the source of information is unclear or the headline sounds like the newspaper's opinion, then attribution is mandatory. That's one of those rules that doesn't bend. Compare these headlines from the same event but different papers: "Reagan knew of contra funding" and "Senator asserts Reagan knew of arming contras." The critical difference is that the second headline contains a source, which is critical.

When needed, attribution works best at the end so that it does not impede the message. Compare:

Authentic letter from American hostages to home asks, 'Free us'	'Free us from this terrible situation,' hostage letter asks

The headline with the attribution at the end reads better. The first headline buries the news at the end. With attribution, the challenge to the writer is to avoid writing similar-sounding headlines such as these:

> Bottled water contains
> arsenic, N.Y. officials say
>
> Upstate valve accused
> leak, NRC official says

Since the same person wrote those, he could have avoided the repetition by using a different form of attribution.

> N.Y. officials find
> arsenic in water
>
> NRC aide cites missing
> valve as cause of leak

Putting an abundance of modifiers in front of a noun can muddle any headline. "Windfall profits tax phaseout pushed back" hides the verb and leaves the reader wondering if "phaseout" might not be it. (The verb is two words, "phase out," but readers don't always spell when they read.) The writer would not have had a problem if the writer had used present tense: "President delays windfall phaseout." Given that a tax on windfall profits was a major news item at the time, the reader would understand the rewrite without tax and profits.

When writing multiline heads, some headline writers attempt to make each line stand on its own. That way the reader is not jerked along, unsure how the headline fits together. To write such headlines, the writers avoid "bad breaks," or the splitting of a phrase whose parts cannot stand alone. One example:

> Pat leaves White
> House very sad

If the reader reads the headline line by line, the reader is jarred.

> Pat leaves White

The possibilities at this point are endless and the reader may stop to figure them out or the reader may go to another story or the reader may read the second line as a unit unto itself.

> House very sad

The emphasis has now switched from Pat to the House. The House of Representatives? Will the reader re-read? No.

A more typical example involves the splitting of an infinitive between lines.

> Senate rejects plan to
> end free prescriptions

Some editors frown on such breaks and urge their writers to avoid them. Some editors and professors consider the preceding rule nothing but superstition. Certainly common sense should remain the primary rule in determining headline clarity. Obviously, this is a bad break:

> Tanka aide admits taking $2
> million bribe for boss on TV

And an absolute taboo in the category of bad breaks is this:

> Psychologist Erich
> Fromm dead at 79

Names should never be split between lines of a head.

Headline writers have created their own slang (called "headlinese") when they have needed a short word to take the place of a big word that won't fit. Here are some examples of headlinese, all to be avoided: *ups, raps, meets, nips, OKs, pens, nabs, fells, hikes, eyes, airs, inks, nixes, taps, tabs, solon, accord, pact, axes, looms, sets, rips.* The test of a headline word is this: If it is common to everyday conversation, use it; people will understand it.

Because headlinese is uncommon, it is seldom clear, as one 9-year-old discovered one day after looking at "A's down Yankees." "Does that mean the Yankees lost?" she asked. When the reader has to ask, the headline is no good. Given the use of horizontal layout in which headlines are easier to write because they go across the page instead of down in narrow vertical columns, writers can more easily avoid headlinese. In horizontal layout no writer can have an excuse for this: "House axes tax slash; vows

$ probe." That has an Attila-the-Hun quality to it, which makes it hard to read.

The following headline is almost hard to believe: "Wrestler nipped in state finals." Does it mean the wrestler was bitten? Some headline writers opt for words such as *cut* for *reduction* and *Mideast* for *Middle East*. But "Troop cut seen in Mideast fray" defies explanation because of the headlinese.

Not all slang, of course, should be avoided. In this headline, the use of up, as slangy as it is, provides a snappy cadence the headline would otherwise lack:

> Federal aid to cities up,
> but not up with inflation

Headlines that begin with verbs confuse the reader and are best avoided. What is the reader to make of "Charge man with murder?" Who charged the man with murder? And this headline, although it has a national tabloid essence to it, actually comes from a staid small-town daily: "Has her house burned but her cheer's back." Because the headline begins with a verb, it sounds as though the woman intentionally burned down her house, which was not the case.

Just because a headline should not begin with a verb does not mean it should lack a verb altogether. Verbs are the locomotives of thought, and without verbs thoughts go nowhere. The following doesn't budge: "Growing awareness in U.N. of Third World independence."

A headline must be clear. Fathom this: "Egyptian fat cat class expansion charged." If you figured from that the rich are getting richer, you have more patience than most readers. Can you figure this one: "Pix Nixed in Cineplex Snit"? This one may be easier: "Prose Pros Nix Phrase Maze." Consider this: "False sex scandal rumored." Why would anyone bother to spread a rumor about a "false sex scandal"? How far would such a rumor get?

Colon headlines create problems because of the multiple use of a colons. Consider these three colon headlines:

> Heinz, Green: Similar views on national issues
>
> Vorster: No urban black rule in South Africa
>
> Hearst: 'Rebel in search of a cause'

In the first, the colon functions as an equals sign or replaces a verb. The headline says Heinz and Green have similar views. But in the second, the colon functions as a signal for an attribution tag. In other words, Vorster is making the statement about black rule. Thus, the third headline must be a direct quotation from Patty Hearst. Wrong. The direct quote is about Hearst, not by her. The confusion results from the multiple functions of the colon. Here are some more:

> Public: Strong work force needed to keep U.S. great
>
> Suspect: 'I messed things up' in other kidnapping attempts
>
> Studies: Saccharin users face low risks
>
> Social Security: Everyone's involved but few understand system
>
> Austerity threatens Newgate: historian

Some editors wisely ban colon headlines while others insist that their use be clear and consistent throughout the paper. To achieve consistency means not mixing some of the preceding usages. That seems to be the only way to avoid confusion.

Like leads, headlines should be specific. The tip-off to a say-nothing lead is the word "discuss" as in "City Council Wednesday night discussed raising taxes." The same word tips off the reader to a say-nothing headline as in Candidates discuss Social Security proposals. A better headline would tell what the candidates said. Similarly, this headline, "U.S. Supreme Court upholds FCC stand," says nothing because the reader does not know what the FCC's stand is.

Question headlines deserve the same gimmickry label given question leads. Don't try to con the reader into a story with a question headline, such as "Cigarettes harmful to infants?" After all, the headline should be telling the story, not raising questions. "Smoke harms infants, doctor says" would be an acceptable rewrite.

Uncommon words should be avoided.

> Androgynous
> management
> suggested

After reading that headline, this one, with its long word for dies, doesn't look so bad.

> Councilman
> succumbs
> at meeting

Obviously, *succumbs* was picked to fill out the line. That's padding, which should be avoided.

Labels usually fail as headlines because they merely sit atop a story and do nothing. They turn off the reader. Something like "Today's weather" says nothing. What about the weather? That's what the headline should answer.

Single quotation marks take the place of double quotation marks in headlines because the double marks are space consuming and unattractive in headline type.

Forget the style rules when using numbers in headlines. In some newspapers, no number is spelled out; always use the figure. In other newspapers, the loneliness of the figure 1 has earned it special status — spell out when used alone. Regardless of the rule, when using the pronoun one, spell it out.

And does not appear often in headlines. Instead, the comma substitutes.

> Woman shoots husband, drunken friend

If *and* is used, the ampersand is a legitimate substitute at most newspapers. It takes less space.

Headlines, of course, follow the rules of grammar. Logic doesn't take a backseat just because a writer can't make a headline fit. This is a poor head: "Resident injured in fire, destroys home." It sounds as though the resident destroyed the home. "Resident injured as fire destroys home" makes sense.

IN ERROR THEY GLARE

A newspaper's most vulnerable spot is the headline. The qualified privilege that extends to a reporter's story does not protect the headline writer. Good attorneys caution editors that a libel-safe story means nothing if the headline fails.

Letters to the editor often reveal reader unhappiness with misleading headlines. Usually, the writer begins by saying: "The story was accurate, but ... " and then goes on to complain how the headline distorted the story and gave a lasting misimpression. So true. If the reader takes in nothing but the headline and the lead, the headline is sure to be remembered. One study of reader satisfaction found that headline accuracy was the single most important predictor of satisfaction with a newspaper.

Reader satisfaction aside, courts have found in favor of plaintiffs in libel suits even when the story was accurate and the headline writer's intention was not to slur anyone. This headline, "Bid specs reported 'rigged'," cost a newspaper $10,000 even though the writer was trying to say the specifications favored (were rigged in favor of) some manufacturers over others, not that anyone was fraudulent (which is what *rigged* suggests). Intentions don't count.

A thoughtless headline can deflate any claim of fairness and objectivity when it seems to take sides. For example, "Student protests mar decade's start" was the headline on a story recapping the 1970s. Perhaps it is matter of perspective, but some would argue that had it not been for the student protests, a senseless war would have gone on longer than it had. The merits of that point aside, the headline should have been neutral. Changing *mar* to *mark* would have done that. In another case, when protesters were arrested for trespassing at the Statue of Liberty, a headline writer convicted them before they faced a judge: "Protesters trespass on Statue of Liberty." Since trespassing is a crime, the people must first be convicted before one can say they trespassed. Another headline writer declared a legal decision at the outset of a lawsuit: "Fallout victims sue government." The second paragraph of the story calls them "alleged victims of nuclear fallout." The court will decide, not the headline writer.

Headline errors also create problems for reporters. Many readers believe that reporters write the headlines on their stories, so when a headline contains an error, the reporter gets blamed. This creates problems between reporters and sources, with the sources believing that the reporter is not playing fair.

Headlines thoughtlessly placed on a page can combine to give an unintended meaning; for example, stories about prostitutes and a political candidate that appear side by side so that the one headline reads into the other in this fashion:

Prostitutes identified   Watson runs for office

Even if the reader realizes that Watson is not one of the prostitutes, the damage has still been done.

Headlines containing grammatical or semantic errors are embarrassing. When a woman who had been severely beaten emerged from a comma of two weeks and spoke, one headline writer said:

"Comatose jogger speaks to family." The writer didn't realize that comatose means in a coma and unable to speak.

Spelling errors are bad enough in stories, but in headlines they're out there where everyone can see them. When some fraternities decided to hold nonalcoholic parties, a headline writer noted: "Frats set 'dryer' parties into effect." Good news, parents: Your sons are doing their own laundry. The right word is *drier*. This headline, "Writer dies who wrote war declaration," is awkward because the relative clause (*who wrote war declaration*) does not immediately follow the noun (*Writer*) it modifies. And this one abuses the language: "Defense Plays Good Despite Flutie's 447 Yards." *Well, well, well*. The defense plays well.

Then there's the two-faced headline, such as these from a school board's proposal to restructure the system for students in grades 7 through 12. "School board considers regrouping secondary students into 2s," one headline said, suggesting that all students would be paired off. Said another: "Secondary students may undergo change." One editor quipped: "To what? Primary students." And, if you don't like the results of a trial, express your feelings in a headline such as this: "Jury hung in Mesmer murder case." Now that would be a story. What kind of deal is involved in "Mubarak offers U.S. bases"? Has the president of Egypt been given the right to give away U.S. bases? No, he offered bases in Egypt to the United States. The headline says it both ways.

The more seriously flawed two-faced headline is the one with a ribald meaning. Here are two: Dick should veto studs, Carson says" and "Dick will fill vacancy, court rules." The reader is expected to know that "Dick" is a governor's first name, but that isn't clear. The headline writer would have served all readers better with "Gov. should veto studs, Carson says" and "Gov. will fill vacancy, court rules." The same headline writer also wrote: "Delinquent water, sewage customers are fingered." The writer meant they were *named*. The sexual connotations aside, the writer misused "sewage," which is what the system gets rid of. The writer meant "sewerage," which means the system and for which there are customers. After all, who would want to buy sewage?

One two-faced headline that never saw the light of print: "Leaking is a Washington habit." The same, though, can't be said for "Doctor discusses disease with lucky victims" in which the "lucky" means the victims who didn't die. A copy editor for the late *New York World-Telegram* wrote this headline and readout:

Ford lays off 50,000 men
as strikers cut off parts

Action halts
nearly all
production

The way to keep such headlines from getting into print is to ensure that every headline is read by someone other than its creator.

WRITING SEDUCTIVE HEADLINES

A good headline is alluring. It doesn't smack the reader over the head but instead seduces the reader into reading the story. A good headline stimulates readership. A good headline is a pleasure to read even though the reader may not say, "That was a good headline." In fact, the reader never notices good headlines. Good headlines do not call attention to themselves but to the stories they accompany. Copy editors can learn to write good headlines. Headline writing is the same as the finishing polish on a jewel. The attitude of the headline writer helps determine the quality of the headline. A dated headline from *Editor & Publisher* expresses the quality of the headline writer: "Wanted for The Rim: Man Who Writes Like a Poet."[3] The headline is the copy editor's signature on a story.[4]

On a story about a shortage of beef, a writer grabbed the readers with "Don't beef — there isn't much." Who could complain? When a home economist announced that, despite rumors, the price of hamburger was not going to $2 a pound, a writer caught in the spirit offered: "$2 per pound burger report pure baloney." When NBC and the Nebraska Educational Television Network settled a dispute over logos, one headline announced "All's well that N's well," the dispute having been over the similarity in the stations' N-styled logos. On a story about the high level of tax revenue that a state had reaped in one month: "In Pa., April is the richest month of all." At another time, the Associated Press reported that residents filing their returns around April 15 wouldn't get their refund until July 4, thus sparking this headline: "IRS: In by the 15th, out by the

---

[3] Ed Bacon, "Wanted for The Rim: Man Who Writes Like A Poet," *Editor & Publisher* (April 27, 1968), pp 68-69.

[4] My local newspaper, the *New Mexican*, lists at the bottom of most section fronts the name, phone number and e-mail address of the section editor and the name and e-mail address of the person who designed the section and wrote the headlines.

Fourth."

When a U.S. president who had just been shown in photographs slipping on a piece of ice outside the White House later said something he shouldn't have, a headline writer touted the story with "President slips on his tongue." The headline worked because the image of the president slipping on the ice was still fresh. Remember "show and tell" in grade school? One newspaper story suggesting that television programs in which people at home shopped for goods offered on the air wasn't doing too well got this headline: "Shop-at-home program fails to show and sell."

The copy editor bent on writing good headlines does not quit after the first attempt. Second-rate headline writers would accept the following on a story about the R-factor, which tells how well insulation insulates: "Energy department gives insulating tips." For the reader, the headline guarantees instant sleep. Knowing that such a headline would have a high yawn factor, the writer produced: "Insulating means learning the fourth R." Intriguing.

The headline writer goes beyond the obvious to produce a good headline. When a judge ruled that police could not cross municipal boundaries in hot pursuit of speeders and the newspaper produced a story saying the police were not happy with the ruling, a headline writer wrote: "Police cool to ban on hot pursuit." The writer of the story praised the headline writer, who replied: "But it was the obvious head." Likewise, a profile on Jim McKay, among other things the host of a television program called "Wide World of Sports," cried out for more than this headline: "Jim McKay: his wide world."

To be understood, a headline should not require the reader's familiarity with another medium. The headline writer who relies on the reader knowing some television jingle or watching some television program could write a poor headline if the reader never watches television. However, such a headline is fine if the reader understands the intended meaning without getting the secondary meaning. This headline, about the Milwaukee Brewers, a baseball team, is an example: "The Brewers That Made Milwaukee Famous." Seen on a sports page, that headline makes sense. But to those who are familiar with the pitch for Schlitz beer, the headline reveals more because Schlitz advertised itself as "The beer that made Milwaukee famous." The reader who doesn't know about Schlitz beer still understands headline. Those who know the Schlitz motto appreciate the headline more.

A blogger with a literary background, writing about the death of someone he considered a hero, titled the piece "Earth, Receive an Honored Guest." By itself, it makes sense. But anyone who is familiar with the poetry of W. H. Auden knows that it comes from the poem he wrote on the death of Yeats ("In Memory of W. B. Yeats"):

> Earth, receive an honored guest;
> William Yeats is laid to rest

Then there are the missed opportunities. On the story of a dog that escaped from his owner's car after a fatal accident on an interstate highway, the headline writer wrote:

> Owner searching for dog lost in deadly crash

A drop head said:

> 'He's my boy,' owner says of pet missing since rollover

Accompanying the story was a photograph of the missing dog. His name? Romeo. The headline that should have been on the story:

> Romeo, Romeo, where art thou, Romeo?[5]

The drop head and photograph fill in any blanks — and I don't think there are any. It was just a missed opportunity.[6]

A good headline writer relies on the story, the situation, the opportunity. *The New York Times* one day published a story about how long a person would take to fill out federal forms. The story began on the front page with this headline, "An Average Reader Finishes This Article in About 2 1/2 Minutes," and continued to an inside page where the reader was greeted with this headline on the continuation: "You Have About 2 Minutes Left." The headlines are clever and relevant.

Headline writers always need to be careful that they are not being more clever than clear. The standard headline with a strong verb serves most stories. Few stories in a daily newspaper would benefit from cleverness, so don't attempt to make every headline more than it should be. Mixed metaphors and strained puns detract from headlines. This one, "Curtain rises on Bears' question marks," drew this comment: "Keep curtain risers on the Arts Page and question marks in the grammar books

---

[5]Shakespeare wrote: "Wherefore art thou ... ," but *wherefore* means *why?*
[6]Alas, Romeo was found dead a few days after the accident. He had been hit by a car.

and that way you won't mix them." The way to measure the headline with a pun is to submit it to the groan test — if another reader groans, scrap the headline.

Depending on the size of the newspaper, a copy editor can write from 10 to 30 headlines a day. The advice of Elwood M. Wardlow, an associate director at the American Press Institute, is for headline writers everywhere: "Remember well: Headlines sell."[7]

Caption Writing

Captions rank right behind headlines in what is most highly read in a newspaper. They convey information in a few sentences and cannot suffer from ambiguity. They serve the reader much the way headlines do, and for that reason copy editors should give them as much attention.

A good caption with a photograph completes the thought the photograph starts or provides something the photograph doesn't, such as a name. The caption gives the photograph context and explains anything not immediately clear to the reader. Just like a story, a caption requires strong verbs, the kind that denote action not passivity. A caption is usually written in the present tense because it describes the photograph the reader is looking at. That immediacy best comes across in the present tense. Frequently, a time element does not appear in a caption, especially if a story accompanies the photograph. If a time element is needed, it does not appear with the present-tense verb in the opening sentence. It appears in another sentence or in a subordinate clause.

Editors who write captions always have the photograph before them as they write. Wise editors want to see what they are writing about and know they can avoid mistakes that come with writing about something they cannot see. A chief editor, for example, may crop a photograph and not advise the copy editor who then writes the caption from memory. The newspaper will look silly if the caption mentions someone or something cropped from the photograph.

Examine the photograph on the next page. What questions does it raise? Now read the caption to see if your questions have been answered.

What is the main focus of the photograph? Since there's action, it is the helicopter taking off — and that's what the first sentence of the caption

---

[7]Elwood M. Wardlow, "Writing Headlines," *presstime* (September 1986), pp. 16-17.

A helicopter carrying one of the victims of a two-car collision on N.M. 68 north of Embudo Station on Thursday afternoon takes off for the University of New Mexico Hospital in Albuquerque. According to State Police, a southbound SUV driven by Becky Segola crossed the centerline and collided with a northbound Toyota sedan driven by Ervin Fresquez. Segola and Fresquez's passenger, Joyce Herrara, were airlifted to UNMH. The accident is under investigation, according to State Police Lt. Juan Jose Martinez. (Photograph taken by the author and published in the Albuquerque *Journal's* Santa Fe/North edition Oct. 6, 2006)

is about. It is not about the accident, but the main action in the photo. The accident is secondary and is explained in the next two sentences.

Caption writing, like headline writing, has its own set of rules, some of which duplicate other aspects of newspaper production. Some editors would distinguish between captions written for photographs that accompany stories and photographs that stand alone (such as the helicopter photo caption). Captions on photographs with stories should avoid duplicating the headline, but, rather, should further explain the story.

Some other caption guidelines that can apply either to photographs with stories and photographs standing alone:

> 1. *As noted, use the opening sentence to describe the photograph and write it in the present tense.* Unless you can find a clever way to subordinate the

time element, don't use it, because the sentence will not make sense with a present tense verb and a time element, which will function as past tense. In describing the action, don't state the obvious. Rather, explain what is happening.

2. *Identify every recognizable face in a photograph.* The standard form is to say (from left to right) but a more interesting way cites some form of action a person is taking: (smiling), (frowning), (walking away).

3. *A caption writer should not editorialize.* Present the facts as neutrally as possible and let the reader make the judgments. The caption writer should not attempt to put himself in the mind of the people in the photograph and tell what the people are thinking.

4. *Make sure the caption is consistent with the story.* Don't have a caption saying 20 people died in an accident and a story saying 10. And don't spell the same word differently. In the caption of a photograph of a wrecked plane, the writer said the plane belong to "Japan Airlines." The photo showed the company's name painted on the fuselage: "Japan Air Lines." Which is correct? the reader asks.

5. *Be honest about the source of a photograph.* If the dictator of a country provides a photograph of his torture-free prison after having been accused of conducting torture in the prison, note that the dictator provided the photograph. It would probably be necessary in such a situation to state that the dictator would not allow news photographers inside the prison. Another time to reveal the source comes when the newspaper is using a file photograph. When the mug shot of an 85-year-old person who just died makes the person look 55, the newspaper should indicate the age of the photograph. That's usually done by noting the year the photograph was taken.

6. *A camera can lie and the perspective it provides might not be honest, so explain such distortions in the caption.* This applies especially if a telephoto lens (which makes subjects appear closer to each other than they are) or an extreme wide-angle lens (which distorts) is used.

7. *Rewrite wirephoto captions.* They are turned out rapidly and sometimes as an afterthought. Check captions against stories, which are sent later in the cycle than the photograph. The story may have updated information; in fact, check for the latest story. A thoughtful copy editor who takes an extra minute to do the job well can always improve such a caption.

Headlines and captions are important parts of the news package and copy editors pride themselves on writing good ones.

Chapter 14

RESPONSIBLE JOURNALISM

Two topics that come together well in journalism are ethics and libel. They are intertwined and overlap. Ethics is a set of rules or standards that govern how journalists should practice their craft, while libel focuses on how the law will hold them accountable for the results. No one who wants to be a journalist should step into a newsroom without some sense of ethics and libel. In fact, this chapter only whets the appetite.

A PRIMER ON ETHICS

Morality is usually defined as the rightness or wrongness of an action or behavior. Ethics, then, is a set of moral principles that underlie a person or group's behavior. Many professional groups have formal codes of ethics, and violation of these codes can bring censure or even removal from the group. Attorneys, for example, can be disbarred for violating some of the rules in their code.

But, unlike attorneys, journalists aren't members of a licensed profession, and, thus, unethical behavior can go unpunished. In many cases, the punishment involves a litany of hand wringing on various blogs and in a journalism review or two. In fact, as various journalistic groups have struggled to devise codes of ethics over the past century, they have also had to wrestle with the First Amendment, for implicit in any formal punishment of someone who practices journalism is its potential for infringing on that person's First Amendment rights.

Unethical behavior manifests itself in journalism in many ways. The Society of Professional Journalists' Code of Ethics[1] says, "Journalists must be free of obligation to any interest other than the public's right to know

---

[1] SPJ is not the only journalism-related organization with a code of ethics. Among others is the Society for New Design, whose one-page code emphasizes accuracy, honesty, fairness, inclusiveness and courage.

the truth." The code then goes on to list areas where journalists need to exercise caution. Among them:

Freebies. Journalists are discouraged from accepting anything that might compromise their integrity. "Nothing of value should be accepted," advises the code, noting such things as gifts, favors, free travel, special treatment.

Divided loyalties. The SPJ code warns against divided loyalties, which can come about when a journalist holds a secondary job or public office or is involved in a political organization. Urging journalists also to avoid any personal behavior that might create a conflict of interest, the code reminds its adherents that journalists serve the public first.

Source validation. Some journalists suffer from the notion that because they possess information, it should be published. But the SPJ code advises caution when it comes to news communications from private sources as opposed to public records, urging that such information be substantiated.

Public business publicly arrived at. Journalists are encouraged to pursue news that is in the public's interest and to stand firm for open government openly arrived at. Implicit in this paragraph is the notion that journalists should not sit in on closed government meetings with the promise not to publish what they learn.

Confidential sources. The code urges journalists to protect their confidential sources, which has sometimes meant a journalist has had to go to jail rather than reveal a confidential source. The other side of this matter, though, is whether journalists too readily use confidential or anonymous sources.

Plagiarism. The code says "plagiarism is dishonest and unacceptable."

Other sections of the code discuss accuracy and fair play. What the SPJ code and other codes come down to is an attempt to establish a high level of general moral behavior both in the gathering and publishing of news. No code can anticipate every questionable situation a journalist might confront. As Ben Johnson says in another SPJ publication:[2]

---

[2]Ben Johnson, "The Problem of Collecting and Presenting Information," in Manuel Galvan (ed.), *Solutions Today for Ethics Problems Tomorrow*, (special report by the Society of Professional Journalists, 1989).

Be prepared to handle each situation on a case-by-case basis. Few ethical rules should be drafted that make clearly right and wrong determinations. Most cases are invariably somewhere in the middle.

Still, we have an idea of past practices that journalists have frowned upon. In addition to the ones noted in the SPJ Code of Ethics, those practices include listening in on private meetings, stealing documents, not properly identifying oneself as a journalist, and fabricating stories. A survey by the American Society of Newspaper Editors produced a list of problems. They included made-up quotations, false documentation to support an in-depth article's conclusion, reporters working on the side with governmental or public relations agencies, not crediting another news outlet as the source of a story, and accepting payment to speak before groups the reporter might later write stories about.

Another ethical concern arises innocently in the day-to-day business of journalism. Journalists assume too frequently and too readily that everyone they talk to understands how the news media work. Thus, when a journalist calls a source and starts asking questions, the source, especially if it's someone unaccustomed to dealing with the news media, might not realize that what he or she is saying will be published. It is a journalist's obligation to protect unsophisticated sources from their own naiveté. This is a good procedure:

Reporter: I'm writing a story for publication/broadcast about such and such and I want to ask you a few questions and will most likely quote you by name in the story.

At the end of the interview, the reporter always takes the trouble to confirm some information.

Reporter: Before I leave/hang up, I want to verify some things that you said. Do you have a minute or so for me to do that?

Obviously, such an approach is not necessary with public officials, especially public officials who work with the news media on a daily or almost daily basis. They know what journalists do and need no coddling. But many people are thrown into the maelstrom of a news event only once in their lives and, lacking preparation, have no idea how to deal with the news media. An ethical journalist does not take advantage of someone's inexperience with the news media. Juveniles are especially vulnerable and should be treated, no pun intended, with kid gloves. The more sensitive the story, the more cautious the journalist needs to be. Even photographs can be problematic if the juvenile can be identified. Never use a photograph of anyone identifiable to illustrate a story if the person in the photograph has nothing to do with the story.

What it comes down to is how you would like to be treated if you were the subject of a news story. That's the way you should treat others. You can still get good stories when behaving ethically.

COVER THE NEWS

Imagine you are a reporter for a major newspaper stationed at one of the paper's bureaus. It is Sunday and police in your area have been searching for a man involved in a shooting. You learn that police have zeroed in on the man's whereabouts, and you go to the scene.

Police have surrounded a house and ordered you to stand beyond the roadblock. You do. Bored, you direct traffic. You take some photographs and you make sure your snub-nose .38 is in its holster. At some point, you look up and see the suspect walk out of the bushes near you and head toward the police, who are looking the other way. The suspect is holding a shotgun over his head, apparently a sign that he is going to surrender.

Believe it or not, the reporter involved in that situation eventually took out his gun and "covered" the suspect as he walked toward the police. (He also took three photographs.) Eventually, the reporter warned police that the suspect was near and they turned around. The suspect immediately surrendered.

The problem here is that the reporter, instead of covering the news, became part of the news. He even wrote a sidebar about his adventures, which appeared on the front page of the next day's paper. The story that didn't get done, though, was the one about how badly the police had handled the situation. That story didn't get done because the reporter who should have been covering the police was too busy playing police officer.

Cover the news. Don't make it.

PLAGIARISM

The SPJ Code devotes one sentence to plagiarism. You would guess that would be enough, since anyone who has ever taken an English course should know what plagiarism is. Plagiarism is always a potential problem in journalism given that journalism is the craft of fashioning stories second-hand using (usually) first-hand sources. Attribution is the best safeguard against plagiarism.

Plagiarism means the borrowing — without credit — the writings or ideas of others. Roy Peter Clark of the Poynter Institute[3] has come up with seven procedures that "now seem dangerous and unprofessional." His list: "robbing the morgue,[4] abusing the wires, lifting from other newspapers and magazines, looting press releases, hiding collaboration in the closet, cribbing from the books, scholarship and research of others, recycling your old stories." In each instance, attributing information to its appropriate source removes the problem. The morgue is a special problem, a problem compounded by the fact that most newspaper's morgues are now electronic and that journalists can access another newspaper via the World Wide Web. It's so easy to copy and paste something and not indicate whence it came or take credit for it.

One of the more egregious and recent examples of that occurring was attributed to Jayson Blair of *The New York Times*. In a 7,000-word correction — really an investigation of what Blair had done — the *Times* reported that he "misled readers and *Times* colleagues with dispatches that purported to be from Maryland, Texas and other states, when often he was far away, in New York. He fabricated comments. He concocted scenes. He lifted material from other newspapers and wire services. He selected details from photographs to create the impression he had been somewhere or seen someone, when he had not."[5]

Even for the well-intended reporter, it is easy to pick up and use verbatim language from an old story and not see the problem unfolding before your eyes. A good journalist wants to write well and interestingly and to use original language. Avoid clichés. Avoid jargon. Write it as it has never been written before. Be original. Then you won't plagiarize.

When dealing with the morgue — yours or another newspaper's — don't remove elements that tell what your source is. If you remove the identifying information, you are liable to assume the material is yours and use it without credit. If, by the way, you use something verbatim, put the information in quotation marks. The preference, though, is to paraphrase, using original language. But verbatim or paraphrased, it must be attributed.

The wire services present an interesting problem. They transmit news, with the understanding that the client will credit them if the client uses the news in the form transmitted. But if the client decides to rewrite the information, the client has no contractual obligation to attribute it.

---

[3] http://www.poynter.org/
[4] The "morgue" is journalese for the newspaper's library.
[5] "Times Reporter Who Resigned Leaves Long Trail of Deception," *The New York Times* (May 11, 2003).

Problems have arisen when journalists have lifted verbatim parts of a wire story without credit. Scrupulous editors will advise readers when stories carrying staff bylines include information from a wire service.

Rather than deal with the temptation or the accident of borrowing from another news medium, some journalists prefer not to read other newspapers, listen to the radio or watch television until their stories have been written. That may work under deadline conditions, but that doesn't preclude reading a day-old newspaper and subsequently borrowing from it. And so the news media have become more conscious about even attributing which news outlet served as the initial source of a story, even when competitors are involved.

Columns also present a special problem. A columnist reads someone else's column and then writes a similar column. The similar column mimics the idea of the original but does not use the language. It is still plagiarism, and columnists have lost their jobs doing that. Again, the injunction to be original can save many a writer.

When you're not original, say so. There's no shame in acknowledging that an idea came from someone else. When Dennis Hetzel, then the publisher of the *York Daily Record*, borrowed a column idea, he concluded the particular column this way:

> (So I won't be accused of plagiarism, I must thank Jack Keith, managing editor of the Bellingham, Wash., *Herald*. Keither wrote a similar column that made many of the points I've made today.)

It's true Hetzel's readers probably would never know about the other column, published nearly 3,000 miles away. But Hetzel is a responsible journalist and acknowledging the source is part of his routine. It also establishes Hetzel's credibility with readers. They see how he behaves and they can infer that he makes his staff behave the same way.

A quirkier area involves using direct quotations. Take as an example sports columns in two different newspapers published a few days apart in which the direct quotations were the same. The first column suggests that the statements quoted in that column were made exclusively to that writer. But what if the comments were made at a news conference? Then the direct quotations are fair game, some would argue, and one columnist may borrow from another column without attribution. Perhaps not. If the journalist wasn't present when the statements were made, he or she is better off attributing them to a source than running them without attribution and implying first-hand work.

The attribution advice also holds when rewriting news releases.

There's nothing wrong with saying, "In a news release, the president of Company X said ... " Good journalists routinely attribute information taken from Web sites and blogs. Similarly, when more than one journalist works on a story, all who contributed should get credit, even if only one — the writer — is listed at the top of the story. If not listed at the beginning, the others should be credited at the story's end.

Journalism is not the work of experts. A journalist writing about child abuse is a journalist, not a psychologist. So the journalist relies on experts for information. It happens every day. Relying on others is part of what a journalist does. So the journalist needs to ensure that the experts get the credit. The way to ensure that there's no confusion about who gets credit is to keep good notes. When you sit down with a book or report that you may want to borrow from, first write down in your notebook what the source is. That is better than mistakenly using the information unattributed or trying to find the source later.

A journalist also needs to be careful about recycling his or her work without acknowledging the recycling. This is not a problem for beginning journalists who are writing routine stories. It is a problem, Clark points out, when a writer moves from one news outlet to another, takes his files with him, and then recycles a story from the previous job. Clark calls borrowing from yourself "a low-grade ethical problem."

As a freelancer, a sportswriter wrote these paragraphs for a magazine:

> The fundamental economic theory of supply and demand.
> There are thousands of teachers, but only one Dan Marino. If a math teacher leaves a school system the system won't fall apart; a replacement of near equal caliber can be found. When the Dolphins lose Marino, they go from being a good team to an average team.

About a year later the writer joined a newspaper staff and wrote a story on the high salaries athletes receive. It contained this:

> Again, the law of supply and demand answers that issue.
> There are thousands of teachers, but only one Larry Bird. If a high school coach math teacher leaves the [name] City Schools, it won't fall apart; a replacement of near or equal value can be found quickly. However, if Bird is injured, as he was two years ago, then the Boston Celtics go from being an elite NBA team to an average team.

Asked about the similarity, the writer readily acknowledged that he had rewritten himself. He saw no problem, because he was the writer. But beyond the lack of originality in the second piece, there is also the issue of who owns the content of a publication. In some cases, a publication buys freelance work and purchases one-time publication rights. But a newspaper is a different animal and, in most cases, owns the copyright to published work, because the newspaper pays the writers. So not only is this an example of an ethical problem, it also reflects a potential legal problem.

What the beginning journalist needs to develop is a hyper-sensitivity to using other's work and re-using his own, to know when it is proper and when it is not, and to attribute accordingly. There is no shame in attributing information.

SENSITIVE STORIES

The editor advises the reporter to get as many details as possible when covering the story and to "show, don't tell" when writing it. But just what does the editor mean? That may be good advice in a feature story about a local veterinarian's handling of stray dogs, but does it apply to a triple murder?

Some stories require sensitive treatment. Sometimes, explicit writing is not the best approach. Take, for example, a story provided by the late Dick Smyser, founding editor of the *Oak Ridger* in Oak Ridge, Tenn. The story comes from the *Anchorage Daily News* and reports the charging of a suspect in a triple murder. The story goes into graphic detail about the murder scene. This is about the rape and murder of a mother and three daughters. The story even contains this paragraph: "They came upon a grotesque scene, according to court documents filed in the case Friday." Not content with reporting just that, the reporter describes the condition of each victim, from the knife wounds to the damage done by the brutal rape.

The managing editor apologized to the readers, who then responded with a flurry of mostly condemnatory letters. Generally, readers condemned the newspaper for a lack of taste. The graphic detail was not necessary. Some readers also recognized that the detailed coverage would create a problem for the defendant in getting a fair trial.

Smyser argued that journalists need to appreciate that some subjects — sex, race, religion, tragedy, damage suits (medical malpractice, especially) — are inherently more sensitive than others. In a list of guidelines Smyser — who became an itinerant journalism professor — used in his classes, the last one serves as a guide when dealing with sensitive subjects:

Ask one basic question in each situation: Explicitness to assure that the full story is known, understood? Exploitation — details, tone, emphasis not really to report but rather to excite, titillate? Explicitness, yes; exploitation, no.

Race and Sex

As Dick Smyser noted in the previous section, stories dealing with race and sex create sensitive situations. The nonchalant handling of a subject's race or sex can raise questions about a news outlet's impartiality and credibility. Crime stories are especially dicey when they give the race of the suspect but not the race of the victim. The suspect is a minority and the reader should infer that the victim is white. Better to avoid identification by race at all. So few criminal suspects are identified by the general public, that a written description serves more to indict an entire race than to alert the public to a particular suspect.

Problems with race are not limited to the police beat stories. Here is an excerpt from a feature story on a bouncer in a college town bar:

> He's a Korean, 6 feet and 1 inch tall, and he tips the scales at 285 pounds. He's ticklish. He has a silly giggle.

What does his race have to do with his job as a bouncer? Nothing. The writer saw the bouncer as something exotic and was probably saying more about herself when she inserted the bouncer's race into the story in such a prominent way. Later on, by the way, the story reveals that the bouncer was born in Korea and the story is accompanied by his photograph.

A journalist must also be sensitive to writing that suggests women derive their standing from men. A woman once lamented to a friend about an article on her husband's hobby of raising honey bees. She was referred to as the "honey queen," as though she had no significance other than being married to the honey king. Yet, she was working full time and, like her husband, had a Ph.D. Some sexist writing is more subtle. Despite the effort by journalists to use neutral terms, how many times have you heard the phrase "spokesperson" applied only to females while "spokesman" is exclusively applied to men. Using neutral language does not mean neutralizing women only.

Sexist language is another problem. Consider this lead:

> PETERBORO, Ontario (UPI) — A pretty blonde co-ed was evicted from her apartment for her noisy lovemaking sessions with a steady stream of boyfriends.

The story could have been written without the sexist references to "a pretty blonde co-ed." Supposing she would have been ugly? Language characterizing a person's physical condition is generally irrelevant. Avoid judgmental writing. Also note that "blonde" is a noun and, thus, is spelled incorrectly in this example. The correct spelling for the adjective form is without the "e."

References to a person's sex should only be made when necessary and then to the sex of everyone in the story. The best approach is to treat people as individuals rather than as members of a race or by their sex.

AGE

As noted later in this chapter, some people cringe when their ages appear in a news story. That's no problem. The problem arises when a journalist characterizes someone's age and suggests that because of the person's age the person fits a certain stereotype. Referring to someone over 70 as "doddering" is but one example. A student newspaper once referred to a 32-year-old as "middle aged." Well, if you're 20, perhaps. But just as a 32-year-old should not be relegated to a stereotype, neither, for that matter, should the 20-year-old journalist or anyone else.

This is an another example — the lead on a murder story:

> A 60-year-old woman who sold dresses out of her home was stabbed to death early Tuesday by an assailant the elderly woman apparently let into her Natrona Heights apartment, the police said.

"Elderly" is a state of mind; 60 isn't elderly.

ANONYMOUS OR UNIDENTIFIED SOURCES

Suggesting that anonymous sources or unidentified sources are an ethical problem may come as a surprise to budding journalists who see anonymous sources cited day after day. But not all editors are happy with using anonymous sources and from time to time editors inveigh against them while some reporters are willing to go to jail to protect them.

What's the problem?

Anonymous sources strike at the credibility of the news outlet. The attribution tag "according to a high White House source who declined to be identified for publication" doesn't give the reader or viewer much to go on when deciding how valid that person's information might be. Why doesn't the person want to be named? Does the source have an axe to grind? Did the unidentified source who told a newspaper columnist that a judge had traded his vote for a political favor have a hidden motivation? (The judge won a libel case, as you'll learn shortly.)

The problem with anonymous sources, despite all the protestations of journalists, will not go away. In some cases, they are merely evidence of a lazy reporter who won't make the second telephone call to verify information and get a named source on the record. Instead of accepting something from an anonymous source, you should first attempt to put the person the record. Failing that, try to find a source that can be named. Failing that, explain in the story why the source is anonymous. For example:

> The source would not be identified because he is not authorized to speak for the State Department.

But the best advice: Get sources on the record. That will help keep you out of jail.

JUST THE FACTS

A student of mine once turned in a feature story about steroids. The lead focused on a young man named Jim, who used steroids. But toward the end of the lead, the writer revealed that Jim was a figment of her imagination, that she had made him up even though there were a million people like him. Then as now, the argument against making anything up remains. If any part of the story is made up, how can a reader be certain if the entire story isn't made up. Why can't the journalists write about real situations? Why does a reporter have to make anything up? Given all the good stories waiting to be uncovered, journalists don't have to make anything up.

Journalists deal with facts. They put them together in the hope that the facts lead to larger truths. Novelists use their imagination to spin stories that they hope lead to larger truths. It is not the outcome that gets measured but how journalists and novelists arrive at the outcome. A novel can be dismissed because of a weak imagination, but a news story should never be able to be dismissed because it's not based on fact.

PHOTOGRAPHS

A distasteful or unethical story must be read before anyone will react to it. A newspaper can publish such a story but few may notice because the story hides among the advertisements and carries a bland headline that attracts no attention. A photograph, though, requires none of the effort of reading. It can be taken in with a glance and its impact imparted immediately. A photograph needs no headline, and a reader does not have to read five or six or seven paragraphs into a photograph to learn the details. The photographic story appears in an instant — one sweep of the eye usually makes the story clear.

What does the reader make of a series of photographs that show (1) firefighters searching a creek for the body of a boy who fell through thin ice, (2) one firefighter carrying the boy's body to the shoreline, (3) and the dead boy's mother tearfully watching the unsuccessful rescue attempt? Is this series of photographs intrusive? If the photographer trespassed on the woman's property, she could make a claim that her privacy was violated. But what if the photographer shot the scene from a distance, did not poke a camera in anyone's face and did not behave obnoxiously while trying to get the photographs? Did the newspaper still invade the family's privacy? Are the photographs newsworthy?

How about the newspaper that publishes a photograph of the body of a woman who has been hit by a train? Her body lies across the tracks and the camera angle makes it appear she was decapitated. The dead woman was suffering from mental illness. In this case, many journalists would agree that the photograph added nothing to the printed account of her death — it merely heightened the family's anguish.

The *Poughkeepsie* (N.Y.) *Journal* also received criticism for publishing the photograph of a man who had been shot and was near death as paramedics attempted to save him. The photograph shows a man who was shotgunned in the stomach and who died about four hours later. But what if the man had not died? Would that soften the impact of the photograph? Would it mean something else to readers to know that the victim was under indictment on a drug charge? In other words, does the victim's possible criminal background make a picture of his dying fair game for publication? What, instead, if he had been the mayor of Poughkeepsie? What if he had been a nobody? Also, what of the man's family? Must they be subjected to such a photograph? Editors must consider many things before deciding to publish such a photograph.

In Fort Myers, Fla., the *News-Press* published a photograph of an injured child and her distraught family watching paramedics work on her while a helicopter prepares to land and take the child to a hospital. The child, who had gone into a street to retrieve some books she had dropped and been struck by a car, was alive when the *News-Press* published the photograph. She died a few days later. Only one complaint reached the managing editor, and that was to say that the photograph was in poor taste. On the other hand, a police sergeant and a paramedic both praised the paper for publishing the photograph because they felt it worked to promote safety. Whether or not such photos do is a question that journalists continually struggle over.

Editors on an 18,000-circulation daily once had to decide on publishing a so-so photograph of a woman trapped in her wrecked automobile. They easily rejected the photograph. The driver in this case had been the subject of a police chase, had been in three minor accidents before her big crash and was legally drunk. The police planned on pressing charges. The editors felt that by publishing the photograph they would be adding to the person's problems, so they chose to publish just a story. Publishing the photograph would not have served the public interest.

It is not, however, an invasion of privacy to publish a photograph of a current accident that occurs in public. Publishing it months or years later, however, could be an invasion of privacy because the photograph is no longer news (i.e., current). As noted earlier, newspapers have been successfully sued for using photographs to illustrate an article when the photograph was unrelated to the article.

More clear-cut examples of privacy invasion arise with photographs on people on private property and shot at a distance with a telephoto lens, which enables the photographer to see something not visible to the eye of a passer-by. Most journalists argue that such photographs are not ethically obtained. Publishing them compounds the sin. Long-distance photographs worth using might show illegal activities and, thus, have news value. Make sure the newspaper's attorney approves publication.

Editors supporting the publication of photographs later considered by some to be an invasion of privacy defend the publication on the ground that the photograph serves a greater good. When Stan Forman of the Boston *Herald-American*[6] photographed a fire escape breaking away from a building and casting two people to the ground, one to her death, the resultant flurry included an inspection of all of the city's fire escapes. Some editors used that to defend publication of the sequence, which won a Pulitzer Prize. Some editors use the same defense in publishing gory accident photographs. People will drive more carefully after seeing such photographs, the editors argue. But are the effects of these photographs diminished by the fact that readers become jaded from seeing so many

---

[6]Now the *Boston Herald*.

accident photographs?

Other editors would argue that they're not in the social good business, just the news business. They say they publish photographs because they are news and not because they might solve some social problem. On the other hand, if an editor publishes a photograph with a greater good in mind, might not the same editor withhold a photograph because it might represent a greater evil? Editors must avoid a childcare mentality when editing newspapers. The major criterion for any photograph is its inherent news value. A photograph of a body crumpled up after falling 10 stories lacks the news value of a photograph showing the body falling, unless the victim is newsworthy (a public official), in which case any photograph might be used.

Such a situation occurred on January 22, 1987, when the treasurer of Pennsylvania, R. Budd Dwyer, called a news conference the day before he was to be sentenced for his role in a kickback scandal. Instead of announcing his resignation, Dwyer pulled a .357 magnum from a manila envelope, inserted it in his mouth and shot himself. The photographs available to newspapers across the country included Dwyer pulling the gun, Dwyer just as bullet came out the top of his head,[7] and Dwyer bleeding from the nose and mouth, his body slumped on the floor. The photo most favored by editors surveyed by the Associated Press Managing Editors was one of Dwyer with the gun in his right hand and his left hand extended toward the photographer in a gesture that says "keep away." The choice for most was not to show the actual suicide or the aftermath.

But the *Philadelphia Inquirer* used photographs of Dwyer with the gun in his mouth and his body on the floor seconds later. Then editor of the editorial page, Edwin Guthman, explained in his Sunday column that using only the photograph of Dwyer waving reporters away "would not really convey what had happened." Guthman, who was responding to readers' complaints, said that the senior editors who made the decision to publish the photographs noted the public circumstances of Dwyer's suicide. "In agony," Guthman wrote, "Dwyer was trying to make an appalling statement, and, however deranged he may have been, we did not want to tamper with the force of what he was attempting to convey."

Case-by-case judgment arises in many decisions on the selection of news photographs. In the early 1960s the Associated Press transmitted a photograph of a Vietnamese monk who had doused himself with gasoline

---

[7] A scene then imitated in the movie "No Way Out."

and then lit a match. The photograph shows the monk in flames. Some editors rejected the photograph because they published morning newspapers and did not feel it appropriate for a breakfast audience. The same editors undoubtedly would not use it in an afternoon paper because it would offend the dinner crowd. Other editors used it because the act of self-immolation showed the emotion of protest in Vietnam at that time. That was its news value. It showed something people in the United States would never have understood in words alone.

A later Vietnam photograph, this one of a police chief executing a suspected Viet Cong officer with a pistol shot to the head, appeared on the front page of *The New York Times* and *The Washington Post*, among others. (The *Times* had rejected the monk photograph.) NBC showed footage of the execution but cut away when the footage showed the corpse and blood rushing from the head of the corpse. The NBC producer made a decision between news and gore; he edited out the gore and kept the news.

Some editors would argue that distance between the reader and the event makes the photograph easier to use. A newspaper would reject the photograph of a local woman's body lying on railroad tracks but might show the photograph of firefighters removing the body of a youngster, his face clearly showing, from the waters of a river where his school bus had plunged — in Spain.

Overall, editors must ask themselves if any photograph, no matter the content, contains enough newsworthy elements, adds insight to a problem or puts a story into context to make it publishable. If the photograph has a voyeuristic value rather than a news value, the editor has good reason to reject it.

A Primer on Libel[8]

Do you remember when you were a kid and somebody called you a name, say "a left foot from Tuckahoe"? Your equally brilliant rejoinder was: "Sticks and stones may break my bones, but names will never hurt me."

---

[8]This section of the chapter reflects, in part, my experience as an expert witness in defamation cases. Generally, what I have done in those cases was to testify on behalf of the plaintiff or the defendant about the standards of good journalism. What juries needed to know is what constituted the good practice of journalism before deciding if the newspaper had been negligent. My testimony had nothing to do with the practice of law, but the practice of journalism.

That's not true. In the eyes of the law, calling people names can be harmful — to their reputation and your boss's pocketbook. It's called libel, and, succinctly put in the *Associated Press Stylebook And Briefing on Media Law,* "libel is injury to reputation."

One point budding journalists need to understand is that it doesn't matter who says something libelous. If a journalist uses the libelous statement in a print, broadcast or Web story, the journalist can get sued, and if the journalist's company loses in court, it will have to pay damages.[9] A newspaper can be sued for something libelous in a letter to the editor, while the person who wrote the letter may be ignored. In libel suits, the person defamed usually goes after the person or company with the deepest pockets. Juries are always willing to punish newspapers, whereas appellate judges usually reduce or reverse jury decisions. The largest jury award, $222.7 million against *The Wall Street Journal,* was reduced by the trial judge to $22.7 million, and the case was eventually resolved in favor of the newspaper. But even if a news medium wins a libel suit, it still loses, for it has to spend hundreds of thousands of dollars defending its case.

Journalists should always be concerned with not libeling someone. Journalistic practice stems from what the courts have determined to be legitimate defenses against libel. For private persons, i.e., not politicians and other public officials, they are:

> *Is the statement true?* When your newspaper quoted a woman as saying that her doctor had operated on her 12 times for cancer yet she never had cancer, could your attorney prove that the doctor was in fact guilty of malpractice?
>
> *Is the statement privileged?* Official reports and legislative and judicial proceedings have absolute privilege, meaning a witness in a malpractice suit can in fact accuse a doctor of having done something without proving it and not be sued for libel. The news media then have the qualified privilege to report the witness' testimony, as long as the reporting is accurate and fair (e.g., not out of context).
>
> *Is the comment part of fair criticism?* People have fairly free rein to comment on the public performances of people who regularly work in the public eye, people such as politicians, authors, actors, entertainers, composers, writers and so on. So if you're assigned to review a play by

---

[9]*Damages,* by the way, is a legal term and refers to money that a judge orders paid to someone for an injury or loss. The word should not be used to describe the outcome of fires or accidents. That's *damage.*

the local theater group, and you think the lead did not perform well, you may say that.

When it comes to public officials, journalists seem to have had broader latitude. This stems from a Supreme Court decision known as the *New York Times vs. Sullivan* or just commonly known as the Sullivan decision. In this situation, the *Times* published an advertisement that contained 14 fact errors about public officials and police in Montgomery, Ala. The Supreme Court ruled that because the people in question were public officials, they would have to prove that the advertisement was published with a reckless disregard for the truth or with knowledge that it contained false statements. The court wanted to provide an atmosphere for robust debate on public issues, reasoning that has been repeated in other decisions in lower courts.

But that may have taken a slight turn in favor of public officials in late 2006. A jury in Illinois awarded the chief justice of the Illinois state supreme court $7 million because it said a newspaper columnist had written a false statement about the judge and had acted with malice. The columnist, writing for a 14,000-circulation daily, had written that the judge had traded his vote in a decision for a political favor. One juror was quoted as saying that the jury wanted to restore the judge's reputation. By the way, the columnist relied on unidentified sources.

The situation is further confounded by international access to domestic newspaper's Web sites. *The Wall Street Journal* ultimately settled a libel suit launched in Australia a few years ago because of something published on its Web site in New Jersey.[10] At the time, Australia libel law roughly followed British law, which was pro-plaintiff and anti-journalism. But that changed in 2006 when the equivalent of Britain's supreme court, the Law Lords, overturned a libel decision that had gone against the *Journal's* European and U.S. editions. Rather than try to divine a set path to follow, journalists should take from this to always be cautious.

A journalist can defame someone in many ways. Suggesting illegal or improper behavior on the part of someone, especially a professional, can draw a libel suit. Linking someone to unsavory elements in society could prove troublesome in court. Reporting someone has been charged with a crime — and giving the wrong crime — can be libelous. Calling a doctor a "quack" is *libel per se*, a classification for words that are considered

---

[10] R. Thomas Berner, "Libel Laws Jeopardize Aussies' Web Access," *Baltimore Sun* (December 18, 2002), p. 27A. This was also published in the *Charlotte Observer* (December 26, 2002) and the Sarasota *Herald-Tribune* (December 30, 2002).

libelous on their face.

In many circumstances, by the way, a quick and prominent correction or apology can head off a libel suit. All the doctor wrongly accused of operating on a women 12 times wanted was an apology and when it wasn't forthcoming, he sued and won a $300,000 judgment. But all he really wanted was his good name restored to him.[11] A similar situation arose in an early case of a blogger losing a libel suit. The person defamed, a lawyer, first asked for a retraction and sued only after one was not forthcoming.[12]

In Ireland, in an effort to reduce the number of defamation lawsuits, a Press Ombudsman and Press Council were established with the authority to mandate public apologies. In Australia, the Press Council makes nonbinding recommendations, although it does publish its findings regularly in the hope that publicity will help. All manner of press councils exist throughout the world, except in the United States. The United States has no national press council, the argument being that such an organization would conflict with the First Amendment, which forbids regulation of the press. However, some states have voluntary press councils, where complainants give up their right to sue a news organization in exchange for the opportunity to present their case before the council's informal panel of jurors (usually made up of citizens and journalists).[13]

Let's go through a series of situations and see what kinds of problems they might cause.

> You are the opinion editor of your college newspaper and receive a letter condemning the health center on campus and one doctor in particular. The named doctor is accused of having diagnosed someone as having indigestion, yet two days later the person was rushed to the local hospital with a case of acute appendicitis. The letter ends by advising readers not to take the doctor's word for anything.
>
> Fortunately, an apology by the editor saved the college newspaper a lot of money. But what if there was some truth to the charges? One move in a case like this is to wait for the patient to sue and then report the lawsuit. That puts the burden of proof on the injured person, not the

---

[11]I was the doctor's journalism expert. Eventually, the case was settled for much less.

[12]Nora Lockwood Tooher, "Lawsuits Aim at Libelous Bloggers," *The Legal Ledger*, St. Paul, MN (Nov. 2, 2006).

[13]To get an idea about which country or states have press councils, go to www.wanewscouncil.org/world.htm/.

newspaper, and puts the debate into a legal arena, with its umbrella of qualified privilege. Since this was a college health facility, the letter could have been sent to the doctor's superiors in central administration, and their subsequent investigation could have become a news story. The information could have also been forwarded to the local medical society or to state officials.

A story's lead says that police have arrested two men on charges of trying to smuggle drugs to a friend in the city lock-up. The headline says: "Drug smugglers foiled." Although headlines are discussed in detail in Chapter 13, this instance is worth noting. A false headline on an accurate story can land a newspaper in court.

Your newspaper carries a story that the golf pro at the local country club has been fired. He contends he resigned and that your story injured his "good name, credit and reputation." That depends. He will have to prove the injuries, and that will be difficult if he's got a new job at an equal or better salary and a good credit rating. The newspaper better be able to document, through paper or witnesses, that the golf pro was fired.

An FBI agent sues author Peter Matthiessen because the agent feels he was defamed in *In the Spirit of Crazy Horse*, a book about Indian life in South Dakota and especially about a fatal confrontation at Wounded Knee in 1975. After four years, a federal judge dismissed the suit, saying, in essence, that the FBI agent was a public official and that the public had a legitimate right to question the conduct of FBI agents in doing their job. The judge said the book was protected because its author exercised the right of every person to criticize government.

A group of people has organized as the College Town Consumer Protection Agency, and at one of the agency's meetings someone in the audience stands up and condemns the local television repair business by name as "a fraud that never does anything right and overcharges to boot." The speaker offers no evidence and no one has ever sued the repair service. Your television station reports the quotation by showing a videotape of the person speaking. Of course, the person who made the comment might get sued. But more likely the defamed television repairperson will sue the television station that broadcast the comment. Clearly, the news editor had time to think about the comment and made a decision to use it.

Another person at the same meeting suggests that the city attorney, who also has a private practice, is "an ambulance chaser." While it is true that the city attorney is a public person, the speaker was referring to the attorney's private practice. It used to be that calling an attorney "an ambulance chaser" was *libel per se*. At one time calling someone a "communist" was *libel per se*, but the times changed. Remain current.

> Your newspaper publishes a story linking a local businessman and his business to illegal activity. The newspaper argued that the stories were true and that no evidence was offered to the contrary. The newspaper's sources were anonymous. The businessman was awarded $2 million and his business $1.5 million. The newspaper planned an appeal.

Despite the fact that the Sullivan decision established something of a national libel law, all 50 states still have wrinkles in their laws that make generalizations hazardous. It's always smart to find out what the law is in the state you're working in. Not all states, for example, recognize *libel per se*. The plaintiff has to prove defamation. Also, the statue of limitations varies widely from state to state. In some states, if an aggrieved person does not file a suit within six months, the statue of limitations has passed and the person may not sue. In other states, it can be three years. In some states, the clock does not start ticking until the aggrieved person realizes he has suffered a loss because of the defamation, meaning if a person discover three years after the article has been published, he or she then has another three years to file a lawsuit.

Some journalists see the laws of libel as a burden. But a more constructive examination reveals that our libel laws provide extreme latitude. Libel laws protect people who deserve to be protected, both individuals and the news media. Legitimate questions about a person's reputation are the stuff of news stories, and the law protects the news media when reporting on those. But reckless investigation and scurrilous comment, which no responsible journalist should be interested in anyway, have no place in the news media. Libel laws lead to greater accuracy and, thus, credibility for the news media.

The real question in libel is not how does a journalist defend against a lawsuit, but how does a journalist report in a responsible manner so as not to commit libel in the first place? Fair and accurate reporting is a good safeguard. If a private person is criticized in a public forum, seek her out for her response. If the criticism occurs in private, you may still have a story, but you should show it to your lawyer first.

Avoid a rush to judgment. Don't publish in haste only to repent in court. Distinguish between charges against someone and actual guilt. In the United States, a person charged with a crime is presumed innocent until proven guilty. Thus, a person arrested for a crime is arrested *in connection with* a crime not *for* a crime. Good headline writers are careful to state, for example, "Jones held *in* murder," not "Jones held *for* murder." Also be cautious when police say they are looking for someone who is a "person of interest" and give you a name. A "person of interest" is not a suspect and should not be labeled as a suspect as Tom Brokaw of NBC News did with a security guard named Richard Jewell, mistakenly linked to the bomb explosion at the 1996 Olympics in Atlanta. NBC settled with Jewell for $500,000. Other news outlets settled for less, although some lawsuits were still outstanding late in 2006.

The larger advice is this: Stick to the facts. If police arrest someone for something, that's the news. Don't embellish by calling the person a suspect or going off the deep end in reporting all manner of speculation. If the police arrest the wrong person, that's their problem. If you libeled the person in the meantime, that's your problem.

A lawyer for *The Washington Post* once called libel "the grim reaper of loose journalism." Carelessness paves the path to the courtroom. The reporter who nails down every fact is less likely to have problems with libel. Problems with libel can occur not only in the major stories but also in the "little stories," such as accounts of what the police did in the past 24 hours. Make sure you get the full name, age and precise address. Some people squirm to see their ages in print, but it's a wonderful way of distinguishing between two people with the same name. (Additional information on libel directed at copy editors appears in Chapter 10.)

Responsible journalism is the desired outcome in most of the newspapers and television and radio stations in the United States. Responsible journalists behave in a way that does not bring into question their ethical and legal principles. They understand that they have a purpose to report the facts in an effort to get to the truth and that their credibility requires that they do it responsibly. It's the only way.

Appendix A

Sentences and Paragraphs

The thread of every story is the sentence. No writer has room for a false stitch in sewing a story together.

It is far easier to tell what sentences do than to tell what they are. In *Understanding English,* Paul Roberts says definitions of sentences number more than 200, that the short definitions "are either untrue or impractical or both," and that "English sentences are too complicated to be encapsulated in a definition." Roberts titled the chapter he devotes to sentences "Something That Ends with a Period."

Traditional and Nontraditional Sentence Patterns

Traditional sentences contain, at the minimum, a subject and verb, often thought of as the actor and the action. *She smiles* is an example. Sentences also have a subject-verb-object (or object of action) pattern. That is the way people talk, which makes it the ideal pattern for broadcast and print journalists.

```
       s     v      o
   The boy struck the ball.
```

Another pattern is subject/linking verb/complement, in which the complement modifies or describes the subject.

```
       s   lv   c
   She is smart.
```

A sentence reflects the order in which people usually think. People do not separate one idea into sentences. A person who watched a Little League baseball game would not report a player's success at bat by saying:

   The boy.
   Struck.
   The ball.

The journalist would instead put together all the related elements of the player's success into one sentence.

> The boy struck the ball.

If the journalist wanted to explain more, perhaps what happened to the ball, he or she would tell that in the same sentence, because what happened to the ball is the result of the boy striking it.

> The boy struck the ball, which bounced over the pitcher's head and into center field.

The journalist would not say the preceding in two sentences. He or she would not say:

> The boy struck the ball.
> *Which bounced over the pitcher's head and into center field.*

That is not logical. Yet that is the way some novices write. They fail to perceive the logic of an action or thought. They disjoint logic by separating major and subordinate ideas into separate sentences. Often one of the elements cannot stand by itself because it is a dependent clause — a clause that depends on a main clause to give it meaning. The disjointure is a *sentence fragment* (italicized in the preceding example). Editors and professors scorn sentence fragments; good writers avoid them.

Another sentence fragment typical of novices:

> Because the person with a college education will understand dimensions others may miss.

Because is a conjunction that shows a relationship, and that relationship is best shown within one sentence. What follows *because* in the preceding example relates to a prior thought. The thoughts should be joined.

> A college education gives a person a fuller life because the person with a college education will understand dimensions others may miss.

Bad fragments typically have nothing to stand on or to relate to. Writing a sentence fragment is akin to taking a newborn child away from its parent and expecting the child to survive on its own. Such an expectation is illogical. Survival is impossible. Do not disjoint the logic of a sentence. Do not use sentence fragments.

Despite what you have just read, you may have seen sentence fragments in newspapers or heard them on news broadcasts. Your eyes and ears are fine. You may have read or heard sentence fragments in a question-and-answer structure in which the answer was not the traditional sentence structure of subject-verb-object. For example:

> So which gift package did the housewife who has everything pick?
> *The one with the appliances she doesn't need.*

Other examples exist, but most come from the minds of book writers and reviewers, columnists, and magazine and feature writers, not from everyday journalists who write hard news. Regardless, the exceptions are worth mentioning, so when the time to use them arrives, you will know you aren't violating any strict law of grammar. As you study these, note that they have some logic to them and that they are not like the disjointed fragments scorned earlier. The first comes from *The Camera Never Blinks* by Dan Rather of CBS News. (All italics are added.) To the question of how to start preparing for journalism, Rather wrote:

> And the answer is so simple. *With reading, with books, with words.* Education starts there. So does good writing.

Here is another, this one from a sports column by Bill Lyon of the *Philadelphia Inquirer:*

> But you check him out and he doesn't breathe through gills. His feet aren't webbed. *No dorsal fin between his shoulder blades.*

Despite the absence of a subject and verb (in that case, *There is),* the reader carries the thought to completion without any labor. Using sentence fragments as special effects can be overdone. The fragment is effective because it is used sparingly. Very sparingly. Now back to basics. From the traditional patterns explained at the start of this chapter flow an infinite number of variations called simple, compound, complex and compound complex, all important more in function than label.

THE SIMPLE SENTENCE

The best sentence is the simple sentence. It sticks to one idea or action.

> The boy struck the ball.

That doesn't mean, though, that a simple sentence is necessarily short. Through connectives and a variety of modifiers, a simple sentence can become quite long. First, a connective, which creates a compound object:

> The boy struck the ball *and* the rock.

And now a prepositional phrase:

> The boy struck the ball and the rock *at the same time.*

And another:

> The boy in *the blue trousers* struck the ball and the rock at the same time.

And with some modification in front of the subject (in this case, an adjective):

> The *tall* boy in the blue trousers struck the ball and the rock at the same time.

The sentence can be made longer still with a *compound predicate* (the verb and all its complements and modifiers), a pattern not to be confused with a compound sentence.

> The tall boy in the blue trousers *struck the ball and* the *rock at the same time and fell.*

In an early version of this sentence the connective *and* was used to create a compound object, *the ball and the rock*. Now *and* has also been used to create a compound predicate. A five-word sentence has become one of 19 words. But, despite its length, it is still a simple sentence. Here is a simple sentence of 30 words, its length reached through the addition of two participial phrases.

> The clean air bill also covers other air pollution sources, generally giving industrial areas more time to meet standards while offering added protection for areas that now have clean air.

Here's the breakdown:

Basic sentence	The clean air bill also covers other air pollution sources,
First phrase	generally giving industrial areas more time to meet standards
Connective	while
Second phrase	offering added protection for areas that now have clean air.

The preceding is atypical of broadcast journalism because of its length and complexity. A broadcast journalist would convert it to two sentences.

> The clean air bill also covers other air pollution sources. Generally, the bill gives industrial areas more time to meet standards, while it offers added protection for areas that now have clean air.

Such an approach is easier on the ear; the listener can grasp the information more readily.

THE COMPOUND SENTENCE

The compound sentence relates at least two ideas or actions of equal importance. A compound sentence consists of two closely related sentences that might also be written as separate sentences — that is, both ending in a period. Compound sentences are joined with connectives (often called *coordinating conjunctions*) such as *and, but, or, nor, while, yet*. Another connective is the semicolon (;).

> It wasn't the subfreezing playing conditions or a matter of being outplayed; the game was decided by puck luck.

The use of compound sentences prevents tedious writing. When correctly structured, they take the place of two simple *but related* sentences.

> The president is waiting for the bill, but the House has not yet acted on it.

With some revision that sentence could have been written as two sentences.

> The president is waiting for the bill. The House has not yet acted on it.

Compound sentences are mishandled when they are edited into two simple sentences, their relationship broken by a period. For example:

> The magazine's operations director and a woman are missing west of Nassau. A multinational air and sea hunt has been launched.

The sentences are related, not like cousins but like twins, and should not be separated.

> The magazine's operations director and a woman are missing west of Nassau, and a multinational air and sea hunt has been launched.

As before, the length of a sentence has nothing to do with what type of sentence it is. Compound sentences can be short ...

> John hit the ball and Marty caught it.
> He likes to swim in the ocean; she likes to swim in a pool.

... or long ...

> The substance of the Panamanian talks was not made public, but Panama's minister for canals took part in them.

... even too long ...

> Hundreds of off-duty policemen, protesting work schedules and delayed pay raises, picketed Monday at nearly all of the city's 52 station houses while representatives of the Fraternal Order of Police sought, once again without success, to persuade the mayor to agree to their demands for better working conditions.

The best thing to do with an awkwardly long compound sentence is separate it into shorter sentences.

> Hundreds of off-duty policemen, protesting work schedules and delayed pay raises, picketed Monday at nearly all of the city's 52 station houses. At the same time, representatives of the Fraternal Order of Police sought, once again without success, to persuade the mayor to agree to their demands for better working conditions.

Sentences with compound predicates may look like compound sentences, but they are not. Here is an example of each;

Compound subject	*John and Marty* ran to the cabin.
Compound predicate	The revolution *was called "Helter Skelter" and was considered started with the first slayings.*

The Complex Sentence

Not every idea or action in a sentence is as important as another. A secondary idea or action is subordinate to the main idea or action. The important idea or action appears in the independent or main clause, independent because it needs no help in conveying an idea. For example:

> The tall boy in the blue trousers struck the ball and the rock at the same time.

That is an independent clause. By itself it has meaning. But the idea or action in a subordinate clause does not have meaning by itself; subordinate clauses depend on main clauses for their meaning. Standing alone they are the much scorned fragments mentioned earlier.

Creating a Subordinate Clause

To subordinate a clause or clauses, use *that, which, who, because, after, where, although, though, when, if*. (Remember, though, that through elliptic writing the pronouns that lead off subordinate clauses are sometimes discarded. The sentence, however, is still labeled complex.) Here is a complex sentence:

> *When the first pitch was thrown,* the tall boy in the blue trousers struck the ball and the rock at the same time.

The subordinate clause is italicized. It makes no sense by itself. Here are other examples of complex sentences:

> John Smith, *who is 61,* makes a good living predicting the outcome of political campaigns.

> *If his well connected Republican staff members were called upon to lead the investigation,* they would undoubtedly end up looking into the activities of fellow Republicans and other members of the establishment.

One of the most frequent complex sentences in journalism begins with an attribution tag.

> He said *Williams could do the job.*

Such a structure defies the conventional definition that a subordinate clause cannot stand by itself because it has no meaning. In journalism, however, the distinction is that the unattributed sentence is the opinion of the writer, and writer's opinions are not allowed in news stories. The preceding complex sentence could also be written:

> Williams could do the job, he said.

Clauses and Relationships

The failure to use complex sentences is the failure to perceive complex relationships.

> Ford criticized Carter for not mentioning the Humphrey-Hawkins bill. The bill would provide jobs for all Americans who want them. Carter once endorsed the bill.

Three simple sentences do not convey the essence of Ford's criticism. The first simple sentence says nothing; left out is the crucial explanation of what the bill would do and the significance of Carter's silence, The following two simple sentences suggest that Ford's criticism, what the bill would do and Carter's prior endorsement are separate ideas. They are not. There is a very important relationship that must be stated — and a complex sentence is the proper vehicle.

> Ford criticized Carter for not mentioning the Humphrey-Hawkins bill, which would provide jobs for all Americans who want them and which Carter once endorsed.

Incorrect Subordination

One of the pitfalls of subordination is subordinating the wrong thing or something incongruous with the main clause. The wrong thing:

> An 81-year-old Minnesota man was hunting *when he died of a heart attack early today.*

The key point of that sentence is italicized. The news has been subordinated to a less important piece of information. There should be no subordination; the sentence should read:

> An 81-year-old Minnesota man died of a heart attack while hunting early today.

Now the key point is in place; it is no longer hidden.
Incongruous:

> The judge rejected the neighbors' request for $2,500 in damages *although he estimated that a horse drops an a average of* 24 *pounds of manure daily.*

The italicized portion of that sentence has nothing to do with the sentence's main point — the judge rejecting the claim. If you remember that a sentence is a logical pattern, that everything in it is logically related, you won't subordinate incorrectly.

Length

Complex sentences do not have to be long.

> When I am hungry, I eat.

> If I were you, I'd leave.

In fact, complex sentences can be made very long by compounding the subordinate clauses, which was done in the Ford-Carter sentence.

THE COMPOUND-COMPLEX SENTENCE

A compound-complex sentence contains at least two related ideas or actions and at least one subordinate idea or action. Here is an example from *The Washington Post:*

Main clause	Gas would be piped ashore from the sites,
Subordinate clause	which are between 47 and 92 miles off the coast,
Connective	and
Main clause	pipelines would carry the gas from the coast to the country's most lucrative industrial and residential markets.

Note that the subordinate clause adds amplifying information to the first main clause. In this case, the subordinate clause could be dropped without doing harm to the main clause. However, that particular subordinate clause is an example of giving detail at the right moment. Here is one more compound-complex sentence:

> He says the election could be closer because the incumbent is closing the gap, but he says it's going to be Janice Reilly just the same.

Like any other sentence of great length or complexity, the compound-complex sentence does not function well in broadcasting.

Positioning for Clarity

A writer can structure a sentence — say, a complex one — in one pattern (subject verb-object-subordinate clause) and that sentence would serve its purpose. But the writer could move the sentence from one paragraph to another, and, depending on the new sentences around the moved sentence, its pattern might no longer work to full advantage.

A clause at the end of a sentence may, when shifted to the beginning, provide transition to a new subject or give context to the new subject. A qualifying phrase that just hangs on to a sentence needs to be moved to a position that removes a misleading implication. An attribution tag, repeated throughout a story, no longer need appear at the beginning of a sentence. Bury it, but if possible keep it away from the end of a sentence, for sentence beginnings and endings provide good positions for important information. Transitional markers, too, should not come too early or too late to dim their effectiveness.

Subordinate Clauses

Subordinate clauses can appear in various parts of sentences: the middle of a main clause, before a main clause, at the end of a main clause.

> The tax bill, *which is long and complex,* will be voted on tomorrow.

> The president, *who is eager for a rest,* will begin his vacation next week.

You could edit both of those clauses in the interest of tight writing. Broadcast journalists especially would do that in order to keep the subject and its verb together. In broadcasting, writers do not insert long or confusing phrases between subjects and their verbs.

> The long, complex tax bill will be voted on tomorrow.
> The president, eager for a rest, will begin his vacation next week.

The second sentence could also be written:

> Eager for a rest, the president will begin his vacation next week.

Even though the modifying clauses were edited and moved from behind the word they modify to in front, they were still kept as close as possible to what they modify. But you would not shift the clause in the first sentence so the sentence would read:

> The tax bill will be voted on tomorrow, which is long and complex.

The subordinate clause now modifies *tomorrow*.

Qualification

There are many sentence patterns in which the modification can appear at the beginning, middle or end of a sentence and the reader will understand what it modifies. But you should avoid such a loose approach to sentence structure. The writer of the following did not:

> I have never been sick a day in my life, excluding my childhood years.

What is wrong is that the qualification of the main clause is not given first as a warning or tip-off to the reader. The sentence violates truth in writing.

Placing the modifying phrase first immediately gives the reader the qualifications or modifications of the main clause. There is no misleading the reader in this:

> *Excluding my childhood years,* I have never been sick a day in my life.

Sometimes the related clause must appear first; otherwise, what it explains is not clear.

> Nations have responded negatively to the president's statements on human rights because of increased nationalism.

The question is, were the statements made because of increased nationalism? No — and the proper stress makes that clear.

> Because of increased nationalism, nations have responded negatively to the president's statements on human rights.

Remember, though, that because the beginning of a sentence is a good place for vital information, it ought not be wasted on trivia. Unless you are concerned with transition, don't place a time element at the start of a sentence, especially a lead such as this:

> At last night's Cadbury City Council meeting, city manager Tony Sarno presented a draft of a construction contract.

Phrases for Context

Just as important as qualifying phrases are subordinate clauses that provide a context for a direct quotation. When they follow the direct quotation, they force the reader to back up to see what the direct quotation means.

> "That kind of hits us where it hurts," Councilman Josh Labinski said when told the cost-plus fee would be used for housing outside the city.

A better sentence would not make the reader back up; it keeps the reader moving along.

> When told the cost-plus fee would be used for housing outside the city, Councilman Josh Labinski said: "That kind of hits us where it hurts."

Now you have a context for the direct quotation; now it means something. But the sentence's structure suffers because it violates the journalistic practice of not beginning a sentence with a dependent clause. Broadcasters do not allow sentences written for the ear to open with dependent clauses. Newspaper editors, communicating in a different medium, prefer that sentences open with the main thought followed by any subordinate thought. The advice is good. But, like any other advice or rule, you should ignore it when logic says otherwise. Many of this book's sentences begin with dependent clauses because of my feeling that giving qualification first enhances overall sentence clarity.

Here are four sentences, each one structured a different way. Which sentence is the best?

Dr. Lewis Thomas said last night that man must consider the influence of all life on the separate parts of life *if he is to survive.*

Dr. Lewis Thomas said last night that man — *if he is to survive* — must consider the influence of all life on the separate parts of life.

Dr. Lewis Thomas said last night that *if man is to survive,* he must consider the influence of all life on the separate parts of life.

If man is to survive, Dr. Lewis Thomas said last night, he must consider the influence of all life on the separate parts of life.

The fourth sentence functions well. The qualification or context is first, the attribution tag is buried, and the main clause follows. The commendable feature of the second sentence is that it sets off the qualification with dashes, which give emphasis. However, some might see that sentence as choppy because of the abruptness. They, no doubt, would pick the third or fourth sentence.

Transition

One stress that should come at the beginning of a sentence is the signal that tells the reader that what is to follow contradicts or clashes with what he or she has just read. The transition marker *however* is sometimes placed at the end of a sentence to the detriment of meaning.

> The planning commission proposed a four-lane link between the two bypasses. Planner James Dugan said that building the link would cost an extra $20 million, *however.*

However — the tip-off that what is to follow is not in accord with what has just been said — belongs at the start of the second sentence or near the start.

> The planning commission proposed a four-lane link between the two bypasses. *However,* planner James Dugan said that building the link would cost an extra $20 million.

> The planning commission proposed a four-lane link between the two bypasses. Planner James Dugan said, *however,* that building the link would cost an extra $20 million.

Some writers would never put *however* at the beginning because they feel it hangs there too limply to be effective. William Zinsser suggests placing *however* as early as is reasonable (a natural break in the sentence, as in the second of the two preceding examples) so that "its abruptness then becomes a virtue."[1] It's up to your ear or your editor.

---

[1] William Zinsser, *On Writing Well* (Harper & Row: New York, 1976). The quote comes from the first edition. The book, however, is now in its sixth edition and worth having on any writer's shelf.

Appendix B

Conventional Grammar

Nouns and Pronouns

Defining what a noun is can be tricky. Adhering to the traditional definition *(name of a person, place or thing)* leaves little room to maneuver words into a necessary function. If we accept *football* as a noun only, how could we economically describe the field on which the game of football is played?

Linguists say that a word is a noun when it can be used in certain areas of a sentence, as the subject of a verb or as the object of a verb or a preposition. If we break down the preceding sentence according to function, with stress on which words are nouns, we would probably agree on every one. Here is the sentence again — with all nouns italicized:

> *Linguists* say that a *word* is a *noun* when *it* can be used in certain *areas* of a *sentence,* as the *subject* of a *verb* or as the *object* of a *verb* or a *preposition.*

Effect on Verbs

Consider what effect some of the nouns had on other parts of the sentence cited above. For one, the noun serving as the subject of the sentence influenced the verb. *Linguists* is plural (that is, more than one), so the verb must agree with it in number and person. *Person* used to be a confusing label in grammar, especially when applied to verbs. Traditionalists say there are six persons:

Person	Singular	Plural
1	I say	we say
2	you say	you say
3	he, she, it says	they say

But although there are six persons, a writer needs to learn only two verb forms in the present tense. Most verbs in the English language follow the same pattern; that is, add an *s* to form the third person singular, present tense. Disregarding for the moment irregular verbs and other tenses, you need to recognize only two forms: third person singular and all others. The only time you have to worry about a verb ending being influenced by a noun is when the noun is third person singular, present tense. Had *linguist* (meaning only one) been used in the example, the verb would be *says*.

EFFECT ON PRONOUNS

Another word influenced by a noun in the sentence on linguists is the word *it*. Called a *pronoun (I, you, he, she, it, they,* for example), *it* takes the place of a noun. The noun determines whether a pronoun is singular or plural, of masculine, feminine or neuter gender.

> *Carnegie Building* is old; *it* was built early in the 20th century.

In that sentence the pronoun refers to *Carnegie Building,* which is singular. Thus, so is the pronoun. The noun that influences the pronoun is called its *antecedent.* If the antecedent is plural, so is the pronoun.

> *Leaders* of the hospital union said Thursday *they* would defy a restraining order obtained by the city.

They refers to *leaders.* The pronoun agrees with the noun. The most common pronoun error is not having the pronoun agree with its antecedent.

> The girls' cross-country *team* has had difficulty in finding competition because of *their* winning record.

Their should be replaced by *its* to be correct.

> The girls' cross-country team has had difficulty in finding competition because of *its* winning record.

Similarly:

> T. Roger Smith of Kernville told the *commission* the power company will take advantage of *them.*

The correct pronoun is *it.*

> T. Roger Smith of Kernville told the commission the power company will take advantage of *it*.

However, because *it* is neutral and impersonal, some writers use the word as little as possible. To avoid *it*, change the sentence to:

> T. Roger Smith of Kernville told commission *members* the power company will take advantage of *them*.

A plural noun allows the use of the plural and more personal — them. An incorrect pronoun can be funny, as an advertisement from an X-rated movie attests:

> Take *your* lover to see this film
> Before *they* take someone else!! [Italics added.]

A long sentence gives rise to pronoun error because the writer often forgets what he or she is referring to.

> The combination of renovation costs at Elmbank, a feared lack of control over operations and dwindling confidence in dealing with Willow Community Hospital officials finally prompted the Conejos Medical Services Authority to put Elmbank behind *them* and build a new medical center in Conejos.

Them was meant to refer to *Authority* (5 words back), but because *them* is plural, it really refers to the last plural noun, which is *officials* (12 words back). The wrong pronoun changes the meaning of the sentence. To be correct, *it* should replace *them*.

Sometimes pronouns are used in a sentence other than the one in which the antecedent appears.

> Among those rescued was *Mary Storms*, a 22-year-old secretary who had served as a volunteer at the post and married one of the defenders. *She* lost a leg and broke an arm during the bombing. *She* was several months pregnant but lost *her* child. *Her* husband has been killed.

Note, too, that the pronoun agrees with its antecedent in gender (male, he; female, she; neuter, it). In that example all of the pronouns are female because they refer to a woman.

Sometimes pronouns refer to a noun ahead instead of back:

> When *they* got to the stream, the *campers* took off their boots.

Unclear Antecedent

Although a pronoun can refer to a noun in another sentence, the situation gets confusing when there is a noun in the same sentence as the pronoun but the noun is not the pronoun's antecedent. Consider this example:

> A helicopter put Garcia on board. Because of *his* size, one of the crewmen had to make the flight to the hospital on a runner outside the bubble.

The writer intended the pronoun *his* to refer to *Garcia*, but *his* really refers to *one* in *one of the crewmen*. There is no sin in repeating a word when it will remove an ambiguous pronoun.

> A helicopter put Garcia on board. Because of Garcia's size, one of the crewmen had to make the flight to the hospital on a runner outside the bubble.

Also keep in mind that pronouns refer to the nearest noun. Confusion often results when another noun intercedes between an antecedent and its pronoun.

> Britain has agreed to sell to Egypt a highly advanced radar air defense *system* to double *its* holdings of ground-to-air missiles.

Such a sentence might make the reader reread to determine if *its* refers to system or *Egypt* (or, remotely, *Britain*). *Its* belongs to *Egypt*.

> Britain has agreed to sell to Egypt a highly advanced radar air defense system to double Egypt's holdings of ground-to-air missiles

Missing Antecedent

Make sure the pronouns you use do have antecedents. Nothing can be quite as confusing as a pronoun with no clear antecedent.

> Breslin is on the list, he said, because he voted against a federal strip mine bill. Breslin said he did that because he feels *it* is a state, not a federal, function.

What *it* refers to is unclear. Even in the context of the story, the pronoun's antecedent was absent. I'll hazard a guess to make the sentence clear.

> Breslin said he did that because he feels regulating strip mines is a state, not a federal, function.

Too many pronouns spoil the flavor of a sentence, especially if there is no antecedent because the writer used a pronoun to begin with.

> Acting under Jones' implied orders, *they* killed not because *they* had a fear of what Jones might do to *them* if *they* did not but because *they* had a pre-existing hostility toward society.

The sentence would be clearer if it had started like this:

> Acting under Jones' implied orders, *his followers* killed ...

OVERWORKED PRONOUNS

Overworking a pronoun — that is, using the same pronoun several times to refer to different nouns — can be confusing.

> According to police, Dennis, 21, got the cocaine into this country by putting *it* into a condom, tying *it* shut, and swallowing *it*.

To make clear there's been a shift in antecedents, repeat the new antecedent.

> According to police, Dennis, 21, got the cocaine into this country by putting it into a condom, tying the condom shut, and swallowing it.

A similar example:

> Such was the case last week when Mr. and Mrs. Thomas F. Needle of Pine Street filed suit against *their* neighbors, Mr. and Mrs. Donald Smythe, seeking to have *their* horse farm declared a public nuisance.

Dropping the second *their* in favor of using the possessive form of the antecedent makes the sentence clearer.

> Such was the case last week when Mr. and Mrs. Thomas F. Needle of Pine Street filed suit against their neighbors, Mr. and Mrs. Donald

Smythe, seeking to have the Smythe's horse farm declared a public nuisance.

Pronouns in Attribution

Attribution tags, because they can contain an unrelated pronoun, need careful watching, as this example shows.

> Jones, only 5-feet-2, convinced his followers *he* was Christ, he said.

The pronoun in the attribution tag refers to the speaker the reporter is quoting. Maybe the reader will understand the *he* in *he said* does not refer to Jones; then again, maybe the reader won't.

Pronouns are used frequently in attribution tags because the writer does not want to repeat a person's name to the point of monotony. The caution is: Don't use too many pronoun attribution tags. Return occasionally with the person's name or some other clearly identifiable tag so the reader doesn't forget who's speaking. And if two direct quotations are separated by a paragraph that does not refer to the speaker, use the speaker's name in the paragraphs where he or she is quoted. It is disconcerting to meet a pronoun too far removed from its antecedent.

False Antecedent

Pronouns can make murderers out of murder victims.

> Post-mortem stab wounds in the *victims* show that *they* killed with gusto.

> Post-mortem stab wounds in the victims show that *the killers* killed with gusto.

Indefinite Use

Still another problem with pronouns is using them indefinitely when it isn't necessary. Here is an example of a common usage:

> It will be cloudy and warm today.

Of course, there's nothing wrong with:

> Today will be cloudy and warm.

But some writers refuse to be direct, and they fall back on the indefinite pronoun, which creates vague sentences.

> It was figured the pay increases will total $232,131 a year, based on average salaries.

What does *it* refer to? What does *it* mean? What's wrong with

> Pay increases will total an estimated $232,131 a year, based on average salaries.

Finally:

> It used to be that home fire warning devices were available only as part of extensive and costly fire alarm systems.

The *it* does nothing positive; get rid of it.

> Home fire warning devices used to be available only as part of extensive and costly fire alarm systems.

OTHER ANTECEDENTS

Antecedents are not restricted to nouns alone. A phrase or clause can be an antecedent, which is the case in the following:

> Imagine if *the error is made in the lead*. Here are two leads where *that* happens.

The italicized phrase in the first sentence is the antecedent for the pronoun in the second. As long as the result is clear, it is more economical to use a pronoun in the second sentence.

PRONOUN FORMS

The form pronouns take depends on how and where they are being used in a sentence. Learning the various forms so that you do not write *hisself* for *himself* is a matter of rote.

Personal Pronouns

The personal pronouns used as the subjects of verbs are:

Person	Singular	Plural
1	I	we
2	you	you
3	he, she, it	they

When used as objects, pronouns take these forms:

Person	Singular	Plural
1	me	us
2	you	you
3	him, her, it	them

In their possessive form, pronouns look like this:

Person	Singular	Plural
1	my (mine)	our (ours)
2	your (yours)	your (yours)
3	his (his)	their (theirs)
	her (hers)	
	its (its)	

The forms in parentheses are used in elliptic writing when the object referred to is known.

> Is this your book?
> No, it's hers. (No, it is her book.)

The apostrophe is not used to create the possessive form of pronouns. That is a major exception to the convention of making the possessive form by adding 's. If you remember that possessive pronouns are possessive to begin with, you won't add 's. You don't have to make possessive what already is.

Reflexive Pronouns

Reflexive pronouns are used to emphasize a noun.

> The president *himself* will attend the security meeting.

Reflexive pronouns take these forms:

Person	Singular	Plural
1	myself	ourselves
2	yourself	yourselves
3	himself, herself, itself	themselves

Relative Pronouns

Relative pronouns *(who, which, that, what)* relate an independent or dependent clause to a main clause.

> The student *who* loves writing will write all the time.

> The college, *which* already offers 100 majors, is considering adding another one.

> This is the house *that* Jack built.

> I see *what* you mean.

Use *who* to refer to humans, and *that* and *which* to refer to animals and things. Only *who* changes form according to pattern. As a subject, it is who; as an object, *whom;* in the possessive, *whose*. Some writers have difficulty deciding whether *who* or *whom* is correct. In this sentence, *who* is incorrect.

> Who do you believe?

Any time you are unclear if it should be *who* or *whom* in an interrogative sentence, recast it as a declarative sentence to see which function *who* takes.

> You do believe who.

In that sentence, *who* functions as an object and the objective form is *whom*. If that recasting does not work, substitute *he/him* or *she/her*.

> You do believe she/her.

For this example, the objective form *her* is correct, meaning that *whom* is correct in the earlier sentence.

Demonstrative Pronouns

The last set of pronouns, called *demonstrative,* are *this* and *that* with the plural forms *these* and *those.* Generally, *that* refers to something already mentioned and *this* refers to something coming up. (Distance is another criterion. Something close takes *this;* something farther away takes *that.)* The best example of *this-that* usage comes from the late President Richard M. Nixon. Asked a question at a news conference, he often began his response:

> Let me say *this* about *that* ...

This stood for his response to come; *that* for the question already asked. *That* is overused or misused when *it* would carry the meaning.

> He said that *that* is a good proposal.

Change the second *that* to *it* both to avoid the *that that* construction and because *it* satisfies the meaning. The remaining *that* can be deleted in the interest of economical writing.

> He said it is a good proposal.

SEXISM AND PRONOUNS

A form letter acknowledging receipt of a faculty member's letter of recommendation contained two blanks: one for the student's name and the other for the pronoun that would agree in gender. Such are the lengths some people will go to avoid using *he/him/his* as universal pronouns for men and women.

The issue is simple. Do journalists want to use language that assumes maleness? No, they want to be as neutral as possible. *The Associated Press Stylebook* advises that to avoid pronoun bias a writer should use plural nouns to which the neutral *they* can be affixed. For example:

> Job-oriented training may prepare the *student* for *his* first job.
>
> Job-oriented training may prepare *students* for *their* first job.

Other writers, preferring more precise references to individuals, have adopted a *he/she, him/her* approach. Traditionalists consider such a usage awkward and stick to *he/him* as universal pronouns. Some book authors alternate between examples, which results in a scorecard approach when the copy editor tries to ensure a balanced number of references between the genders. Other writers have suggested singular pronouns that are neutral: *s/he, hir, thon*. Like the proverbial snowball in hell, those creations stand little chance. The news agencies have the best solution: Recast into the plural.

Appendix C

MODIFICATION

Modification problems arise when modifiers are misplaced. By now you should have a clear idea of what modification is. You have already seen in Appendix how ideas can be expanded through modification from a basic pattern (subject-verb) into the most complex structure.

POSITIONING MODIFIERS CORRECTLY

The positioning of modification (which can be a word, phrase or clause) is crucial. Consider this:

> They maintain that the highway would create a barrier separating Crystal City from the adjoining residential area.

That sentence tells us little. Why would the highway create a barrier? And what is so significant about Crystal City that it can't be separated from adjoining residences?

What is lacking is modification at the right place, an explanation of the significance of the highway and Crystal City. The significance cannot be explained two paragraphs later, for you have no guarantee the reader will continue reading past the unexplained information. Nor can you explain the significance two paragraphs earlier in the story because the explanation will lack a context. What must be done is not only modifying, but modifying at the right place and time. Here is the sentence as it appeared in *The Washington Post:*

> They maintain that the highway, *sections of which are to be elevated on walls 30 feet high,* would create a barrier separating Crystal City, with *its shops and offices,* from the adjoining residential area [italics added].

Even before we read that the highway would become a barrier, we get a description of the highway, a description telling why the highway would become a barrier. And even before we read what Crystal City would be separated from, we read what Crystal City contains. When we finish the sentence, we know that the people who live in the adjoining residential area will be separated from Crystal City, where they shop and work.

It cannot be stressed enough that modifiers, be they single words, phrases or clauses, must be placed as close as possible to — if not next to — the word or phrase they modify. If they can't be closely placed, rewrite the sentence.

Here is a headline error involving misplaced modification:

> 3 rebels seized
> with a car bomb

That certainly suggests that whoever did the seizing used a car bomb (in place of revolvers?). The fact is, the rebels had the car bomb. Correctly modified:

> 3 rebels with
> a car bomb seized

Some editors, however, would forbid that headline because the prepositional phrase *(with . . . bomb)* is split over two lines — taboo at certain newspapers.

Similarly, the following sign on an interstate highway approaching Baltimore contains misplaced modification:

> No trucks on Edmondson Ave.
> in Baltimore City over 3/4 ton

It should say:

> No trucks over 3/4 ton on
> Edmondson Ave. in Baltimore City

An editor once argued that the important proximity in any sentence is between the subject and its verb, not the noun or verb and its modifiers. That results in sentences like this:

> Opposition was expressed *to this plan* when it was learned the water level of the dam might go up.

Actually, a phrase and a clause are out of place. The italicized phrase modifies *opposition;* the adverb clause *(when ... up)* modifies the verb *expressed.* Putting all modification in its place results in:

> Opposition to this plan was expressed when it was learned the water level of the dam might go up.

Following the "rule" of keeping the subject and its verb as close as possible results in sentences that are more awkward than the preceding.

> A *bill* was introduced in February in the House of Representatives *that stated the methane should belong to the federal government.*

The italicized clause modified *bill,* yet we must read nine words before we find out what the bill is about. Here is a rewrite:

> A bill stating that the methane should belong to the federal government was introduced in the House of Representatives in February.

Now everything is in its place.

Sometimes correcting a modification problem is not a simple matter of moving a clause next to the word it modifies. Sometimes only a full rewrite can save a sentence.

> Generally, the *requirement* in cases in which the family chooses not to have the body embalmed is *that the final disposition of the corpse must occur within 12 to 72 hours of the time of death.*

That sentence contains too much modification and is made worse by the weak verb *is.* The solution is subordination — a complex sentence.

> Generally, when the family chooses not to have the body embalmed, the law requires that the corpse he disposed of within 12 to 72 hours of the time of death.

Now everything is where it belongs; the sentence has a strong verb *(requires)* and is six words shorter than the original. Usually, though, modification misplacement is not as far off base as the preceding.

In improving the placement of modification, you will find that some sentence structures sound better than others.

Here is a misplacement:

> I couldn't let the *opportunity* pass *to work for any newspaper.*

One ragged rewrite would be:

> I couldn't let pass the opportunity to work for any newspaper.

But even though the modifying infinitive phrase is next to the word it modifies, the cluster of verbs *(let pass)* is awkward, primarily because the object of *let* is not close to that verb.

> I couldn't let the opportunity to work for any newspaper pass.

Sometimes all the moving around in the world won't save a sentence. In that ease, try more precise words.

> I couldn't pass up the opportunity to work for any newspaper.

It is important, then, to view the whole sentence and not just parts of it. The proximity of objects to their verbs is as important as the proximity of modifiers to the words they modify.

Dangling and Misplaced Modifiers

All modifiers have that mischievous habit of appearing in the wrong place. When they do, they are dangling or misplaced just hanging there not clearly attached to what they modify. For the most part, their misplacement is more humorous than damaging. If they damage anything, it is the writer's credibility. Readers may pause, chuckle, and then continue. But they will also question the writer's attention to detail. If readers decide the writing is sloppy, they may stop reading.

The problem of dangling and misplaced modifiers often arises because writers want to say too much too quickly and forget how they've started a sentence. They get into a jam because they don't like to write simple and direct sentences, because they are too lazy to rewrite poor sentences, or because they are trying to avoid writing a series of similarly structured sentences. While it is true that sentence variety is desirable, it should not be achieved at the expense of clarity. Here are some examples of dangling modifiers.

> *Running through the woods,* the low branches were not seen by the boy. (That says the low branches were running when it was really the boy.)

As a Unitarian, I want to ask you about your church. (The speaker is not a Unitarian; he is asking a question of a Unitarian. This is a common speech error.)

To win a football game, the ball must cross the goal line. (Actually, it's the team that must get the ball across the goal line.)

Soon to join the journal's editorial board as an associate editor, Sharon Stark's fiction and poetry have appeared in ... (The phrase modifies *fiction and poetry,* not *Sharon Stark.)*

More grievous are modifiers with nothing to modify.

As a devoted computer user, my dusty typewriter hasn't seen light for 25 years.

Missing is the personal pronoun *I.*

As a devoted computer user, I haven't used my typewriter for 25 years.

Not all misplaced modifiers appear at the beginning of sentences.

Pope Paul also forbade cardinals to bring in assistants, *except for those gravely ill.*

The modifying phrase goes with *cardinals* and should follow it immediately.

Pope Paul also forbade cardinals, except for those gravely ill, to bring in assistants.

If that is clumsy:

Pope Paul also forbade cardinals to bring in assistants. He excepted cardinals who are gravely ill.

A misplaced attribution tag can create a dangling modifier.

Referring to the board's fundamental problem, it became evident that a structural defect exists, Williams said.

The best fix for that sentence is moving the attribution tag because the modifying phrase refers to *he*.

> Referring to the board's fundamental problem, he said it became evident that a structural defect exists.

As that example shows, although the error is labeled a *dangling modifier*, the word being modified can be the element of the sentence that is actually out of place. Fixing the error requires moving it.

The second — and more typical — way of correcting a dangling modifier is moving the modifier. The Unitarian sentence suffices as an example.

> As a Unitarian, I want to ask you about your church.

> I want to ask you, a Unitarian, about your church,

Now the modifier is properly placed. Think as you modify and danglers won't hang your credibility.

OTHER FAULTS

Some writers pile a long list of modifiers in front of a noun. The result is a monster.

> *Majority-supported university residence hall* rules that prohibit door-to-door canvassing do not abridge freedoms guaranteed by the First Amendment.

The writer who wrote that could have dropped some of the modifiers and brought in the information in later paragraphs. Thus:

> University rules that prohibit door-to-door canvassing in residence halls do not abridge First Amendment freedoms.

Piling a long title in front of a name is also a modification fault.

> Managing Director of the Central States' Festival of the Arts Alexis Hunt said that the First Lady will visit the festival on Friday.

Better to make the title the subject of the verb and place the name in apposition.

> The managing director of the Central States' Festival of the Arts, Alexis Hunt, said that the First Lady will visit the festival on Friday.

Another problem is created by using a modifier without first introducing information to provide a context. In a first reference to a custody agreement that was being disputed, a writer wrote:

> A 1973 custody agreement ...

Besides suggesting that 1973 was a vintage year for custody agreements, the phrase also suggests there were other agreements, say, in 1970, 1975, and so on. The proper phrasing:

> A custody agreement reached in 1973 ...

There is a difference in meaning, and it was the latter meaning the writer was after. A few extra words are better if they create a more precise meaning.

A similar fault is using a possessive form in first references, resulting in phrases such as "last night's meeting" before informing the reader or listener there was a meeting last night.

Sometimes the close-as-possible guideline is not followed for idiomatic reasons. We begin our mornings with a *hot cup of coffee* instead of a *cup of hot coffee*. Some people would rather wear an *old pair of glasses* than a *pair of old glasses*. And few speakers say they are going shopping for a *pair of new shoes;* they say a *new pair of shoes*. Acceptable or not, idioms should usually be ignored in writing. To my ear an idiom sounds all right when spoken, but to my eye an idiom looks strange when written.

Appendix D

Punctuation

The writer is ready to go All lessons have been learned He sits before his typewriter paper in place and begins to type at first slowly as he thinks about his words but then faster faster as he picks up the pace and his great writing flows Someday these words will be discovered on this dog eared paper in a multiuse library the writer says outloud in a somewhat gleeful somewhat arrogant voice What could be better to be discovered later or discovered now A thought Perhaps though it would help if I knew how to punctuate That way people would understand what I am writing

Establishing Relationships

Punctuation establishes the relationship between words in sentences and paragraphs. The preceding unpunctuated paragraph vividly demonstrates the incommunicative horror that results when standard punctuation marks are not used. The writer who misuses punctuation does so at the risk of comprehension, of diluting a sentence's meaning or changing a word's nuance. A comma in the hands of a klutz is just another punctuation mark; in the hands of someone who appreciates how words can collide, a comma cushions the blow.

Unhappy with some out-of-focus prints he had received, an amateur photographer returned the negatives to a camera store and asked that new prints be made. The clerk agreed. He placed the negatives into a new envelope and wrote on the outside:

> redo
> out of focus

Fortunately, the clerk realized that he had asked the film-developing company to make new prints *out of focus* rather than make new prints because the old ones were out of focus. A comma after *redo* cushioned the words and defined their relationship.

These headlines, punctuated differently, mean different things.

| Nicaraguan troops fire at crowd, wounding 10 | Nicaraguan troops fire at crowd wounding 10 | Nicaraguan troops fire at crowd-wounding 10 |

The first says the troops wounded 10 people; the second says the crowd was wounding 10 people when the troops fired; the third says the crowd has wounded 10 people but not necessarily when the troops fired. The correct punctuation mark helps the reader understand. (The correct headline is the first.)

The difference between a hyphen and no hyphen can be the difference between gang war and a change of heart, between a gang of delinquents that had broken up deciding to re-form or reform. No small difference, yet it hangs on the thread of a hyphen — and the knowledge of someone who knows how to punctuate.

Even the much abused semicolon, misplaced, alters meaning. Compare the following:

> The drinks are free; unfortunately, the pizza isn't.

> The drinks are free, unfortunately; the pizza isn't.

There's a third possibility, albeit incorrect, one common with novice writers — no semicolon at all.

> The drinks are free, unfortunately, the pizza isn't.

How will readers know which meaning the writer intended?

Finally, the much overused dash can be used to make meaning clear. Consider the following photo caption, where the dash is needed:

> HOME STRETCH: These runners, students and townspeople, near the finish of a 10-mile race held to raise money for Sun Day.

On first reading, the initial comma suggests a series of people runners, students and townspeople. The second comma helps show the apposition, but not strongly enough to avoid a second reading. What is really meant is that the runners comprise students and townspeople, and dashes in place of commas would make that immediately clear.

> HOME STRETCH: These runners — students and townspeople — near the finish of a 10-mile race held to raise money for Sun Day.

If you've ever examined something written two or three centuries ago, you will notice that writers then punctuated more than we do today. The style at that time was to write longer sentences, which in turn required more punctuation. Modern style demands briefer sentences that need less punctuation. However, less punctuation does not mean no punctuation at all. Rather, it means a precise use of punctuation.

THE PERIOD.

End of Sentence
The period indicates the end of a declarative sentence.

> Officials are baffled about the cause and nature of the disease.

It also indicates the end of an imperative sentence.

> Give me your notes.

The period also appears at the end of a polite request that sounds like a question.

> Would you give me your notes.

Abbreviation
The period is used in abbreviations.

> The Middlemen Inc.
> J. C. Penney Co.
> U.S. government
> Harrisburg, Pa.
> Los Angeles, Calif.

It also serves as a decimal point.

> 1.3 percent
> $2.5 million

With Quotation Marks

The period ending a sentence usually appears in front of an ending quotation mark.

> He called the mayor a "redneck."

With Parentheses

The sentence-ending period appears outside a closing parenthesis when parentheses enclose only a word or fragment.

It is a rare newspaper usage (although *Editor & Publisher* follows that style).

A period appears inside when parentheses enclose a complete sentence.

> He called the mayor a "redneck." *(Redneck* is a derogatory term.)

Ellipsis

When the period is used in a series of three (...), it indicates the omission of some words in a direct quotation. The series of three periods is called an *ellipsis*. (The plural form is *ellipses*.)

> To be, or not to be ...
> Whether 'tis nobler in the mind to suffer
> The slings and arrows of outrageous fortune,
> Or to take arms against a sea of troubles ...

Journalists, of course, don't usually quote Hamlet. Often they quote people whose statements were spoken only to them or to a small group, and the public has no idea if something is omitted from a direct quotation. In those circumstances journalists don't usually indicate omissions because the reader won't know what the ellipsis signifies. Here is a direct quotation from a news story:

> We expect the IRA to hit back at any moment. ... The terrorists have already publicly stated they plan a bombing campaign far worse than anything they have done before.

There is no reason for the ellipsis. What reader would know what was missing? Furthermore, the reader probably wouldn't care. If you do use an ellipsis, remember that it is three periods and is in addition to the final punctuation of the sentence. See the IRA quotation, above, for an example.

THE QUESTION MARK ?

This mark appears at the end of a question. Not using it when it is needed can alter the meaning of a sentence.

> Know what's happening.

That is a command telling you to know what is happening. The question mark makes it a question.

> Know what's happening?

Whether or not the question mark appears inside or outside the quotation mark depends on whether the question mark belongs to the quoted matter or the entire statement.

> "Is the mayor going to run for re-election?" council member Pearson asked.

> Did you see the movie "All the President's Men"? When Bill asked me that, I replied: "No, did you?"

Putting the question mark inside the quotation mark in the first sentence of the above example would change the title of the movie to

> "All the President's Men?"

EXCLAMATION MARK !

The exclamation mark is an indication of intensity or excitation.

> Watch out!

Had that been a calmly made statement, such as a piece of advice, a period would have been used.

> Watch out.

The exclamation mark is used cautiously in good writing. Used too much it is weakened — its intensity made meaningless through numerous appearances. In stories the exclamation mark does not appear outside direct quotations because it could be taken as a reporter's opinion.

Jones was charged with murder!

And even within quotation marks it is seldom used. People do not go through life exclaiming many things (unless they have children). My comments do not preclude the exclamation mark's use in a direct quotation, an editorial or a column of opinion.

The Comma ,

The comma is the most widely used punctuation mark, yet some of its uses are hardly absolute. The comma prevents confusion, although misused it can create confusion, as when a writer puts one between a subject and its verb. Here are several sentences whose meanings depend on the comma.

>Robert Williams, junior chairman of the English Department, spoke about Chaucer.
>Robert Williams, junior, chairman of the English Department, spoke about Chaucer.

>On the platform were Victor L. Marchetti, a former CIA officer and six students.
>On the platform were Victor L. Marchetti, a former CIA officer, and six students.

>My wife, Paulette, makes many of the children's clothes.
>My wife Paulette makes many of the children's clothes.

>The highway project list for discretionary funds, approved by the Transportation Commission Thursday, gave link-to-link resuscitation to the Cadbury bypass.
>The highway project list for discretionary funds approved by the Transportation Commission Thursday gave link-to-link resuscitation to the Cadbury bypass.

>The Democrats who run Congress gave him a standing ovation.
>The Democrats, who run Congress, gave him a standing ovation.

>The day was, well, up in the air.
>The day was well up in the air.

>He was first governor of Ohio.
>He was, first, governor of Ohio.

> Most of her story is clear and honest, but before she's done it gets a bit fuzzy.
>
> Most of her story is clear and honest, but before she's done, it gets a bit fuzzy.

The differences between the sentences in each set or the problems with them are discussed throughout this section.

Titles
After names the comma sets off titles or suffixes after names.

> Miriam DeHaas, *the mayor,* celebrated her third year in office by holding an open house.

Suffix After Name
Notice how the comma can change the meaning.

> Robert Williams, *junior,* chairman of the English Department, spoke about Chaucer.

The comma in the last sentence changes both Robert Williams' name and his authority in the English Department. Without the second comma, Williams be comes *junior chairman.* Newspapers do not use junior and senior in those forms, but instead abbreviate to Jr. and Sr. (or jr. and sr.). Furthermore, most newspapers do not set off suffixes with commas. A reporter following the stylebook of the wire services would write:

> Robert Williams Jr., chairman of the English Department, spoke about Chaucer.

Titles as Subjects
The comma also sets off titles preceding names when the title, not the name, is the subject of the sentence.

> The mayor, Miriam DeHaas, celebrated her third year in office by holding an open house.

> Mayor Miriam DeHaas celebrated her third year in office by holding an open house.

> Secretary of State Joseph Shaw appeared before a congressional committee today.

Apposition

The comma sets off modifying words or phrases in apposition to a noun.

> The ceremony, *a contrast to the policies of the past,* had special meaning for Josephine M. Williams, *the college's 32-year-old sociology professor.*

> The second photograph, *a sweeping panorama shot of Viking 2's new neighborhood,* showed an uneven horizon.

> Ed Dunham, a longtime copy editor, spoke to the local chapter of the Society of Professional Journalists last night.

Clarity

The Marchetti sentence in the list at the beginning of this section easily produces confusion. The comma can decide how many people are on the platform.

> On the platform were Victor L. Marchetti, a former CIA officer and six students. (There are eight people Marchetti, a former CIA officer and six students.)

> On the platform were Victor L. Marchetti, a former CIA officer, and six students. (There could be seven people, which is what I would count, or eight, which is another possible count. By my count there is Marchetti, who is a former CIA officer, and six students.)

The following could lead the reader to believe there are three speakers.

> In a speech at Kansas State, Fran Lee, a former consumer editor and a broadcaster said she warned the president against a nationwide vaccination program.

A comma after *broadcaster* makes it clear that *editor* and *broadcaster* modify *Lee*. Likewise, from a nonfiction book the numbers problem appears:

> He, in turn, communicated it to two more people the Governor General, Lord Mountbatten and Field Marshall Auchinleck.

That reads like three people unless you know that Lord Mountbatten was also the governor general.

Restatement

A modifying phrase is often a restatement or further explanation, only from a different perspective. It is still set off with commas.

> The meeting will be held Wednesday, *Nov. 10,* in City Hall.

The italicized portion of that sentence defines Wednesday further.

Don't be fooled into believing that just because a sentence has a connective it doesn't need a comma. Again, the restatement guideline applies.

> The Cadbury Tigers, who have not scored a touchdown in 33 straight quarters, *or since the first period at Clive nine weeks ago,* could not make a 3-0 lead stand up, despite holding Bakersfield without a touchdown.

Without the comma after *quarters,* the sentence would lose its clarity because it would read as though there are two different times.

> The Cadbury Tigers, who have not scored a touchdown in 33 straight quarters or since the first period at Clive nine weeks ago, could not make a 3-0 lead stand up, despite holding Bakersfield without a touchdown.

The reader might wonder which is correct — 33 straight quarters or since the first period nine weeks ago. They are the same thing: the second being a restatement of the first from a different perspective. Only commas make that perfectly clear.

Nonessential Words, Phrases and Clauses

The comma sets off nonessential material (material that can be dropped without damaging the meaning of the main clause).

> The house, *built in 1857,* was sold twice to family members before an outsider bought it.

> My wife, *Paulette,* makes many of the children's clothes.

All the word between the commas does is further identify the subject of the sentence. Paulette can be discarded in the sentence but she will still be my wife.

> My wife makes many of the children's clothes.

In that sentence, my wife remains Paulette. But in the following, with no commas, the word *Paulette* restricts the word *wife*.

> My wife Paulette makes many of the children's clothes.

Without commas, that sentence suggests the existence of my wife Mary, my wife Sue, my wife Anne, and so on.

Here are two sentences that are identical except for two commas. The commas change the meaning.

> The highway project list for discretionary funds, approved by the Transportation Commission Tuesday, gave link-to-link resuscitation to the Cadbury bypass.

> The highway project list for discretionary funds approved by the Transportation Commission Tuesday gave link-to-link resuscitation to the Cadbury bypass.

The first sentence says a list for discretionary funds exists and that it was approved Tuesday. The second suggests more than one list exists and one of them was approved Tuesday.

Similarly, the Democrats are the majority party in the House; they control the House.

> The Democrats, who control the House, gave him a standing ovation.

But if only some of the Democrats in the majority control the House, then the clause is essential and goes unpunctuated.

> The Democrats who control the house gave him a standing ovation.

That suggests that not every Democrat stood and applauded — just the ones in power.

The misuse of a comma has caused debate in the U.S. Senate. In 1977, when Paul C. Warnke was before the Senate as President Carter's nominee to be the country's chief arms control negotiator, a comma became headline news. From the floor of the Senate, Sen. Henry M. Jackson of Washington pointed to a statement Warnke had made in 1972.

> Under those circumstances, it seems to me, Mr. Chairman and Senator Cooper, that the continuation of the missile numbers game is in fact a mindless exercise, that there is no purpose in either side's achieving a numerical *superiority, which is not translatable into either any sort of military capability or any sort of political potential* [italics added].

As punctuated, what follows *superiority* is a nonessential clause and it can be dropped without doing damage to the meaning of the sentence. Jackson told his colleagues there was a contradiction in the 1972 statement and he asked Warnke for a clarification. Warnke replied, in writing,

> I specifically stated that numerical superiority *which is not translatable into either any sort of military capability or any sort of political potential* has no purpose [Warnke's emphasis]."

As punctuated, the italicized portion of the preceding is an essential clause and cannot be dropped without changing the meaning of the sentence. Warnke blamed the comma problem on a sloppy typist; Jackson said it was an intentional distortion, magnified by the alteration of the original sentence. The comma aside, the statement could have been clear from the start had Warnke used *that* to lead off an essential clause (if that's what he intended) or *which* to lead off a nonessential clause (if that's what he intended). But because *which* is sometimes used for *that*, the solution for this case lies in correct punctuation.

Parenthetical Expressions
The comma distinguishes parenthetical expressions.

> The day was, *well,* up in the air.

Without the commas, the condition of the day changes.

> The day was well up in the air.

Commas also make the difference in these sentences.

> "This is a good budget for our investigation," the congresswoman said; any cut, *in my opinion,* will weaken what we are trying to do."

"This is a good budget for our investigation," the congresswoman said; any cut *in my opinion* will weaken what we are trying to do."

Another way of not cutting the congresswoman's opinion is to use parentheses, although it is a second-rate approach.

"This is a good budget for our investigation," the congresswoman said; any cut (in my opinion) will weaken what we are trying to do."

Dates
The comma sets off the year in a complete date.

July 4, 1776, is the birthday of the United States.

However, a comma is not needed in month-year combinations, such as *July 1776*.

Addresses and Ages
Addresses, names of towns, and ages, when placed immediately after a person's name, are set off with commas.

William Marconi, 39, of 310 March St., Cairo, Ill., died today of congestive heart failure.

Transition Markers
The comma sets off standard transition words at the beginning of sentences and in the middle of sentences.

Nevertheless, the president's change of heart on foreign aid will do little to endear him to his party.

The president's change of heart on foreign aid, *nevertheless,* will do little to endear him to his party.

However is also set off by a comma when its meaning indicates that a contradiction or contrary information is to follow.

This car is just the right size for our family. *However,* I don't like the color.

But when *however* means *no matter how,* it is not set off by a comma.

> *However* great he may have been, historians will never rank him with the greatest.

> *No matter how* great he may have been, historians will never rank him with the greatest.

Here is one final example of transitional markers with commas. In this case, as in many other examples, the absence of commas changes the meaning.

> He was, first, governor of Ohio.

The story goes on to explain that *he* was later a senator and then a newspaper publisher — all within recent history. But the absence of commas sends the time back approximately two centuries.

> He was first governor of Ohio.

Introductory Phrases
A comma sets off long introductory phrases at the beginning of a sentence.

> *In an attempt to learn more about the crowds at football games,* the students conducting the study asked fans, coaches, players, league officials and any other persons who were at the games to answer 15 questions.

Introductory Modifiers
The same principle applies to introductory modifiers, such as a verbal, verb clause or prepositional phrase (which begins the preceding example).

> *Running through the woods,* Jack tripped over a rock in the middle of the path. (verb clause)

> *With much less fear than we had expected,* Tracey bravely entered the hospital for an ear operation. (prepositional phrase)

> *Blindfolded,* the kidnap victim could not tell where his abductors drove him. (verbal)

> *By using three steps,* we can get to the room before they do. (prepositional phrase)

Here are four more sentences whose italicized portions are misleading or unclear because of a missing comma. Correct versions follow in parentheses.

> *To eat the survivors* of the plane crash had to dig up roots. (To eat, the survivors of the plane crash had to dig up roots.)

> After the large coal mines *closed the economies* of the towns died. (After the large coal mines closed, the economies of the towns died.)

> If *I published my mask* would disappear. (If I published, my mask would disappear.)

> Most of her story is clear and honest, but before *she's done it* gets a bit fuzzy. (Most of her story is clear and honest, but before she's done, it gets a bit fuzzy.)

In all four examples a verb or verbal is involved. Because the reader might read the word after the verb or verbal as the object of the verb or verbal, the comma is necessary.

Sometimes clauses not appearing in their normal place in a complex sentence are set off by a comma, although the decision to use them should depend on clarity, not convention.

> If I were you, I'd take the job.
> If I were you I'd take the job.

> When we were young, we played stickball.
> When we were young we played stickball.

Modifiers in a Series

Modifiers in a series take a comma if you can substitute *and* without changing the meaning. In such cases, the modifiers have equal rank.

> The long, drawn-out meeting ended when the chairman collapsed.

That sentence could also be written:

> The long *and* drawn-out meeting ended when the chairman collapsed.

In the following, a comma is not needed between modifiers because they are not equal.

The boys wanted to spend a *five-week summer* vacation with their father.

When you have doubt, insert *and* and see if the sentence still makes sense.

The boys wanted to spend a *five-week and summer* vacation with their father.

That sentence makes no sense so the modifiers of *vacation* need no punctuation. Commas also substitute for *and* in other places.

Go *and* see it.
Go, see it.

Try more *and* shorter stories.
Try more, shorter stories.

The last sentence would be nonstandard usage without the comma. The comma-for-and convention also applies to headlines.

Trojans, Rams face tough teams.

Contrasting Ideas

Contrasting ideas are set off with a comma or commas. Sometimes, clauses not appearing in their normal place in a complex sentence are set off by a comma, although the decision to use them should depend on *clarity, not convention.*

The *mayor, not the vice president of the council,* will preside at tonight's meeting.

The student wants to study *literature, not grammar.*

Natural gas, not oil, may provide the richest payoff in the Atlantic Ocean.

Connectives

Newspaper style usually omits the comma before a connective in a short compound sentence.

The president eats breakfast alone and his wife eats with the children.

> The congressman would like to visit our town but his schedule for that day is full.

Long Compound Sentences

However, as in the case of items in a series, the comma should always be used for clarity, especially when you are connecting sentences with *and*, or for reader convenience when you are connecting long sentences.

> At all evening meals, the mayor *serves the wine and his wife* serves the meat.

The reader may have to read that sentence twice to understand that the mayor does not serve *the wine and his wife*. The description of a movie on television provides another example.

> Chicago underworld boss Al Capone plots *to kill Bugs Moran and the famous St. Valentine's Day Massacre* in which seven of Moran's men are gunned down in a warehouse is recreated [italics added].

The problem develops because of a verb followed by its object, then a connective, and then a noun that could be read as another object of the verb. It reads as a compound object. These don't.

> At all evening meals, the mayor serves the wine, and his wife serves the meat.

> Chicago underworld boss Al Capone plots to kill Bugs Moran, and the famous St. Valentine's Day Massacre in which seven of Moran's men are gunned down in a warehouse is recreated.

Usually, a comma is not used in a simple sentence with a compound predicate, as it is in the following misuse.

> The judge found that the husband has assumed parental responsibility, and has shown an interest in his children.

There is no need for a comma in compound modifiers joined by *and*.

> The home of the husband and his girlfriend is normal, and morally satisfactory in every respect except for the absence of a marriage certificate.

Elliptic Use
The comma is used in place of a verb to show the verb is being repeated.

>Williams had 35 marbles; Smith *had* 10, Jones *had* 5, and Wentzel *had* 2. Williams had 35 marbles; Smith, 10; Jones, 5, and Wentzel, 2.

Direct Address
Direct address is set off from the rest of the sentence by a comma. Try the first example without.

>It's time to eat, Amy.
>Amy, it's time to eat.

Placement with Quotation Marks
Commas always appear inside quotation marks.

>"This is a very austere budget," the city manager said.

Attribution Tag
A comma gets a lot of use in direct and indirect quotations by setting them off from the speech or attribution tag.

>Kusion said, "We need a vote on this proposal tonight or it will be too late."

>"We need a vote on this proposal tonight," Kusion said, "or it will be too late."

>"We need a vote on this proposal tonight or it will be too late," Kusion said.

>"City Council must vote on this proposal tonight," Kusion said. According to Kusion, City Council must vote on this proposal tonight. City Council must vote on this proposal tonight, according to Kusion.

>City Council, according to Kusion, must vote on this proposal tonight. (Attribution tags are not normally placed between a subject and its verb.)

A comma is not needed, though, in an indirect quotation when the attribution tag is the beginning and (really) the main clause in a complex sentence.

> Kusion said City Council must vote on this proposal tonight.

If you remember that the preceding is a complex sentence — a main clause and a subordinate clause — you won't put in a comma. Reporters often discard the pronoun that would begin the clause in more formal writing.

In a similar vein, a comma is not used to separate a partial quotation from the rest of a sentence.

> According to Lee, dogs give humans, "a present they'll never be able to get rid of."

That sentence does not need the comma after humans.

> According to Lee, dogs give humans "a present they'll never be able to get rid of."

The partial quotation is the object of the verb. A comma is not placed between a verb and its subject or object. The quotation marks don't change anything.

If the direct quotation is a question or (perish the thought) an exclamatory sentence, the appropriate mark is used *without a comma.*

> "Do you honestly believe we need this bypass?" council member Williams asked the mayor.
> "Yes!" the mayor screamed.

The unnecessary comma would appear as such:

> "Do you honestly believe we need this bypass?", council member Williams asked the mayor.
> "Yes!", the mayor screamed.

If the order of the sentence quoting council member Williams is reversed, a comma or a colon could be used.

> Council member Williams asked the mayor: "Do you honestly believe we need this bypass'?"

> Council member Williams asked the mayor, "Do you honestly believe we need this bypass?"

Masquerade

Sometimes the comma masquerades as a punctuation mark in a series when it is really setting off a phrase in apposition. How many people were arrested in the following?

> Scotland Yard today announced the arrest of 10 alleged slayers, seven Irish terrorists and three Palestinians.

If you said 20, you are wrong. Try 10. Also try a dash or a colon.

> Scotland Yard today announced the arrest of 10 alleged slayers — seven Irish terrorists and three Palestinians.

A similar example:

> Bulgaria has already concluded friendship treaties with at least two other Western countries, the United States and Canada. (That's four countries.)

> Bulgaria has already concluded friendship treaties with at least two other Western countries: the United States and Canada. (That's two.)

Clarity

There are countless examples of how a dropped comma can change or fuzz the meaning of a sentence. I misread the following sign in my oral surgeon's office.

> Because of the nature of *oral surgery appointments* are for the approximate time only.

> Because of the nature of oral surgery, appointments are for the approximate time only.

The place of a person's death can hinge on a comma.

> The American Legion Auxiliary of Mapleville Post 261 will hold a memorial service for Mrs. Mary C. Linn, *who died Sunday at the T.F. Williams Funeral Home* in Mapleville today at 7:30 p.m.

> The American Legion Auxiliary of Mapleville Post 261 will hold a memorial service for Mrs. Mary C. Linn, who died Sunday, at the T.F. Williams Funeral Home in Mapleville today at 7:30 p.m.

A comma can make a difference to a vote-counter.

> The tally shows Wilson with *1,526 delegates more than the 1,505 needed to win the nomination.*

(That gives Wilson 3,031 delegates, but he really had 1,526 — or 21 more than needed to win the nomination.)

> The tally shows Wilson with 1,526 delegates, more than the 1,505 needed to win the nomination.

Erroneous Omission

Sometimes reporters write such involved sentences they forget to punctuate nonessential clauses at both ends.

> TMSA's decision apparently ends more than three years of on-again off-again negotiations among several parties, including TMSA, the county commissioners and the hospital authority (which owns Sunbank) aimed at finding an answer to the problem of how best to use Sunbank.

A comma is needed after the parenthetical phrase. But because that is such a long sentence, it should be made into two.

> TMSA's decision apparently ends more than three years of on-again off-again negotiations among several parties, including TMSA, the county commissioners and the hospital authority (which owns Sunbank). The negotiations were aimed at finding an answer to the problem of how best to use Sunbank.

Instead of a Semicolon

Usually a semicolon is used in a compound sentence when a connective is not used. But when both sentences are very short and their forms are similar, a comma suffices.

> The people lost, the bureaucracy won.

> If the door is closed, don't knock, don't bother me.

THE SEMICOLON ;

The semicolon's primary function is to separate complete but coordinating sentences (called *compound* sentences) that are not joined by a connective.

> The house is big enough; I think there's room for everyone.

> It wasn't the subfreezing playing conditions or a matter of being outplayed; the game was decided by puck luck.

> Among unanswered questions, Foege said, are: "How did it get to the people; why didn't it spread among individuals; were other factors needed for it to spread?"

Some writers — newspaper and otherwise — will put in a period where a semicolon could be used and go on to a new sentence. That doesn't make the preceding examples wrong or uncommon. In fact, they are very good examples of situations in which the period might jar the reader because it would disjoint tightly related ideas.

One place in newspapers where the semicolon is called for is after an attribution tag that separates two coordinating sentences. Often a reporter will make an attribution tag do double work, letting it refer to a statement just made and a statement to follow. Misuse occurs when a comma appears in the place of a semicolon.

> "It was an even game," Jones said, "I felt both defenses were strong."

Correctly punctuated, that sentence would read

> "It was an even game," Jones said; "I felt both defenses were strong."

> "It was an even game," Jones said. "I felt both defenses were strong."

Conditioned as they are to attributing, some journalists are afraid to allow a direct quotation stand by itself because they fear the reader will not tag it correctly. In stories with only one speaker the fear is unfounded. The quotation marks make the attribution clear.

With a Series

A second necessary use of the semicolon is with items in a series in which some items have apposition. Count the number of people in this sentence.

> Present at the party were John Jones, the butler; Mary Smith, a private secretary; two attorneys; Bill Jackson, a former judge; Paulette Harpster, a maid and a horse trader.

Now in this one.

> Present at the party were John Jones; the butler; Mary Smith; a private secretary; two attorneys; Bill Jackson; a former judge; Paulette Harpster; a maid; and a horse trader.

By using semicolons to clarify the ambiguities of possible apposition, the writer shows 11 people at the party, not six.

In the following examples note how the semicolons neatly keep sets of related items separate from other sets of related items.

> In addition to the congressional pay increases, other pay raises include: vice president, chief justice, House speaker, from $65,000 to $75,000; associate Supreme Court justices, $63,000 to $72,000; cabinet members, $63,000 to $66,000; majority and minority leaders in Congress, $52,000 to $65,000; district judges, $42,000 to $54,000.

> The provost said that recommendations will be made in 11 areas: the purpose and place of the college; enrollment, admissions and probable distribution of students; mix and quality of students; scope of academic offerings; quality of teaching; research effort and emphasis; direction and scope of public service; faculty personnel policies; college governance and administrative organization; student housing; and funding efforts, including tuition policies.

> Their roles on the paper were typical of their relationship: Apte the last-dealing businessman, Godse the outraged editorialist; Apte the chairman of the meeting, controlling its flow, Godse the fiery orator; Apte the formulator of their political schemes, Godse their vocal proponent.

Note that in the second example semicolons appear where commas are normally slotted. That happens because very quickly a comma is needed in a series *(enrollment, admissions and probable distribution and students)*. Thus, the writer started with semicolons in place of commas.

Placement with Quotation Marks

Semicolons always appear outside quotation marks. For newspapers that don't italicize or boldface book titles, this is correct for titles:

> Some of the better modern authors and their books are Tracy Kidder, "The Soul of a New Machine"; Jonathan Schell, "The Fate of the Earth"; John McPhee, "Coming into the Country"; Tom Wolfe, "The Right Stuff."

THE COLON :

The colon is used to show a relationship. Think of it as an equals sign — whatever follows it is equivalent or similar to what precedes it or is an explanation of what precedes it.

> With the outbreak of war, another style of dress is common on campus: green army fatigues.

> Students' grades in writing courses reflect a dramatic change: The basics are being taught again in high schools, which shows up in better written term papers.

Note the difference in capitalization. The initial letter that follows the colon in the first example is not capitalized while it is in the second example. When what follows a colon is a complete sentence (subject-verb construction), the initial letter is capitalized. When what follows a colon is a series or list, do not capitalize the initial letter.

> You have three choices: the Army, college or work.

The colon is also used to separate a long introduction from a direct quotation that follows.

> The president did not speak during the applause. After the crowd had quieted, he resumed: "I stand here today to explain my energy plan in full."
>
> He said he was confronted by Mrs. Jones, who told him: "I did it. I hope he doesn't die."

THE HYPHEN -

The difference between the hyphen and the dash is a difference in function: a hyphen connects, a dash separates. The two create problems because some people use them interchangeably. However, they not only function differently, but they are also not the same length. The hyphen is - while the dash is — (often created by typing two hyphens).

In a Compound Modifier

The hyphen is used in a compound modifier that precedes the word or phrases it modifies.

> The new department store was particularly crowded Saturday because of a one-of-a-kind sale on free-standing mirrors.

If the hyphen were dropped in the second modifier, a reader might misread the modification and believe the sale involved free *standing mirrors*.

The hyphen is extremely crucial when a noun and a verb function as a compound modifier. Without the hyphen a person might read the noun as the subject of the verb.

> U.S. run truce
> quiets Lebanese
> and Israeli guns

Granted the verb *run* does not agree with *U.S.* in number, but the addition of the hyphen would clear all doubt.

> U.S.-run truce
> quiets Lebanese
> and Israeli guns

Do not hyphenate when the compound modifier is an adverb and a participle. For example:

> the heavily guarded road; the well built fort; the happily married couple; the well known composer

Readers understand the function of adverbs; it is unlikely they will get confused without the hyphen. That is why the hyphen should be used only when necessary for clarity. In football, some players are *running backs* and play in the *running-back position*. That is not the same as the *running back position*, which sounds like somebody running backward. Likewise, there is a difference between a *child teaching expert*, which suggests a child teaching an expert, and a *child-teaching expert*, an expert who teaches children.

With a Prefix

The hyphen is also used to attach a prefix to a proper noun. It is *anti-American*, not *antiamerican* or *antiAmerican*. Similarly, you should use the hyphen when the prefixed word might be misread. A favorite example of one editor is *anticrime*, which he says could be mispronounced as *an-TICK-re-mi*. Another tongue twister; *antimale*. No, it's not the opposite of tamale. The following eye baffler appeared in headline type: multiemployer.

With a Repeated Vowel, for Word Distinction

When a vowel is repeated in the prefixing process, use a hyphen, as in *re-election*. That convention, however, isn't absolute, as *cooperation* shows. (But you need the hyphen in *co-op* lest you write *coop*.) Sometimes a writer uses the hyphen when adding an ending to a word to create a new word.

> One listener complained that reception was "echo-ey."

The reader might have difficulty with the hyphenless word *echoey*. Similarly, the reader would have difficulty realizing you meant *co-inmates* if you wrote *coin- mates*.

The hyphen distinguishes between two words that look the same. Hence, you *recover* from an illness but you *re-cover* a book; you *recount* a story but *re-count* the results of an election. To duplicate a painting is *re-creation*, which you might do for *recreation* if contact sports aren't for you. Likewise, you might *resent* it when your grades are missent, but you'll be happy when they're found and *re-sent*.

Imagine if one of those words was hyphenated at the end of a typewritten line of copy, with *re-* on one line and the rest of the word on the following line. What does the person setting type do if the word fits on one line? Will the person know the difference? Rather than hope so, the person writing on a typewriter should not hyphenate any word at the end of news copy (computers don't require end-of-line hyphens). If anyone or anything is going to make a mistake, such as *the-rapist* for *therapist*, let it be the computer.

Other Uses

Self is followed by a hyphen when it begins a word. Likewise, the hyphen is used in some compound nouns, such as *chess-player* and *well-being* and a host of others that are in any dictionary. Some compound nouns also function as verbs; then the hyphen is not used. The noun *fade-in,* to mention one of many, is *fade in* as a verb. (Some compound nouns, following the traditional process of many of our words, are written solid — *breakout, shutdown* — *but* the verbs remain two words — *break out, shut down.*)

Most prefixes (which precede a word) and suffixes (which follow) are not hyphenated when attached to words (except proper nouns). *All* as in *all-star, ex* as in *ex-governor* and *non* as in *nonrestrictive* seem to be the only hyphenated ones. As a prefix, *in* is not hyphenated *(insatiable)* when it means *not.* But it is hyphenated in such constructions as *in-service,* where it does not mean *not.* As a suffix, it is *sit-in* and *break-in.* Most other prefixes and suffixes are not hyphenated.

Clarity

The hyphen can make a difference in a headline or sentence that begins with the article *a.*

> A-bomb   A bomb
> explodes   explodes
> in city subway   in city subway

And it can make a difference in those words that function as nouns when hyphenated but function as verbs when written as separate words.

> Break-in weather
> won't ease crisis
>
> Break in weather
> won't ease crisis
>
> Gallup reports
> church-going up
>
> Gallup reports
> church going up

In the following example, the lack of a hyphen creates confusion, but not until you've read about half of the sentence, at which time you must start again to get the meaning.

> After tax earnings last year were reduced by about $2.3 million because of interest not recorded on some loans.

Read the sentence again with a hyphen in the compound modifier *after tax* and you'll get the message.

> After-tax earnings last year were reduced by about $2.3 million because of interest not recorded on some loans.

In the following a hyphen would make the sentence clearer by creating a paired noun.

> Still pictures were allowed only before the president went on television.

> Still-pictures were allowed only before the president went on television.

Without the hyphen, the first sentence appears to need a comma.

> Still, pictures were allowed only before the president went on television.

But what is meant is *still-pictures,* the kind you see in newspapers or have in the family album.

The hyphen is also usually used in constructions like this:

> The people paid the 50-cent fares.

Without the hyphen, the sentence could mean the people paid *50 one-cent fares.* Likewise, don't hyphenate *50 dollar bills* if you mean *50 one-dollar bills.* The hyphen would mean *$50 bills.*

The hyphen is also used to show a person with two jobs or identities.

> Harry Sneer, head coach of the Cadbury Tigers, discusses with *producer-hostess* Mary Rubin ...

And:

> When the two-hour show began in February 1969, *actress-interviewer* Mary Todd was co-host.

This example shows how a hyphen can change a meaning.

> The 6-foot man eating shark was killed. (the man was)
>
> The 6-foot man-eating shark was killed. (the shark was)

Suspensive Hyphenation

Suspensive hyphenation is the tying of two prefixes to one word by using hyphens.

> The 20- and 30-degree temperatures common to this area do not suit me.

Theodore M. Bernstein suggests, however, that writers avoid the opposite construction.

> University-owned and -operated airplanes are always an issue at budget hearings.

There's nothing wrong with repeating *university*. It makes the sentence clear.

> University-owned and university-operated airplanes are always an issue at budget hearings.

Ages

The hyphen is also used in ages functioning as compound modifiers and nouns.

> Tracey, an 8-year-old girl, won the prize for 8-year-olds.

The hyphen is used in fractions (four-tenths, eight-tenths) and in numbers when the first word ends in *y* (seventy-five, sixty-eight).

Broadcast Copy

In broadcast copy the hyphen appears between letters of abbreviations when the letters should be read individually. A broadcast newswriter would use the hyphen like this:

>   Y-W-C-A
>   C-I-A
>   F-B-I
>   U-C-L-A
>   U-S Information Agency
>   U-S Supreme Court

Where there are hyphens each letter is pronounced. The newspaper equivalent is the period, although the period is not used as much in abbreviations as it once was.

THE DASH —

The dash is used for emphasis, usually to set off material a writer wants to stress.[1]

> Journalists tend to overuse the dash, sometimes making it do the work of the colon or parentheses.
>
> With the routine business out of the way, the chairman introduced the two candidates — T.X. Stein of Clive and Leonard E. Tressler of Cadbury — and began the interview by asking the first question.

Lengthy Apposition
The dash is used in lengthy lists in apposition to a noun.

> Members of the trustee advisory committee — Michael Baker Jr., chairman; Harry R. Ulrich, Ralph Hetzel, Walter J. Conti, Helen Wise, Samuel F. Hinkle and J. Lewis Williams — will screen persons for the provost position. (*Note the use of the semicolon.*)

Stress
The dash is also used to stress a word or phrase at the end of a sentence.

---

[1]Before computers were introduced, most typewriters did not have a key for a dash, so two hyphens were used instead. Since most word processing programs now contain a key or a command for the dash, the practice of using two hyphens is less prevalent. However, the autoformat function in Microsoft Word will automatically produce a dash when two hyphens are typed.

> A 25-year-old Visalia man was charged Tuesday with possession of cocaine and attempting to conceal it — in his stomach.

The dash also completes or sums up an involved sentence.

> The senator said the amendment failed on the floor for two reasons — he had failed to make a last-minute check of its pledged voters and he could not counter the feeling that the bill would not work.

As a Colon

Journalists often use the dash where a colon could work as well. The contributing factors fall in three groups natural conditions, the type of materials used and the design elements of the day.

Or where parentheses might also fit.

> Under apartheid the "coloreds" — people of mixed race considered neither black nor white — live apart from the other races and have more advantages than blacks, but fewer than whites.

Misused

Occasionally dashes are used where commas are better.

> Proving assault will be difficult — T.L. Holt, the chief of police, said — because the alleged victim had no marks on him when he made the charge.

Lists

Dashes are used by some journalists to indicate a continued subject and verb throughout a list, although the more common style is bullets.

> The Council also:
> — voted not to meet next week.
> — postponed action on May Day plans.
> — set June 21 as the date for a public hearing on the proposed sidewalk ordinance.
> — told James H. Andrews he could proceed with his plans to clean up Walnut Spring Park as part of a Boy Scout project.
> The Council voted to:
> — keep meeting the first Monday of the month;
> — call special meetings when necessary;
> — ban smoking in the meeting room.

Because continuity from line to line is desired, some editors punctuate all but the last line of such a list with semicolons. Others prefer periods. Whichever, it is a matter of newspaper style, not some convention of punctuation.

PARENTHESES ( )

Information enclosed within parentheses is usually an explanation, a qualification or an example. Such information is not usually crucial to the main thought of the sentence. Journalists use parentheses to enclose explanatory information where it is immediately useful.

> Scientists believe that if the icebreak drift begins soon, it will contribute to the first worldwide experiment of GARP (the Global Atmospheric Research Program).
> Most ethologists (students of animal behavior) contend that genetic patterning determines how all creatures except humans behave.

Other Uses

A journalist will use a parenthetical insert to call attention to something the journalist wants stressed, as John Sherwood of the late *Washington Star* did in an interview with Theodore A. Wertime, a Smithsonian research associate.

> The affluent American way of life as we knew it (he uses the past tense) is already over.

And from a front page story:

> Ten men were in the mine when the explosion occurred at 4:40 p.m. Pacific Coast Time (7:40 p.m. Eastern daylight time).

Parentheses also set off information that is not part of an official name but is necessary for complete identification.

> Warren (Pa.) Times Observer
> Tamaqua (Pa.) Historical Society

Sometimes editors will insert two or three paragraphs of local information into a wire story. The information is set off by parentheses in the following manner.

> Todd accused Hill of choosing this weekend to call a strike because Hill knew 35 percent of the drivers would have pulled off the highway for the holiday weekend.
>
> (No protesting or striking truckers were reported at the Bald Eagle Truck and Auto Plaza at the Milesburg interchange of the Keystone Shortway this morning.
>
> (Milesburg state police said truck traffic on the Shortway appeared to be normal today.
>
> (They said it generally tapered off a bit over long holiday weekends)
>
> Early reports on truck traffic were mixed.

The convention is the same one used for direct quotations continued uninterrupted over two or more paragraphs — a parenthesis at the beginning of each new paragraph and a parenthesis also at the end of the last paragraph.

One place a parenthetical insert does not belong is in a lead. If information is worth being in the lead, then it is worth showing off, not hiding within parentheses — a structure that disrupts the lead's flow.

> The present New Mexico Power Company line could be improved without any sizable expansion (which would considerably lower the cost), a Taos Planning Commission member said last night.

The parenthetical information rates its own sentence, perhaps leading off the second paragraph.

> Holding down on expansion would also lower the cost, William Kitchen said last night.

Abuse

Despite the valuable function of parentheses, journalists use them sparingly. In addition to disrupting sentence rhythm, parenthetical inserts are considered nonessential and can be discarded. The good writer doesn't want to hide information inside parentheses, as this writer did:

> Other large expenditures in the taxi budget are drivers' labor ($1,330); gasoline and oil ($23,400); dispatching services ($22,000); maintenance ($11,800); insurance ($7,850).

The parenthetical information in that sentence is part of the main information and should not be hidden.

Other large expenditures in the taxi budget are drivers' labor, $41,330, gasoline and oil, $23,400: dispatching services, $22,000; maintenance, $11,800; insurance, $7,850.

BRACKETS [ ]

Brackets indicate to the reader that a reporter or editor has inserted something into quoted matter. The reporter or editor may do this to substitute a name for a pronoun where the antecedent is unclear or to give additional information to the reader.

> "I don't think he [Zelenski] has been on top of the situation the way a public official should be," the candidate said.

Some editors would discard the pronoun in the interest of rhythm, but no rule governs the usage.

> "I don't think [Zelenski] has been on top of the situation the way a public ...

In the following sentence, the material inside the brackets provides additional information:

> "I think the secret to this team's success [Baltimore is 6-1] is that we don't have any one guy we rely on," the coach said.

Other Uses

When reporters quote a grammatical error or misuse of the language, they tell the reader by doing the following.

> "After what I read in that newspaper, I'm going to sue them for slander [sic]," the council member said.

The council member apparently meant *libel*.

Abuse

The problem with brackets lies in their intrusive nature and their overuse. At one time journalists were conservative about inserting anything into quoted matter. Instead, they paraphrased any statement that otherwise needed bracketed inserts for clarity. Unfortunately, that is no longer true. It now seems that journalists the country wide are competing to see how many miles of bracketed inserts they can work into a story.

Here are two paragraphs from a 14-paragraph story.

> "[Dallas Coach] Tom Landry is a genius. Why do you think he has a shifting offense? Well, it's to confuse the defense."
>
> "It's a lot like the Cowboys' [offense] except they put [Roger] Staubach back in the shotgun. With Fran, we don't have to because he can get back fast enough [to pass]."

If journalists stopped acting like tape recorders, they wouldn't create such messes. Instead of bracketing, clarify and paraphrase.

> Tarkenton called Dallas coach Tom Landry a genius. "Why do you think he has a shifting offense? Well, it's to confuse the defense."
>
> Grant compared the Vikings' offensive strategy to the Cowboys' and found the only difference in the Cowboys' use of quarterback Roger Staubach in the shotgun. "With Fran, we don't have to because he can get back fast enough" to pass.

Is there a rule for the use of brackets? No, but it helps to remember that clarity rules the written word. Too many bracketed inserts grind the gears of clarity. Use bracketed inserts sparingly.

THE APOSTROPHE '

The apostrophe indicates possession.

> the president's spokesman; the king's English

Generally, it is not necessary to add 's to show possession when the singular noun ends in s. *Charles'* is acceptable.[2]

The apostrophe also shows omitted letters in contractions.

> wouldn't for would not; don't for do not; can't for cannot; she's for she is; he's for he is (avoid he's/she's for he has/she has); it's for it is; won't for will not

The apostrophe also indicates the omission of the current century in a date.

---

[2]The AP stylebook has an extensive discussion on the use of the apostrophe. Please consult it for more details.

> Spirit of '76
> a child of the '50s

The plural of singular letters is formed by adding 's.

> mind your p's and q's
> dot all the i's, cross all the t's

Some editors don't use the apostrophe to form plurals of capital letter abbreviations and acronyms or numbers. They favor POWs over POW's, GIs over GI's, and '50s over '50's.

When referring to the years during an entire decade, AP style excludes the apostrophe (1960s, 1980s, etc.), which follows the rules on how to make a word plural (by adding an "s"). *The New York Times*, on the other hand, includes an apostrophe (1960's, 1980's), which can be confused with a possessive. In AP style, the apostrophe is reserved for the possessive

> The best song of 1971 was "Theme from Shaft"; 1972's was "The Morning After."

QUOTATION MARKS " "

When journalists quote someone, that is, report the person's words exactly (or as exactly as it is humanly possible to transcribe), the person's words are enclosed in quotation marks.

> "People who don't apply themselves can never become great mathematicians," a math professor said recently.

The misuse of quotation marks makes editors scream. One misuse is called *orphan or fragmentary quotations*. To understand the misuse, you must first appreciate the convention of using quotation marks around single words to signal an ironic or sarcastic use, a misuse, a shading of meaning or a slang use of a word.

Here is a sarcastic use:

> "When you remove all the fancy words from my opponent's campaign 'promises,' you'll see he really hasn't committed himself to do anything," Sen. Smith said.

Promises is not what Sen. Smith meant. He was denigrating his opponent's campaign statements by suggesting they weren't what his opponent said they were.

In the following sentence, quotation marks surround a misuse of a word:

> The editor told the cub reporter to get a lot of "quotes" for his story.

What the editor meant was *quotations; quote* is a verb used as a noun only in newsrooms.

Here quotation marks surround a shading of meaning:

> Back in 1970 there were four men on the Supreme Court who took the "absolute" view of the First Amendment.

Relative to the other justices, the four were absolutists. But there has never been a pure absolutist on the Supreme Court, at least in First Amendment decisions.

Quotation marks are also used around slang:

> As a consumer advocate, Lee is constantly on guard against being "taken" and is now in court with 14 cases.

And around coined words:

> The budget problem has been "overmediated," the economist said.
> The economist believed that the problem had received too much coverage in the news media. Labor problems can be overmediated, perhaps, but the word has nothing to do with intensive news coverage.

Usually, the quotation marks around slang and coined words are dropped in subsequent references.

Sometimes writers use quotation marks around a single word or short phrase to make it clear that they are using some else's words, not their own.

> An "astoundingly" large number of children are mistreated by their parents, and a new study of child abuse says mothers are more likely to do the mistreating.

Considering all of the uses that have been cited above, the journalist who places quotation marks around single words risks confusing the reader. For example:

> The mayor said he is "angry" with council member Blair.

If the mayor is indeed angry, drop the quotation marks so the reader doesn't believe the word is misused. If the mayor is being facetious, make the context clear and use the quotation marks. It is puzzling to read news stories of someone's retirement or resignation that include this phrase:

> The resignation was accepted with "regret."

Single quotation marks are used in place of double quotation marks in newspaper headlines. In a story, they are also used to indicate a quotation within a quotation.

> The speaker said: "It was Hamlet, I believe, who said, 'To be or not to be.' Well, that is the question facing us tonight."

Quotations continued from one paragraph to the next are used in the following way:

> "We're not necessarily looking for a direct tie," Hillard said.
> "Those cases may be another disease that we have to thoroughly investigate. [No closing quotation marks.]
> "They wanted to call it a sort of virus or flu."

Finally, there is this warning on something quotation marks don't do — they don't get a newspaper off the hook in a libel case.

> "She's a no-good whore," Petyak said of his daughter-in-law, the former Mary T. Meade.

While it is true that the speaker can be sued for libel, so can the newspaper. Quotation marks don't change that fact.

Appendix E

A Condensed Stylebook

This newspaper stylebook is based on the stylebook jointly developed by the Associated Press and United Press International, which you are encouraged to consult. The author's own style rules are so marked.

abbreviations Some titles before names are abbreviated, unless they appear in direct quotations. Abbreviate Dr., Gov., Lt. Gov., Rep., the Rev., Sen. and most military titles such as Gen., Col., Capt., Lt., Adm., Cmdr. When courtesy titles are necessary, use Mr., Mrs., Ms. (see **courtesy titles**).

Using the first three letters, abbreviate the months of the year (except May, June, Sept.) only when used in dates, such as Oct. 12 or Oct. 12, 1984, but October 1984.

Abbreviate the names of states in city-state combinations (Joplin, Mo.) with the exception of Alaska, Hawaii, Idaho, Iowa, Maine, Ohio, Texas and Utah. (see **state names**).

addresses Abbreviate in numbered addresses (326 W. Broad St.) avenue, boulevard and street but not alley, drive, road, terrace and others. Spell out when no number is given (West Broad Street).

Always use figures such as 8 Pilsdon Lane rather than Eight Pilsdon Lane.

Numbers used as street names are spelled out: First through Ninth, above ninth uses figures (15th Street).

Directions that are part of an address are abbreviated (1015 S. Terrace Ave.) but are spelled out if no number is given (South Terrace Avenue).

ages Use figures at all times, even if the age is a single digit (Tommy Thompson, 5, eats an ice cream cone for photographers...)

a.m., p.m. Always use lowercase letters. Since a.m. means morning and p.m. means afternoon or tonight, avoid redundancies such as 9 a.m. this morning, 2 p.m. Wednesday afternoon, 10 p.m. tomorrow night.

Bible When referring to the Christian Bible, always capitalize. In other references, lower case, such as:

The wire services' stylebooks are the bible at this newspaper.
Never capitalize biblical.

capitalization In general, follow a downstyle approach in which only proper nouns, names and formal titles before names are capitalized. Titles after names or standing alone without a name are never capitalized.

Work titles or job descriptions are not capitalized:

At the game's end, quarterback Fran Tarkenton threw a touchdown pass to wide receiver Ahmad Rashad.

Common nouns that are part of proper nouns but are being used in subsequent references are lower case: The Republican Party but the party.

century Always lowercase (21st century). Spell out first through ninth and use figures thereafter.

The 22nd century, by the way, begins on Jan. 1, 3001, not Jan. 1, 3000, which begins the final year of the 21st century.

city council/governmental bodies/legislature Capitalize full names such as Houston City Council, the Tucson Fire Department, the Iowa Legislature and capitalize second references to them when it is clear what is being referred to. Houston City Council becomes the City Council, the Tucson Fire Department becomes the Fire Department and the Iowa Legislature becomes the Legislature.

Condensed further, though, it is the council, the department.

congress When referring to the U.S. Senate and House of Representatives or to a foreign body that includes congress in its name, capitalize. Lowercase congress when it is not part of an organization's name or when used as a second reference to a group or as a substitute for convention.

congressional districts Always use figures and capitalize: the 3rd Congressional District, the 23rd Congressional District. But use lowercase in subsequent references: district.

congressman, congresswoman Neutral sex references include: House member, senator, but not congressperson. (author's entry)

constitution Capitalize whenever referring to the U.S. Constitution. When referring to other state's or nation's constitutions, capitalize only with the state or nation's name: the Oregon Constitution, the French Constitution.

An organization's constitution is always lowercase.

constitutional Always lowercase.

county Capitalize in names of counties and county government units: Schuylkill County, the Clive County Sheriff's Department. Subsequent references in a clear context always take capital letters: County Sheriff's Department.

Lowercase county when it stands alone or as a subsequent reference to a proper name.

courtesy titles Avoid courtesy titles. A person's sex or marital status has nothing to do with that person's newsworthiness. However, apply courtesy titles to situations where confusion might result, such as when writing about a married couple and referring to one of them. Does the reference to Jones mean Mr. Jones or Mrs. Jones (or, if preferred, Ms. Jones)? Then a courtesy title is needed. (author's preference)

datelines Newspapers use datelines only on stories from outside the newspaper's immediate circulation area. Generally datelines consist of a city name followed by the state (abbreviated per style): Laramie, Wyo. Well known cities do not need a state. Los Angeles does not need Calif., for example.

State names are not used in newspapers published in that state unless the city name by itself might cause confusion: Washington, Pa., Cairo, Ill.

In roundup stories, state names might be necessary within the story proper to make references clear: Altoona, Iowa, and Altoona, Pa.

dimensions/weights Always use figures, but spell out feet, inches, yards, meters, pounds, grams, ounces.

The newborn baby weighs 8 pounds, 7 ounces and was 21 inches long.

The only exception to metric abbreviations comes with millimeter (use mm) when used in reference to film widths (35 mm) or weapons (50 mm).

directions/regions Lowercase compass points when standing alone. Capitalize regions known specifically by direction, such as the West, the South, the Middle West, the East, the Northeast, the Southwest.

Lowercase general directions when part of a proper name, such as southern Texas, unless the section is well known, such as South Philadelphia and Southern California.

distances follow the general number rule: Spell out one through nine and use figures for 10 and above. The proud parents of the 8-pound, 7-ounce, 21-inch baby took their child on her first trip — a five-mile drive to Grandma's.

fractions Below 1, spell out; above, use figures or convert to decimals. To convert 31/4, into a decimal, divide the 4 of ¼ into the 1 and affix the answer with a decimal point to the whole number: 3.25.

hurricane Capitalize when part of a storm's name. A storm is not a hurricane unless the sustained wind speed is 74 miles an hour. Lesser blowing attempts are called tropical storms.

Although hurricanes have female and male names, all subsequent references to them are made with the neutral pronoun it.

incorporated Although seldom needed in a corporation's name, when used incorporated is abbreviated and capitalized Inc. Do not set off with commas: NL Industries Inc.

initials When a person chooses to be known by his or her initials, respect that usage. Use periods but do not space between initials because video display terminals and typesetters use space codes as guides in justifying lines and a space between initials could place them on separate lines.

it/she Modern usage does not use gender pronouns to refer to neutral objects. Ships, nations and hurricanes are it not she.

names/nicknames Refer to people as they prefer to be known, such as J. Edgar Hoover and Jimmy Carter (whose full name is James Earl Carter Jr.).
The same guideline applies to nicknames, except when the nickname is intended as derogatory ("Fats" Olson).
Some people acquire nicknames because their given names are uncommon. Thus, Amandus Lutz was always known as "Bud," which he preferred.
Nicknames are set off with quotation marks except on the sports pages, where nothing is used.

No. Always the abbreviation for number when referring to rankings. The No. 1 ranked football team in the pre-season poll finished No. 19.

numbers Generally, spell out one through nine and use figures for 10 and above.
Numbers at the start of a sentence are spelled out if the result is not ungainly, such as: One thousand six hundred fifty-two students collected money to help fight cancer last year. The sentence works better this way: A total of 1,652 students... However, don't carry that rule to extremes. It's all right to begin a sentence Five people... A total of five wastes words.
For exceptions to the general numbers rule, see addresses, ages, century, congressional districts, dimensions/weights, fractions, No., temperatures.

party affiliation Three possible approaches form the basic application of this guideline:
Republican Sen. Susan Collins of Maine said...
Sen. Susan Collins, R-Maine, said... (note punctuation and abbreviation)
Sen. Susan Collins said... The Maine Republican also said
The choice often seems based on what goes best with the rhythm of the sentence.

pope/pontiff Capitalize pope only in a formal title, but never when used alone. Pope John Paul II visited... The pope saw several... Pontiff is not a formal title and is always lowercase.

post office Do not capitalize; the correct name is U.S. Postal Service although post office may be used when referring to the building where mail is distributed from.

president Capitalize only when part of a title, such as President Lincoln. When standing alone, lowercase.

race Identification of anyone by race should be avoided. Consider the subjects of stories as individuals rather than as members of a race and copy will avoid unnecessary racial references. (author's preference)

seasons Unless part of a proper name, the seasons of the year are always lowercase.

slang Don't use.
People may use slang when they talk, but when they read, they expect precision, not flippancy, in the words they read. Given the generational differences among many slang words, their use impairs communication.

spouse When referring to marriage partners in general, use spouse to avoid the implication that only men occupy work roles and women are only housewives.

state names Always spell out state names when they stand alone, but, with the exception of eight, abbreviate when used with town and city names in datelines and stories. Accepted abbreviations are: Ala., Ariz., Ark., Calif., Colo., Conn., Del., Fla., Ga., Ill., Ind., Kan., Ky., La., Md., Mass., Mich., Minn., Miss., Mo., Mont., Neb., Nev., N.H., N.J., N.M., N.Y., N.C., N.D., Okla., Ore., Pa., R.I., S.C., Tenn., Vt., Va., Wash., W.Va., Wis., Wyo. (Do not use U.S. Postal Service abbreviations; they are confusing.)

temperatures Except for zero, all temperatures are given as figures. Use the words minus or below zero to report such temperatures. Do not use a minus sign. Temperatures, by the way, are not hot or cold. They are high or low.

time element Except when referring to the current day (the day of publication) use the day of the week. Thus, a Thursday newspaper would refer to Wednesday and Friday where appropriate, not yesterday and tomorrow.

United Nations/U.N. Use United Nations as a noun; use U.N. as a modifier. The United Nations met today to debate a U.N. resolution.

United States/U.S. Use United States as a noun; use U.S. as a modifier. The United States sends many U.S. products overseas.

vice president As a formal title, capitalize; standing alone, lowercase.

women/men The two sexes are equal and should be treated as such. Copy should not assume a group of people is all male or female; copy should not refer to a woman's physical appearance (attractive) or a man's (muscular); copy should not use a woman's family relationship (mother of five).

In other words, treat men and women with equal respect and with a total lack of condescension and stereotyping.

Appendix F

Glossary

advance a story written and made available to an editor days before its publication date. Typically, such stories are features that do not have to appear immediately.
advertising the solicited and paid-for sales pitches that appear in a newspaper. The revenue from advertising helps pay the bills but the work of the editorial department attracts the audience for the advertiser.
Associated Press, The a news-gathering cooperative.
attribution the identified source of information in a story.
access in computer language, a verb meaning to locate and process.
bleed the editing process of removing words and phrases as a way of reducing the length of a story rather than cutting paragraphs from the end.
blind lead one in which the main character or place in a story is identified generally rather than specifically.
brite a light-hearted or humorous story.
broadsheet the format/size of a standard newspaper.
box a border surrounding a story or other page element.
budget a list of top stories. Also called "directory," "digest" or "schedule."
bullet a dot used at the beginning of each paragraph that is part of a list. Some editors use dashes.
bulletin a rapidly sent message that tells of an usually significant or dramatic change in a story or quickly tells of an important happening that probably will be a developing story.
bureau a subordinate office of the main newspaper office.
butcher a pejorative term used to describe a copy editor who does graceless work and makes stories worse rather than better.
byline at the beginning of a story the name of the reporter who wrote the story or of the wire service that provided the story.
caption the words used to complement a photograph.
circulation the number of newspapers sold, usually discussed in terms of number of newspapers sold in a day. Advertisers are charged rates according to a newspaper's circulation and one with a large circulation can charge more for an advertisement than one with a small circulation.
cliché a phrase used so many times it has lost the warmth and glow of originality. Avoided in good writing; removed in good editing.
column (a) a row of type, any length. (b) a short essay expressing a viewpoint.
cutline (see caption)
database an electronic library that can be accessed from a computer.

deadline the final moment in any department of the newspaper after which productive, economical work can no longer be accomplished.

discretionary time periods of freedom when readers can do as they please; generally considered competition for newspapers.

edition a press run's worth of newspapers, not a day's worth. An edition is usually focused on a particular locale (city edition) or time of day (early edition). (see zoned edition)

evergreen a virtually timeless story.

feature a human interest or soft news story written in a narrative or other non-news style.

filler short items used to take up space when a longer story comes up short.

focus group a gathering of newspaper readers brought together in an unsystematic fashion by a researcher looking for subjective analysis of a particular newspaper and for questions around which to build a readership survey.

graphic a visual element designed to enhance the communication of a story. Drawings more than photographs qualify as graphics, although when editors refer to "graphic elements," they include photographs.

gutter the vertical white space between columns or pages.

hard news news that occurs and is reported within a 24-hour or shorter cycle; information that is timely. (see soft news)

headline the larger type appearing (usually) above a story and telling what the story is about.

headlinese slang or words in headlines that one would not use in normal conversation.

issue a single copy of a publication or the entire publication for a particular day; not to be confused with edition, which is a particular production within an issue. The local edition of Monday's issue contained fewer than the normal number of typos.

journalese the jargon of journalism; not fit to print.

jump as a verb, the process of continuing a story from one page to another; as a noun, the continued matter.

lead the beginning of a story. Depending on the story type, it can be the first paragraph or several paragraphs. Sometimes the word is spelled "lede."

library a newspaper's collection of reference works and the newspaper's own stories. Older journalists call it the "morgue."

libel anything published or broadcast that defames a person.

localize the process of rewriting or editing a wire story so the angle of interest to the newspaper's audience appears at the beginning of the story.

news the timely content of a newspaper.

news hole the amount of space devoted to the news, usually determined as a percentage of total space after the advertisements are dummied.

Newspaper Fund a nonprofit foundation supported by various newspapers and news organizations and dedicated to encouraging young people to consider careers in journalism. Two programs provide internships for minorities and students interested in copy editing.

Newspaper Guild a union whose members include journalists. At some newspapers members of the advertising staff also belong to the Guild.

newsprint the paper on which a newspaper is printed.

obit journalese for "obituary." An obituary is an account of a person's death and facts about the person's life.

ombudsman a member of the newspaper staff whose main function is to process reader complaints against the newspaper and to serve as an in-house critic of the newspaper.

peg a story's *raison d'etre*; the main point on which the story hangs.

publisher the chief officer of a newspaper. The publisher oversees all phases of the newspaper, although the publisher does not get involved in day-to-day decisions in any one department.

Pulitzer Prize journalism's most prestigious honor bestowed annually on the best journalists and newspapers (and plays and books).

readership survey a systematic study of audience feeling toward the content of a newspaper or magazine.

sidebar a story related to a major story, but keying on one special point.

soft news the timeless or feature content of a newspaper that usually has some relationship to a recent news event. Also, often a derisive term for stories of mass appeal but not of mass benefit.

standing headline a headline used unchangingly day in and day out to identify a type of news. Verboten when used as the main headline on a story. For example, "Weather" as a standing headline lacks the communicative strength of "Hurricane expected." Standing heads should not be used in place of an original headline.

stet a printer's term (derived from the Latin *stare*) to advise the person setting type to disregard a correction or to let a word stand as is even if it appears incorrect. The word has no use in a computer system, but every generation of copy editors should know about it for nostalgia's sake.

style the prescribed way of processing ambiguous or ambivalent usages in a news stories. Style should always be consistent.

tabloid a newspaper format that is half the size of a standard newspaper. Also a phrase used to describe sensational newspapers.

time element usually the day of the week a news story takes place. Today, this morning, and days of the week are acceptable time elements. Some newspapers allow the use of yesterday, tomorrow, and last night, but AP does not.

transition a word or phrase that tips the reader to a change of subject in a story.

typo a typographical error.

United Press International a privately owned news-gathering organization.

zoned edition an edition of a newspaper that includes a page or section emphasizing news of a small area within the newspaper's larger circulation area.

INDEX

A

A Night to Remember, 130
accuracy, 22, 74, 142, 155, 204, 235, 245, 246, 264
advertising, 18, 39, 144, 147, 345, 347
African-American, 182-184
ageism, 182
American Press Institute, 151, 240
American Society of Newspaper Editors, 247
Amish, 27
anecdote, 42, 43, 96, 131
anonymous source, 255
anonymous sources, 246, 254, 255
Associated Press, 27, 65, 72, 89, 98, 129, 156, 161, 237, 258, 260, 290, 339, 345
attribution, 8, 9, 71-73, 76, 87, 88, 90, 91, 97, 99, 170, 194, 199, 201-203, 229, 230, 233, 248, 250, 254, 274, 276, 279, 286, 297, 298, 317, 321, 345
attribution tag(s), 73, 97, 99, 170, 194, 199, 201-203, 233, 254, 274, 276, 279, 286, 297, 298, 317, 321
Auden, W. H., 239

B

beat(s), 7, 22-24, 34, 37, 39, 73, 98, 99, 107, 120, 123, 173, 202, 253
Bennett, Lance, 24
Berkman, Robert I., 41
Bernstein, Theodore M., 148, 328
bias, 42, 48, 290
biases, 42, 43, 52

Blair, Jayson, 249
blind lead, 87, 89, 90, 345
Broadway, 141
Burke, Edmund, 18
byline, 75, 345

C

Caesar, Julius, 17
Capote, Truman, 130
caption(s), 9, 13, 65, 141, 142, 151, 160, 170, 182, 185, 186, 204, 217, 221, 223, 240-243, 302, 345
censorship, 17
Chancellor, John, 23
Chicago Tribune, 136
city directory, 53, 143, 157, 164
city editor, 13, 143, 144, 147, 152, 153
Clark, Roy Peter, 249
clichés, 101, 189, 249
code of ethics, 245, 247
column, 17, 29, 143, 169, 177, 205, 223, 250, 258, 269, 306, 345
columnist, 159, 160, 169, 177, 178, 184, 185, 213, 250, 255, 261
Commission on Freedom of the Press, 21
communications, 19, 21, 88, 95, 246
computer, 18, 53-55, 83, 110, 112, 117, 152, 205, 297, 325, 345, 347
conflict, 22, 23, 26, 129, 131, 132, 246, 262
Congress, 4, 28, 63, 132, 159, 161, 207, 306, 322, 340
Connery, Thomas, 20, 21

copy editing, 13, 147, 151, 162, 163, 346
copy editor(s), 8, 13, 65, 141-144, 146, 147, 149, 151-165, 169-176, 178-182, 185, 186, 189-193, 195-201, 203-206, 208, 209, 211-215, 221, 225, 228, 236-238, 240, 242, 243, 265, 291, 308, 345, 347
courthouse, 50, 54, 136, 179
curiosity, 7, 33, 34, 36, 38, 61, 106

D

damages, 143, 171, 260, 275
Dante's *Inferno*, 49
database, 45, 54, 158, 345
Day of Infamy, 130
deadline(s), 8, 63, 64, 83, 92, 96, 101, 108, 109, 120, 142, 143, 151, 153, 154, 162, 206, 213, 217, 250, 346
defamation, 171-173, 259, 262, 264
dependent clause, 7, 92, 268, 278, 289
devil's advocate, 48
dialogue, 98, 118, 131, 134, 164
digital camera, 53
direct quotation(s), 37, 45, 73, 74, 76, 81, 98, 99, 105, 154, 157, 160, 161, 169, 189, 194, 195, 199, 200, 201, 203, 204, 233, 250, 278, 286, 304-306, 318, 321, 323, 332, 339
direct quotes, 73, 98, 105
documents, 7, 45, 49, 50, 53, 54, 72, 106, 110, 130, 247, 252
dog bites a man, 22, 59
Drake, Donald C., 50, 135-137
Dwyer, R. Budd, 258

E

Eberhard, Wallace B., 22, 60
editor(s), 8, 13, 14, 17, 19, 20, 24-27, 29, 33, 36, 37, 40, 41, 52, 59, 60, 62-65, 67, 68, 77-79, 83, 86, 91, 93, 113, 118, 123, 138, 141-149, 151-165, 169-178, 180-186, 189-193, 195-201, 203-206, 208, 209, 211-215, 217, 220, 221, 223-225, 228, 231, 233, 234, 236-238,
[editor(s), *continued from previous column*] 240-243, 247, 250, 252, 254, 256-260, 262, 263, 265, 268, 278, 280, 291, 294, 297, 304, 308, 325, 331, 333, 335, 336, 345-347
Elizabeth I, Queen, 17
Encyclopedia Britannica, 54
essay, 129, 160, 183, 345
ethics, 2, 9, 174, 245-247
ethnic, 24, 151, 166, 182, 184, 185
ethnocentrism, 182
expert witness, 259
eyewitnesses, 42, 183

F

fair comment, 171, 173
fair play, 246
falling action, 129, 131
feature, 8, 13, 27, 37, 40, 66, 67, 81, 103-105, 108, 109, 113, 120, 121, 131, 132, 134, 145, 178, 196, 228, 229, 252, 253, 255, 269, 279, 346, 347
feature story, 27, 66, 67, 81, 103-105, 108, 120, 121, 134, 228, 252, 253, 255
feature writing, 13, 131, 132
Federal Depository Library, 54
"Final Salute," 135, 136
"Final Salute," 135, 136
Finger Lakes Times, 105
first person, 73, 113
First Amendment, 7, 18, 69, 245, 262, 298, 336
flashback, 131, 137
fly on the wall, 53, 108, 130
focusing statement, 47
foreshadowing, 108, 131, 134
Fourth Estate, 18
Franklin, Benjamin, 18

G

Gannett, 59
gender, 24, 282, 283, 290, 342
gobbledygook, 154
Google, 45, 54

graphics, 64, 65, 148, 151, 346
Gross, Paget H., 42
Gutenberg, Johannes, 19
Guthman, Edwin, 258

H

Hall, Max, 129, 130
Haney, Daniel, 98
Hansen, Kathleen A., 38
headlines, 9, 61, 65, 141-143, 147, 151, 160, 173, 191, 223, 224, 226-240, 243, 263, 302, 315, 337, 346
Heisler, Todd, 136
Herald-American, 257
Hersey, John, 130, 131
Hiroshima, 130
historical background, 94
historical lapse, 95
Hodges, Louis W., 175
Hollywood, 130, 141
homophobia, 182
human interest story, 27, 30
Hutchins Commission, 21
Hutchins, Robert M., 21
hypothesis, 40, 43, 123, 124

I

In Cold Blood, 131
in-depth article, 123, 126
independent clause, 273
Indian, 184, 199, 263
indirect quotation(s), 71, 73, 99, 317
information, 7, 9, 13, 14, 17-20, 23, 29, 30, 33, 34, 36-42, 45, 53-55, 57, 60, 62, 66, 68, 69, 71-73, 75, 77-79, 83, 87-89, 91, 95, 97, 98, 109, 110, 116, 120, 124, 129, 130, 132, 135, 136, 146, 152, 160, 161, 170, 173, 179-181, 192-194, 197, 199, 200, 203, 205, 206, 211, 214, 220, 228, 229, 240, 242, 246, 247, 249-252, 254, 255, 263, 265, 271, 274, 276, 278, 293, 298, 299, 312, 329, 331-333, 345, 346

international, 14, 19, 27, 28, 60, 62, 63, 115, 120, 147, 196, 261, 339, 347
interview, 38, 39, 41, 45-50, 56, 57, 67, 109, 116, 143, 247, 329, 331
interviewing, 39, 47, 53, 55, 137
inverted pyramid, 77, 78, 95, 191, 199, 208, 209

J

jargon, 189, 249, 346
Jewell, Richard, 265
Jones, Mark, 110, 113
journalism, 4, 9, 13, 14, 17, 18, 20-22, 24, 33, 36, 41, 42, 48, 52, 59, 69, 71, 84-86, 99, 113, 118, 123, 129-131, 143, 145, 146, 149, 162, 164, 174, 175, 245, 247, 248, 251, 252, 259, 261, 262, 265, 269, 271, 274, 346
journalist(s), 13, 17, 18, 20-27, 30, 33, 39, 40, 42, 43, 45, 50, 52-54, 56, 57, 69, 71-74, 76, 83-86, 96, 98, 101, 108, 109, 113, 120, 123, 129, 131, 137, 145, 157, 162, 165, 175, 18, 182, 199, 204, 205, 208, 211, 214-218, 245-247, 249-254, 260-262, 264, 265, 267-269, 271, 276, 290, 304, 308, 321, 329-335, 337, 346, 347
juvenile(s), 54, 247, 248

K

Kidder, Tracy, 57, 323
Kihss, Peter, 143

L

language skills, 13
lead, 7, 22, 29, 34, 40-42, 46, 50, 54, 59-61, 64-67, 71, 72, 75, 77-81, 83-95, 101, 105, 130, 133, 135, 136, 138, 144, 146, 152, 156, 159, 181, 182, 184, 189, 191-198, 208, 214, 219, 223-225, 228, 233, 235, 253-255, 261, 263, 264, 273, 278, 287, 308, 309, 311, 332, 345, 346

libel, 8, 9, 141, 143, 151, 171-173, 177, 234, 235, 245, 255, 259-262, 264, 265, 333, 337, 346
libel per se, 261, 264
library, 4, 19, 22, 29, 40, 41, 45, 54, 55, 109, 110, 249, 301, 345, 346
Lieutenant Columbo, 46
Lord, Walter, 130
Los Angeles Times, 27
Luce, Henry R., 20

M

malice, 261
Marchetti, Victor L., 306, 308
Mary, Queen, 17
mass market, 19
mass media, 14, 129, 184
Matthiessen, Peter, 263
Mennonites, 28, 66
Milwaukee Journal, 36
morgue, 249, 346
Moscow, 27
Murrow, Edward R., 20

N

narrative, 8, 129-135, 137, 138, 209, 228, 346
narrative nonfiction, 8, 129-135, 137, 138
Native American, 184
NBC, 20, 23, 237, 259, 265
New York Times, The, 14, 20, 25, 26, 60, 61, 123, 136, 142, 143, 148, 158, 163, 174, 182, 183, 229, 239, 249, 259, 261, 335
news, 2, 7-9, 13, 14, 17-25, 27-30, 33, 34, 37, 39-42, 45, 47, 54, 59-65, 67-69, 71, 72, 74, 77, 78, 80, 81, 83-89, 92-95, 98, 103-105, 108, 113, 119-121, 123, 129, 130, 133, 135-137, 141, 143-149, 153, 163, 164, 171, 172, 176, 177, 182-186, 191, 193-197, 200, 204-206, 211, 213-215, 220, 223, 226, 228, 230, 236, 242, 243, 246-260,

[news, *continued from previous column*] 262-265, 269, 274, 290, 291, 304, 311, 325, 336, 337, 345-347
news conference, 176, 250, 258, 290
news editor, 143, 144, 147, 263
news junkies, 14
news media, 2, 7, 17, 21, 24, 25, 28, 42, 47, 54, 63, 69, 113, 145, 176, 177, 182, 184, 205, 247, 250, 260, 264, 336
news releases, 39, 250
newscasts, 88, 95, 153
newspaper(s), 13, 14, 18-29, 37, 39, 41, 47, 50, 54, 59, 60, 62-65, 67, 68, 72, 76, 83, 94, 97, 99, 103, 113, 118-120, 123, 131, 135, 137, 141-149, 151, 153, 155, 158-161, 164, 170-183, 181, 189, 191, 196, 197, 201, 203-205, 208, 211, 216, 218, 223, 224, 226, 228, 229, 234, 235, 237-242, 247-252, 254-265, 269, 278, 294, 296, 304, 307, 313, 315, 321, 323, 327, 329, 331, 333, 337, 339, 340, 341, 343, 345-347
newsroom, 8, 24, 41, 47, 49, 142, 144-147, 149, 153, 245
newsworthiness, 59-61, 341
newswriter, 22, 78, 81, 85, 328
newswriting, 13, 22, 60, 87, 97, 101, 104, 191, 208, 209, 218
no-content lead, 85
no-news lead, 85, 87, 88
note-taking, 7, 50, 55, 56
notebook, 46, 52, 55-57, 107, 251
notepad, 46, 53, 56

O

Oakland Tribune, 177
obituaries, 8, 29, 62, 103, 119, 120, 123, 180, 226
obituary(ies), 8, 29, 42, 54, 62, 103, 119-121, 123, 157, 164, 180, 216, 226, 347
observation, 7, 45, 49-53, 109, 155
off-the-record, 41
op-ed, 144
Orlando Sentinel, 36

Otto, Jean W., 17, 20
Oukrop, Carol, 174

P

Pagano, Bernard T., 42
paragraphs, 8, 9, 22, 71, 74, 76, 78, 79, 84, 89, 91, 94-97, 100, 105, 108, 133, 135, 156, 157, 159, 182, 183, 192, 194, 197-201, 203, 205-208, 223, 251, 256, 267, 286, 293, 298, 301, 331, 332, 334, 345, 346
paraphrase, 73, 98, 154, 204, 249, 334
past tense, 72, 100, 133, 228, 242, 331
Patton, George, 134
Pentagon Papers, 60, 69
person of interest, 265
Philadelphia Inquirer, 27, 50, 135, 137, 258, 269
photo editors, 13
photograph(s), 9, 13, 22, 26-28, 41, 64, 65, 117, 147, 173, 174, 178, 185, 204, 239-242, 247-249, 253, 255-259, 308, 345, 346
photographer, 136, 147, 256-258, 301
physical characteristics, 52, 53
Pitts, Beverly, 84
Pittsburgh Press, 40
plagiarism, 9, 246, 248, 250
point of view, 131, 145, 183, 196, 201
police beat, 34, 173, 253
police blotter, 34, 35, 37
pompous (writing), 8, 154, 170
Portrait of Hemingway, 130
portrayal of women, 182
Post and Courier, 35, 36
Poynter Institute, 249
press council, 262
printing press, 17
profanity (using in stories), 8, 161
profile, 29, 40, 108-110, 113, 119, 121, 136, 138, 238
Pulitzer Prize, 33, 127, 131, 136, 169, 224, 257, 347

Q

question leads, 48, 81, 233
quotation marks, 10, 98, 194, 201, 203, 215, 234, 249, 304, 306, 317, 318, 321, 323, 335-337, 342
quote leads, 81
quote(s), 57, 73-75, 81, 96, 98, 99, 105, 136, 138, 157, 169, 180, 202, 203, 233, 247, 280, 304, 333, 335, 336

R

race, 9, 138, 145, 151, 156, 182, 183, 186, 252-254, 302, 303, 330, 343
racism, 24, 182, 184
rape, 173-176, 180, 252
Rather, Dan, 269
Reagan, Ronald, 135
recorder, 53, 57
reporter, 13, 19, 26, 29, 30, 33, 34, 36-43, 45-56, 59, 64-66, 69, 75-79, 83, 87, 89, 93, 104, 105, 109, 119, 123, 129, 134, 137, 141-143, 145, 146, 148, 151, 152, 154-156, 158-164, 166, 169, 173, 176, 178, 180, 181, 183, 185, 195, 200, 201, 203, 212, 215-217, 219, 235, 247-249, 252, 255, 265, 286, 307, 321, 333, 336, 345
reporting, 4, 7, 13, 14, 20, 24, 25, 33, 37, 40-43, 45, 52, 53, 55, 68, 83, 85, 104, 108-110, 120, 123, 124, 127, 130, 137, 142, 143, 146, 148, 156, 161, 162, 171, 176, 179, 181, 220, 252, 260, 261, 264, 265
reputation, 38, 171, 172, 260, 261, 263, 264
resolution, 28, 129, 131, 343
Rich, Carole, 84
rising action, 129, 131
Roberts, Paul, 267
Ross, Lillian, 130
Rummler, Gary, 36
Rumsfeld, Donald, 74

S

Saddam Hussein, 73
Salsini, Paul, 83
scene, 34, 53, 59, 76, 77, 105, 116, 131-133, 135, 175, 211, 212, 248, 252, 256, 258
Schmich, Mary, 136
Schneider, Andrew, 40
Schudson, Michael, 19
senior citizens, 29, 185
senses, 52, 132, 137
sentence(s), 8, 9, 64, 65, 71, 72, 74, 76, 79, 83, 84, 89, 92, 95-97, 99, 110, 119, 135, 136, 154-156, 158, 160-162, 165, 172, 178, 179, 185, 189-194, 199, 200-208, 211-214, 218, 220, 221, 224, 240-242, 248, 267-285, 287, 289, 294-298, 301-323, 326-333, 336, 342
sex, 9, 22, 78, 120, 145, 151, 164, 177, 182, 183, 186, 219, 232, 252-254, 340, 341
sexism, 9, 182, 184, 290
sexist references/writing, 253, 254
Shakespeare, 109, 116, 239
Sheeler, Jim, 135
shorthand, 55
simple sentences, 74, 272, 274
Smyser, Dick, 252, 253
social responsibility theory of the press, 21
Society of Professional Journalists (SPJ), 85, 86, 245-248, 308
source(s), 7-9, 14, 23, 24, 36-43, 45, 46, 48, 49, 53, 54-57, 59, 60, 66, 71-76, 81, 83, 88, 98, 109, 123, 124, 137, 155, 157, 164, 169, 173, 180, 203, 229, 235, 242, 246-251, 254, 255, 261, 264, 270, 271, 345
specific information, 37, 71, 72, 75, 77, 88
sportswriter, 57, 194, 213, 216, 251
Star Chamber, 18
Stephens, Mitchell, 30
stereotype(s), 8, 25, 52, 182, 184-186, 254

Stevenson, Adlai, 59
Stocking and Gross, 42, 43
Stocking, S. Holly, 42
style, 8, 13, 67, 72, 76, 103, 122, 123, 142, 146, 149, 151, 165, 170, 171, 176, 191, 199, 200, 208, 219, 234, 303, 304, 315, 323, 330, 331, 335, 339, 341, 346, 347
subject, 14, 42, 45-50, 54, 96, 99, 105, 109, 113, 116, 120, 131, 143, 157, 158, 169, 177, 185, 189, 190, 203-205, 229, 248, 257, 267, 269, 270, 273, 276, 281, 289, 293-295, 298, 306, 307, 310, 317, 318, 323, 324, 330, 347
subsumption, 99, 100, 212
Sullivan decision, 261, 264
summary, 17, 56, 80, 89, 131, 132, 135, 137, 192
Supreme Court, 65, 66, 158, 233, 261, 322, 329, 336

T

tape-recorder, 57
telegraph, 19
television, 14, 20-22, 29, 46, 60, 62, 63, 65, 67, 78, 83, 88, 95, 110, 112, 116, 117, 129, 161, 171, 172, 189, 209, 218, 237, 238, 250, 263, 265, 316, 327
tense, 72, 100, 131, 133, 216, 224, 227, 228, 230, 240-242, 281, 282, 331
tension, 64, 129, 131, 135
The Camera Never Blinks, 269
The Front Page, 23, 27, 77, 239, 248, 259
The New Yorker, 130, 131
thinking, 45, 66, 83, 114, 159, 178, 242
third person, 73, 281, 282
Thornburgh, Richard, 25
time element, 71, 72, 75, 196, 216, 240, 242, 278, 343, 347
TIME Magazine, 20, 21
titles, 72, 75, 100, 144, 146, 147, 207, 229, 307, 323, 339-341
topic, 30, 40, 47, 50, 54, 94, 96, 117, 198, 206
township, 29, 94, 115, 125, 163, 195

training, 146, 290
transition, 8, 95-97, 105, 190, 203, 206-208, 276, 278, 279, 312, 347
Truman, Harry S., 164
trust but verify, 49
typographical errors, 159
typos, 8, 159, 346

U

understanding English, 267
USA Today, 20

V

verb(s), 9, 26, 72, 84, 92, 93, 99, 100, 105, 131, 133, 160, 190-192, 202, 203, 205, 212-218, 224, 226, 227, 229, 230, 232, 233, 239, 240, 242, 267, 269, 270, 276, 281, 282, 288, 293-296, 298, 306, 313, 314, 316-318, 323, 324, 326, 330, 336, 345, 346
verbosity, 9, 211, 213
verification, 38
videographer, 50

W

Wall Street Journal, The, 20, 25, 260, 261

Ward, Jean, 38
Washington Post, 27, 142, 196, 259, 265, 275, 293
Web sites, 21, 36, 54, 131, 251, 261
Wikipedia, 54
Winans, Vanessa, 34
wire news, 27, 59, 149
wire services, 62, 147, 148, 161, 170, 249, 307
Wolf, Doris, 105
Wolfe, Tom, 52, 130, 323
World Wide Web, 20, 209, 249
writing, 4, 7, 9, 13, 17, 25, 33, 41, 47, 50, 52, 56, 57, 71, 73, 77, 81, 83-89, 97, 99, 101, 103, 104, 113, 114, 116-120, 129, 131-134, 144, 146, 147, 149, 151, 162, 164, 170, 175, 178, 182, 184, 185, 189-191, 200, 204, 206, 208, 213, 217-219, 221, 224, 226-228, 230, 237, 238, 240, 241, 243, 247, 251-254, 261, 268, 269, 271, 273, 276, 277, 280, 288-290, 296, 299, 301, 305, 311, 318, 323, 325, 341, 345

X-Y

xenophobia, 182
York Daily Record, 34, 250